Children Writing the Holocaust

Children Writing the Holocaust

Sue Vice

First published 2004 by
PALGRAVE MACMILLAN
Houndmills, Basingstoke, Hampshire RG21 6XS and
175 Fifth Avenue, New York, N.Y. 10010
Companies and representatives throughout the world

PALGRAVE MACMILLAN is the global academic imprint of the Palgrave
Macmillan division of St. Martin's Press, LLC and of Palgrave Macmillan Ltd.
Macmillan® is a registered trademark in the United States, United Kingdom
and other countries. Palgrave is a registered trademark in the European
Union and other countries.

ISBN hardback 1–4039–3511–4

This book is printed on paper suitable for recycling and made from fully
managed and sustained forest sources.

A catalogue record for this book is available from the British Library.

Library of Congress Cataloging-in-Publication Data
Vice, Sue, 1961–
    Children writing the Holocaust / Sue Vice.
        p.   cm.
    Includes bibliographical references and index.
    ISBN 1–4039–3511–4 (cloth)
    1. Holocaust, Jewish (1939–1945), in literature.   2. Jewish children
in the Holocaust.   3. Children's writings.   4. Holocaust survivors'
writings—History and criticism.   5. Holocaust, Jewish (1939–1945)—
Personal narratives—History and criticism.   6. Fiction—20th century—
History and criticism.   I. Title.

    PN56.H55V53 2004
    809'.93358—dc22

                                                            2004043872

10   9   8   7   6   5   4   3   2
13   12   11   10   09   08   07   06   05

Printed and bound in Great Britain by
Antony Rowe Ltd, Chippenham and Eastbourne

Contents

Acknowledgements

Thanks for help of many kinds to Susi Bechhofer, Teresa Bela, Michael Bernard-Donals, Amanda Bernstein, Jeffrey Bernstein, Zoe Birch, Gwyneth Bodger, the late Bryan Burns, Rosemary Cameron, Nicole Campbell, Bryan Cheyette, Lawrence Douglas, Robert Eaglestone, Blake Eskin, Rachel Falconer, Ellen Fine, Emma Finney, David Forgacs, Shirley Foster, Alex George, Susan George, Norman Geras, Felicia Graber, John Haffenden, Flora Hogman, Robert Hope, Debby Hyams, Jerzy Jarniewicz, Kathy Johnson, Jeremy Josephs, Alison Kelly, Robert Krell, Andrew Leak, Judith Levitt, Sue Lukes, Agnes McAuley, Robert McKay, Bob Moore, Deborah Mugan, Duco van Oostrum, Sue Owen, Alan Polak, Matthew Reisz, Andrea Reiter, Hamish Ritchie, Neil Roberts, Carole Roder, Endre Roder, Diane Samuels, Ken Schoen, Ben Smith, Johan P. Snapper, Nicholas Stargardt, Peter Suedfeld, Michael Szollosy, Nechama Tec and Tara Weiszbock; the University of Sheffield Main Library (especially Elaine Dean and the Inter-Library Loans staff); the University of Sheffield Research Fund for a grant relating to this project; The Center for Holocaust Studies at Vermont University; The Hidden Child Foundation, New York; the librarians and staff of the Wiener Libraries in London and Jerusalem; Paula Kennedy, Emily Rosser and the staff at Palgrave Macmillan; Sowmya Balaraman at Integra Software Services, Pondicherry, India. And, finally, to Elizabeth and Anthony Vice; John Vice, Harriet Coles, Florence, Luke and Ellen Vice-Coles; and Pip Vice, John Slaytor, Amelia and Jacob Slaytor.

Introduction

I began this work in response to the controversy over Binjamin Wilkomirski's *Fragments*, which was published as the testimony of a child survivor but subsequently shown to be fiction.[1] I was one of many readers who were so impressed by *Fragments* that they refused to credit early reports that something was amiss with its generic classification,[2] and I was unwilling to believe that its author was not a survivor, nor even Jewish. Some sober reflection after the case was proven showed that there were troubling reasons for *Fragments*' enthusiastic reception – its child's viewpoint meant it was able to rely more on acts of personal cruelty than on the institutional attrition obvious in a text like Chaim Kaplan's Warsaw Ghetto diary *Scroll of Agony*.[3] Further, much of what takes place is specific neither to the Holocaust nor to a Jewish witness, except as the reader makes it so. However, its central narrative conceit, the representation of a child's-eye view, remains striking and impressive. It was because of this child's perspective that I decided to investigate further accounts by and about children during the Holocaust years. I wanted to know how unusual *Fragments* was as a representation of a child's fate during the war years; and how unusual it was to use the disordered chronology and simple language of a child's perspective in order to represent this fate.[4]

I have defined the area of study here as texts written by or about Jewish children during the Holocaust years, for an adult readership.[5] Most of the texts which are about these children are also by them, even if this link is not acknowledged within the text. The novels I discuss, for instance by Louis Begley, Ida Fink and Raymond Federman, are by former child survivors, and concern that experience. I have considered writing by children to include material by or about anyone aged eighteen or younger at the war's end.[6] The one exception to this is Isabella Leitner,

1

whose testimony *Isabella* I discuss as an instance of fragmentary narration. Leitner was deported to Auschwitz in 1944 just before her twentieth birthday, but the protagonist of *Isabella* is represented as someone much younger than this. Analogously, Marga Minco's novel *Bitter Herbs* is self-consciously autobiographical – the characters have the same names as the members of Minco's family to whom the book is dedicated – but the age of the unnamed protagonist is altered from that of the author (who was born in 1920) to that of a younger girl (in her early teens in 1941). Such a change allows the text to gain the effect of a child's 'guilelessness'[7] – not just thematically, but also in terms of narrative form.

The distinctiveness of children's-eye views of the Holocaust takes two main forms. First, accounts by or about children are characterized by a clear range of features. These include defamiliarization; errors of fact and perception; attention to detail at the expense of context; loss of affect; indefinite or divided temporality; irony of various kinds; the confusion of developmental with historical events; charged relations between author, narrator and protagonist; and age-specific concerns with the nature of writing and memory.

Second, children's experiences were often very different from those of adults during the Holocaust years. In the 'sliding scale' of persecution[8] – which ranges from the experience of defamation, going into hiding, imprisonment in ghettos and forced labour camps, to concentration and extermination camps – child survivors are more likely to have undergone persecution short of incarceration in camps (although there are of course exceptions) as the death-rate for children in camps was very high.[9] This fact gives children's perspectives increased obliqueness. Other experiences not shared by adults include those of 'hidden children': these were very young children placed in safe homes or institutions and brought up as Christians, who suffered 'identity disturbances' (in the psychologist Hans Keilson's phrase)[10] which are mirrored in their texts. Older children were able to 'pass for' gentile: although this was easier for women, in Chapter 6, I analyse one text about a teenage girl and one about a teenage boy, both of whom masqueraded as non-Jewish by enacting a performance of Aryan identity.

There were also events in the Holocaust years which for various reasons affected only children. Over 10,000 German and Austrian children were brought to Britain in 1938 and 1939 by the Kinder-transport movement;[11] while the so-called 'Tehran Children' were 900 young Poles who spent a year as slave labourers in the Soviet Union and were taken to Palestine from Iran in 1941. Both occurrences – which belong to the earlier stages of the 'sliding scale' of persecution – have produced many, often conflicting, textual accounts, which I discuss in Chapter 2.

In the chapters that follow, I have not grouped the material I discuss using conventional generic classifications. Rather than divide texts according to their status as testimony, memoir or fiction, I have tried to follow the texts' own forms and structures. Chapter 1 is an analysis of split-time narrative, in which the time of writing alternates with the time of childhood. Although this is not a form exclusive to the representation of children during the Holocaust years,[12] it is taken to an extreme where the Holocaust constitutes the gap between child and adult. This is also true of the narrative forms I discuss in Chapters 3 and 8, on, respectively, experimental attempts to represent lost childhood memory, and fragmentary narration. Here, formal aspects of the texts do double duty in expressing *and* symbolizing memory, amnesia, incomprehension and trauma.[13] In other cases, particularly that of the diaries discussed in Chapter 7, the chapters do follow pre-existing textual genres. Thematic concerns have determined the form of my discussion in Chapter 4, about 'hidden children'. Again, the texts here take on the features of hiddenness and performance that they describe.

I argue throughout this study that children's accounts of the Holocaust are worthy of attention as a matter of perspective, as much as a moral, emotive or memorial issue. Such a structural examination of texts by or about children during the Holocaust also – and perhaps unexpectedly – retains more of the specificity and detail of the children's consciousness and experience. Discussing the child-victims of mass-murder can appear to call upon sentimentality rather than objectivity, although the history of these victims not only has its own rationale,[14] but in itself reveals the Nazis' project to have been genocidal. Children were included in the Nazis' racial murder because they not only represented the threat of future revenge for their parents' death,[15] but were themselves the next Jewish generation.

The subject of children in the Holocaust years may seem to be inspired by, or risk lapsing into, the 'morbid pieties' of which Norman Geras aptly writes in his *The Contract of Mutual Indifference*,[16] something I have been keen to avoid. Such an approach is evident, for instance, in Gabriel Motola's article 'Children of the Holocaust'. Rather than analyse his chosen texts to show what is distinctive about them *as texts*, Motola uses his article to emphasize the injustices undergone by children: 'The texts of children of the Holocaust, by . . . Anne Frank, Danilo Kis, Norman Manea, and, most recently, Binjamin Wilkomirski – reveal a depraved universe whose brutality and despotism finally result in an apocalyptic landscape littered with the bodies of the dead and dying.'[17] Motola's rhetoric shows the danger of using Holocaust imagery metaphorically. It is quite inaccurate to suggest that any of the writers mentioned above represents 'landscapes littered [sic] with the bodies of the dead and dying'.[18] Lawrence L. Langer, in a survey of Holocaust texts which feature images of children, also emphasizes the irredeemable pathos of the situations he presents. His analysis of fictional texts (including Tadeusz Borowski's *This Way for the Gas, Ladies and Gentlemen* and Dan Pagis's poetry) takes the form of asserting that fictive tropes and language amount only to an 'advantage' in enabling the reader's task of 'judging behavior and evaluating motive'.[19] By contrast, in the present work I have focused on the judgement of narrative effects in such texts. The metaphorical invocation of the image of children in the Holocaust frequently falls – or willingly steps – into the trap of morbid piety. The theologian Irving Greenberg, in his essay 'Cloud of Smoke, Pillar of Fire', uses the facts of death in the camps as metaphors in the service of a post-Holocaust theology that would, as he puts it, be 'credible [. . .] in the presence of burning children'.[20] Greenberg's argument in these terms is of course polemical, but it both relies upon and obscures the reality of the deliberate murder of the very young. This is clear in Greenberg's remark that, 'burning children *speak* of the absence of all value' (my italics).[21] A similar use of the trope of 'burning' appears in David Patterson's study of Holocaust diaries, *Along the Edge of Annihilation*. Patterson remarks,

> The wild, burning eyes of these children [of the Holocaust] are eyes that have seen death overtake their companions; they are the eyes of innocents awaiting slaughter, filled with the flames of the crematoria that await them. It is through such eyes that the teenager from the Lódz Ghetto, David [sic] Sierakowiak, beholds one of his classmates.[22]

This passage is not untypical of Patterson's book, and offers both a backshadowing[23] ('awaiting slaughter') and a confused view of a specific figure. Far from viewing his classmates with 'such eyes' – 'filled with the flames of the crematoria' – Dawid Sierakowiak died of starvation and tuberculosis in the ghetto where he had lived.

Literary techniques

Throughout this study, I argue that literary techniques and conventions are adapted and deformed in order to represent not only a child's-eye view, but a child's view of historical atrocities. This has the result that texts representing children's-eye views of the Holocaust are distinct from other kinds of Holocaust literature, and that they are also different from other examples of literature with child protagonists. Although comparisons can be drawn with canonical works, such as James Joyce's *Portrait of the Artist as a Young Man* (and Raymond Federman's *The Voice in the Closet*, in Chapter 3), I argue that the historical context of these Holocaust texts undermines the grounds for such comparison. Above all, what characterizes the texts analysed here is the temporally charged relation between narrator and character. Although the voice of a child is not unmediatedly present in any of the texts I discuss,[24] various methods are used to present the relation between the adult narrator in the present, and the child in the past. Below are some examples of different ways in which testimonial and fictional texts attempt to match perspective and subject.

Irony

Irony of various kinds characterizes children's-eye-view texts about the Holocaust, due to the temporal and cognitive gap between narrator and character. In *Battlefields and Playgrounds*, his novel about a child growing up in wartime Hungary,[25] János Nyiri uses an unusual mixture of deflating irony and faux naiveté which at least partly corresponds to the division between narrator and child focalizer. As in many children's-eye-view texts, naiveté doubles up as a literary technique and a trait of childhood. In *Battlefields and Playgrounds* – as the title suggests – the war is not only set alongside the concerns of the youthful protagonist Józska Sondor (like the author, born in Budapest in 1932), but subordinated to them. Józska thinks of Britain's plan to attack Germany in terms of football: 'It was similar to Ferencváros's off-side tactics, which tired out the enemy forwards before their own side took the initiative. The problem was that it might take months...'; of his mother's boyfriend in terms of the war, as he says at the time of the battle of Moscow: 'Home was less peaceful; Gyula and I tolerated each other's presence, but that was only a truce too'; and the war itself in terms of release from school.[26] Unusually among the kinds of irony we will come across – pathetic irony in Binjamin Wilkomirski's *Fragments*, the irony of ignorance in Éva Heyman's diary – that in *Battlefields and Playgrounds* is the irony of black humour:

'Who's dead?' asked Dávid almost brutally. Mother shook her head.
'Everyone. Oswiecim'.

'Who's that?' I asked, suddenly reassured. At least it wasn't anyone I knew.[27]

Here, Józska still thinks of death in individual terms, and cannot recognize the notion or name of Oswiecim, or Auschwitz, a site of mass death.

Child characters' voices

The only way in which to represent a child's voice in a literary text is through stylization; it cannot be reproduced. Partly for this reason, such an attempt is unusual in texts about children during the Holocaust years. One example of the representation of children's voices, however, is from *Hidden*, a testimony simultaneously by and about Polish teenagers Faiga and Luzer Rosenbluth. Both spent the war in hiding: Faiga, re-named Fela, 'hid openly' by masquerading as gentile, while Luzer, as Lonek, hid away from sight in a barn. Both emigrated to the USA after the war. Although its prefatory comments show that the text is a reconstruction, written by a third person from the stories related by Fay Walker and Leo Rosen,[28] it uses a stylized, present-tense image of teenage idiom. This means that factual detail and commentary on other characters has to be part of the children's discourse: 'Lublin was on the Bystrzyca River, maybe a hundred miles southeast of Warsaw', Luzer observes, in an incongruous mixture of impersonal narration and an imitation of oral utterance (*'maybe* a hundred miles'). This impression of orality conforms both to the genre of oral Holocaust testimony,[29] and, in literary terms, to Mikhail Bakhtin's notion of 'skaz'. Bakhtin defines this as a mode of narration 'that imitates the oral speech of an individualized narrator'.[30] In *Hidden*, Faiga and Luzer are at once narrators and characters, but their first-person testimonies are literally 'oriented towards someone else's speech', as Bakhtin puts it,[31] because of the hidden narrator who has ghost-written their stories. Luzer's inner monologue in the barn consists of a clash of discourses arising from this compositional method:

Yeah, yeah, Mamche ordered me to stay alive, to carry on the family name. (Which is pretty funny, since I've changed my first name to Lonek, to seem more Polish.) But, at this minute, I'm like Esau, so hungry...that he'd sell his birthright to Jacob.[32]

Here, skaz consists both of an image of pre-war Jewish idiom ('Mamche', Biblical references), and contemporary American argot ('Yeah, yeah', 'pretty funny'). Together, they produce not a sample of the child's language itself, but an 'image'[33] of one that never existed.

By contrast, in her testimony of living in hiding in a French convent, Leah Iglinsky-Goodman does at times attempt to reproduce the perspective and language of a three-year-old child in the convent cellar:

> I was all alone in this dungeon place. The giant stone walls concealed frightening monsters, and the ceiling, the floor and the huge wooden door...[34]

However, this effort at reproduction is just as stylized as that in *Hidden*, showing the adult narrator's efforts to convey incomprehension (the walls' concealment of 'monsters' is presented as fact) rather than the child's viewpoint. The closer the text tries to approach this viewpoint, the further away it gets, as shown by the shift from the past tense of the narrator ('I was all alone') to the spatial present-time of the child ('*this* dungeon'): an adult narrator is apparent here, not a child protagonist. Indeed, despite the insistence by the narrator and by Martin Gilbert in his foreword that Iglinsky-Goodman's memory is full of 'gaps',[35] it is rather characterized by a remarkably full and clear recall, of dialogue, facts and detail, which are clearly the result of adult reconstruction.

Adult narrators

Throughout this study we will see a great variety of narratorial experimentation, inspired by the effort to represent a lost historical and developmental world. Here, I mention various texts whose meaning depends on the stylization, inflation or reduction of a narratorial voice. Such a technique, which represents a child's perspective, is generally more successful than efforts to represent the child's voice. Two memoirs – Cordelia Edvardson's *The Burned Child Seeks the Fire*, and Karen Gershon's *A Lesser Child* – use third-person narration to convey an abrupt severing of ties between past and present.[36] In both cases it is focalization through the child's eyes that establishes the link between child character and adult narrator. Both memoirs are about the reconstruction of childhood rather than simple representations of it.

Gershon left Germany for Britain in 1938 as part of the Kindertransport movement, at the age of fifteen; although her two sisters survived the war, her parents Paul and Selma Loewenthal were killed.[37] In *A Lesser Child* the limited developmental view of a child is matched by the restricted historical view of someone living in Germany in the 1930s. For instance, the child interpreted her parents' behaviour according only to the familial scenarios of paternal philandering and maternal hysteria. Kate's father often stayed out late, but

The cause of Selma's anxiety at such times *may not have been*, as Kate believed, his philandering, but his reckless tongue: he would tell political jokes without caring who might overhear him. When she observed her mother weeping in his arms, this *may not have been*, as she believed, evidence of a reconciliation after a quarrel. Paul may have been trying to comfort her when she was in despair over their worsening circumstances.[38] (my italics)

As the verbs of reconstruction show ('may not have been'), there is an overlap between what Dominick LaCapra calls 'structural or existential trauma' – here, the child's Oedipal view of her parents – and the 'historical trauma' of specific events.[39] Such a historical perspective can only be supplied with hindsight. However, awareness of historical trauma is not only the province of an adult view, as we can see in an episode from *The Burned Child Seeks the Fire*. Like the unnamed child in this memoir, Edvardson was born in 1929, the illegitimate daughter of the 'half-Jewish' German writer Elisabeth Langgässer and a Jewish father whom she never met. Although she was brought up as a Catholic, the child was deported to Auschwitz in 1943, partly as the result of her attempts to protect her mother.[40] The 'existential' trauma of the child's familial relationships is inseparable throughout *The Burned Child* from its historical dimension, particularly because the child is seen as more Jewish than her mother. The child remembers that a family friend called her a ' "filthy Jewish brat" ' when she was about nine. Only with some effort, which appears to take place during the process of writing, does the adult narrator recall the incident fully:

What was he so mad about? She no longer knows. But she does! It occurs to her – wasn't that how it was? – that the girl and the blue-eyed son had played forbidden games and been caught. Yes, that's how it was. Yes, she was a filthy Jewish brat.[41]

Beneath the historicized, racial slur lies a sexual transgression. However, again the two are not separable, as the word 'forbidden' suggests: these 'games' represent both an existential *and* a historically specific affront. The child understands Jewishness by its connection with 'filthy' sexuality, as opposed to Catholic 'purity', as she thinks of herself: 'A filthy Jewish brat: what is that, anyway? Does it mean [. . .] playing forbidden games? But she's really a pious little Catholic girl who took her first communion several years ago.'[42]

Although Gershon's and Edvardson's memoirs both use novelistic techniques, they are non-fiction. By contrast, in Bogdan Wojdowski's 'auditory'[43] novel *Bread for the Departed* we see the reduced narrator of the polyphonic novel, in Mikhail Bakhtin's phrase. *Bread for the Departed* is about the Warsaw Ghetto, seen through the eyes of David – like Wojdowski himself, aged twelve in 1942 – who is represented in the third person. Precisely because of its historical setting, the novel takes on extreme polyphonic form, as described by Bakhtin: it consists of '*a plurality of independent and unmerged consciousnesses and voices ... each with its own world ...* contradictory in its values'.[44] Polyphony in *Bread for the Departed* has a partly memorial function.[45] The presence of so many clashing accents – in the sense of both 'values' and dialects[46] – is 'explained' by the listening but uncomprehending presence of the child David, and allows the role of the conventional third-person narrator to be taken over by the characters. For instance, David tries memorizing English grammar by repeating it to himself before falling asleep:

The present tense and the past tense of the verb *to be*.
'I am, you are, she is. She is. We are, you are, they are.'
'I was'.[47]

David's fear of death, and his fate after the novel's end in 1943, are not spelled out by the narrator, but conveyed indirectly through the recitation of a school lesson.

In her memoir *Landscapes of Memory: A Holocaust Girlhood Remembered*,[48] Ruth Kluger – who was born in Austria in 1931, and deported to Theresienstadt, then to Auschwitz and Gross-Rosen between the ages of twelve and fourteen – uses the spatial layout of the text to represent her struggle *in the present* with memory and historical events. For instance, the adult Ruth glosses her mention of the Hitler Youth boys' 'daggers' with a parenthesis about a former member, now a university colleague, who told her that these were ' "good for cutting bread, that's all" ' (6), which the narrator does not accept: ' "That's a dagger for sure, I think" '. Later in the narrative the older Ruth returns parenthetically to this issue when writing of 'the boys ... in their short pants and their Hitler Youth daggers (or bread knives with motto)' (53), affirming her own view by placing her colleague's view in mocking parentheses.

Kluger's parentheses show that the past exists literally within the present. They represent the corrections to memory that the adult Ruth cannot utter; on several occasions, including the dagger episode, she remains silent when confronted with incorrect or outrageous statements.[49]

After quoting what her father told her seven-year-old self about shops destroyed on *Kristallnacht*, Ruth represents her memory in two levels: 'I merely made a point of remembering his words. (See, I still know them)' (19). In general, the parentheses aim to 'bridge the gap' between knowledge and memory (a distinction also made in Saul Friedländer's *When Memory Comes*), particularly in the case of *memories* Ruth has of her father, whom she *knows* to have died in Auschwitz. In this case, memory may be accurate but is also unreliable due to the 'discrepancy between actual, normal, petty sentiments and the horrendous suffering of which childish memory is innocent' (28). As the original German title – *weiter leben*, 'still living' – suggests,[50] it is the notion of mass death that causes memory to falter.

Finally, I will mention the experimental use made of an adult narrator by the Romanian-born novelist Norman Manea. The stories in his collection *October Eight O'Clock* which concern the war years are written in the first person from the viewpoint of a child, but the discourse throughout is that of an adult. The tropes of a child's viewpoint – naiveté, incomprehension, missing facts – are adopted, but not in an effort to reproduce a child's voice (the boy speaks only once directly). Instead, they constitute a very 'adult' absurdity and surrealism.[51] For instance, in 'The Sweater' an unnamed boy recounts his envy of the multicoloured sweater his mother knits for a non-Jewish girl (naturally she is not described as such: 'The little girl had nothing to do with the curse on us; she was innocent').[52]

The story's historical and geographical setting is not described, but left for the reader to infer: 'The sky might suddenly open and we would find ourselves in a real train, not like the cattle cars they had unloaded us from in this emptiness at the end of the world.'[53] The little girl, Mara, dies, and the sweater is retrieved; but it infects the doctor, who also dies. Although the gaps in this story appear to be the result of the boy's ignorance, they are in fact strategic. The boy describes the doctor's diagnosis of Mara's illness: 'There was nothing else to do but raise his hands and mutter the name of the affliction.' The 'name' of the illness is withheld, rather than unknown. The boy himself succumbs to a 'delirium', which is introduced in its own terms rather than explained: 'I woke up in the coffin, being lowered into the grave next to Mara; then there was nothing.'[54] The story is both realist and allegorical, and the hinge between the two modes is the child's viewpoint. His ignorance is the narrator's fable, as the story's concluding line shows: 'Time itself had sickened, and we belonged to it.'[55] While the boy might well see sickness everywhere, the image is that of a literary adult.[56] Although Louis Begley fills in the gaps of 'The Sweater' from Manea's biography – 'the nameless place is a concentration camp somewhere in Transnistria... the little boy [and] his family are Romanian Jews'[57] – these refer only to the story's realist and not its allegorical identity.

Throughout *Children Writing the Holocaust* I argue that, although literature of the Holocaust from a child's viewpoint is based on historical criteria, it can be described as a literary genre. The questions that I posed at the beginning of this introduction – whether there were many texts written about a child's Holocaust experience, or from a child's perspective – can both clearly be answered affirmatively. Indeed, many writers who are well known within Holocaust studies (Saul Friedländer, Elie Wiesel, Ida Fink) and outside them (Raymond Federman, Sarah Kofman, Georges Perec) have written about the Holocaust years from the viewpoint of a child, but their work has not before been analysed according to its developmental viewpoint. It is to these texts that I now turn.

1
Split Narration

Many texts written from the viewpoint of child survivors of the Holocaust are structured in what is apparently the same temporally split manner. Sections about the traumatic past alternate with sections describing the present: either that of the post-war era, or the time of writing. In Saul Friedländer's memoir *When Memory Comes*, for instance, the past is the product of retrospection while the present is written as it unfolds in the form of a diary; while in both Shlomo Breznitz's *Memory Fields* and Georges Perec's *W or the Memory of Childhood*,[1] the moment of writing is a third moment, distinct from the wartime and post-war times discussed. Such texts are also divided between a child's and an adult's perspective; the past of the Holocaust is the time of childhood, its effects that of adulthood. Unlike 'fragmentary' texts, these texts are chronological although they are not linear.[2] In this chapter, I will examine three child's-eye-view texts structured in this way to see how this particular form is appropriate to the concerns of each.

The effects of temporally split narration can be listed in general terms. First, such a structure places past and present side by side, both disrupting a teleological and backshadowing view of history, and complicating the precedence of either mode.[3] Such disruption is achieved both structurally and through the use of tenses and parallels or, in a term used by Binjamin Wilkomirski in the fictional *Fragments*, the use of 'threads'[4] connecting the two times.

Secondly, temporal splitting also effects a spatial division: locations which have very different meanings are placed alongside each other. In many Holocaust texts wartime Europe is superseded and redeemed by post-war USA (see for instance Naomi Samson's *Hide: A Child's View of the Holocaust*[5]), but in the divided texts an *interleaving* occurs instead: Bratislava with the USA in Breznitz's text, occupied France with Tierra del

Fuego in Perec's, while in Friedländer's case wartime France is set beside Israel in 1977. A further twist is given to this interleaving by Perec's novel. Not only are time and space alternated, but so are fact and invention. In *W or the Memory of Childhood*, Perec's French convent is almost as fictive as the South American island of the interleaved science-fiction narrative.

Thirdly, such a form by its very nature conveys the effect of trauma, by, for instance, efforts to remember in detail, or to forget; speculations and reconstructions from the vantage-point of composition; an awareness of lost or suppressed childhood affect; and reflections on the linearity that has been abandoned.

'Looking back doubtless distorts one's vision' (168): Saul Friedländer, *When Memory Comes*

Saul Friedländer was born Pavel Friedlander in Prague in 1933. His memoir describes the journey of young Pavlíček, as he was called by his parents, from wartime Prague, through France where he spent three years hidden in a convent at Saint-Béranger, to Israel in 1948. Both the young Saul's parents were killed at Auschwitz. Paul (as I shall refer to the memoir's young protagonist, in contrast to the adult narrator Saul) was baptised in the convent as the Catholic 'Paul-Henri', and spent much of his youth avoiding the memory of his parents and his past. *When Memory Comes* traces the process of retrieving a suppressed memory, and tries to reconstruct a thirty-year-old past. The text consists of alternating passages of memoir, about Saul's wartime childhood in Prague and the convent, with passages of a diary kept by the adult Saul in Israel, in 1977.

When Memory Comes attempts to reconstruct Saul's parents as well, an almost impossible task as they remain trapped within the view of the child. Like Elie Wiesel's *Night*, *When Memory Comes* represents the split between past and present selves as one of naming. Just as the Hungarian child Eliezer in Wiesel's memoir becomes the French Elie, so here the Czech Pavel is reborn as Israeli Saul, in a reversal of the New Testament conversion of Saul to Paul (12).[6]

As the title of his memoir indicates, the narrator Saul aspires to full memory despite – and obviously because of – the gaps in what he can remember, and also despite his own expectation of incomplete recall. 'When memory comes' is the reworking of a quotation from Gustav Meyrink: 'When knowledge comes, memory comes too, little by little. Knowledge and memory are one and the same thing' (quoted vi). Friedländer's reversal of Meyrink's link between knowledge and memory is significant; Saul's memory must stand in for and even constitute a knowledge which remains unverifiable[7] – despite his efforts at gaining corroboration for it as an adult (from Vlasta, the nursemaid engaged by his parents, and the nuns who sheltered him in France). The opposition between memory and knowledge both structures *When Memory Comes* and constitutes its concerns: it underlies the division between past and present, child and adult, 'spectator' and victim, Europe and Israel, memoir and diary.

The signs of this effort to substitute memory for knowledge include Saul's habit of backshadowing – that is, seeing the past from the viewpoint of the present – although by definition this takes place only in the sections dealing with the past and not in his diary. He notes, 'I was born in Prague at the worst possible moment, four months before Hitler came to power' (3); and says of his father, 'A bourgeois aesthete perched on the edge of a volcano, he foresaw nothing of what the future would bring' (5). However, neither of these comments blames Holocaust victims in the usual manner of backshadowing;[8] any hint at reproach for his parents' fecklessness in producing a Jewish child in 1939 and fleeing only as far as occupied France is at most ambivalent. As Saul puts it, this was a 'happy period of my life, despite a few *ominous shadows*' (15, my italics): it is implied that these shadows were not perceived as such at the time by the child Paul, and only gained ominous meaning later for the adult Saul. This is clear, for instance, in Saul's description of Jewish students having to leave the schoolroom weekly for separate instruction, 'beneath the gaze of classmates that *today* I suppose was either mocking or amused, but one that I distinctly *remember* as being attentive' (28, my italics). Affective meaning has been added retrospectively to what was remembered simply as a posture.

A similarly amended version of backshadowing also characterizes Paul's first significant encounter with death. The director of his new school dies, and Vlasta explains that he is to be cremated; learning of 'an oven for cremating people' makes the child 'deeply upset' (15). This is a clear instance of a historicized version of Freud's *Nachträglichkeit*, in which later knowledge gives 'belated' meaning to an earlier event.[9] Saul is reading back into the childhood disturbance a later, Holocaust knowledge of people killed in order to be burnt: people who included his own parents. This is not backshadowing, then, but a variety of belatedness, although Saul tries to suggest that there could have been some element of foreknowledge in Paul's upset: the director's cremation haunted the boy's nightmares, partly, Saul claims, due to the child's awareness 'of a growing anxiety round about him which is still, however, difficult for him to identify' (15; see also 113).

Indeed, the very urge to give memory the status of knowledge appears to conform to the logic of *Nachträglichkeit*: with hindsight, mystification is cleared up, the source of a troubling event recognized and restored. But this does not work as effectively with public history as it does with the history of an individual. While the Wolf Man in Freud's case history does come belatedly to understand the sexual meaning of events which took place during his infancy, the same logic cannot easily be ascribed to Saul's view of Paul's fear of cremation.[10] If extra meaning is belatedly given to this fear, it is simply that of historical irony, not recognition or reactivation of anything implicit in the earlier event which Paul was then too young to understand. This radical distinction between psychic and historical *Nachträglichkeit* marks not any dishonesty on Saul's part but the extreme difficulty of reaching any reconciled view of the Holocaust, especially when it interrupts an individual's childhood.

What is most striking about *When Memory Comes* is that it describes a series of extreme and traumatizing events undergone by a young child – separation from his parents, being placed in an alien environment and made to conceal his identity, learning that his parents had been killed – in a reflective and distancing manner. The original shocks of the 'total upheaval' (5) are in some cases described (notably Paul fleeing from the convent back to his parents) but it is left to the text's form to convey the resulting splitting and separation. Saul tries to leave behind the detailed focus of childhood memory and adopt the broader perspective of adult knowledge. For instance, Saul's memory of Paul's love for his nursemaid Vlasta – 'But it is Vlasta whom I find everywhere' (16) – is followed by a conversion of memory into knowledge: 'The influence of the Vlastas of all nationalities on the rapid assimilation of the Jewish bourgeoisie of Europe merits study [as] the essential link between the Jewish child and the world around him' (16).

Paul's memories of his father are similarly transformed into a less affectful view. Paul's view of his father as 'an extraordinary person', more 'vivid' than his mother, becomes Saul's quest for something more than this memory: 'I deduce [...] that [my father] was still familiar, for a time at least, with a Jewish milieu that was still Orthodox for the most part' (5). Yet even this description conveys the difficulty of reconciling memory and knowledge. Paul's view of his father as 'extraordinary' comes, Saul admits, from the unreliable source of memory: 'doubtless because I saw him through a child's eyes'; while Saul's deduction about his father's Jewish knowledge is from external evidence (Saul now knows his father completed his education in Lemberg) and not backed up by his sole evidentiary source, the child Paul: 'yet [my father] bore no apparent traces of such a background' (5). Memory seems to testify more to feeling than to fact, to Saul's dismay. This conforms to Jean-François Lyotard's citation of Freud's notion of *Nachträglichkeit* as a model of how the murder of the Jews during the Holocaust can neither be perfectly remembered (or known), nor forgotten.[11] Lyotard describes the originary event in the 'double blow' of *Nachträglichkeit* as 'a shock without affect': the moment of the event is too overwhelming to be felt. Yet 'with the second blow there takes place an affect without shock': the event is past, but the feeling originally aroused by it remains, free-floatingly. This is akin to Saul's experience of looking back at his lost parents and being unable to unite the affect of his memory with factual knowledge. For Saul, affect itself becomes associated with Jewishness – the lost component of his memory.

The reader of Friedländer's memoir may wonder how successful *When Memory Comes* is in its effort to convert memory into knowledge. The book's title suggests that memory can be the same as knowledge, a synonymy not borne out by the book's divided structure and content. Indeed, despite the healing hoped for from the act of writing itself, Saul emerges as a subject whose time and place of birth have turned him into one radically split, 'a person divided' (62). His diary-writing present in Jerusalem has a more overtly uncomfortable relation to the past than, say, Shlomo Breznitz's American present to his past. The assertion of unlikely links – Saul claims that 'the *same* anxiety is still ever-present' in Jerusalem in July 1977 (at the time of Anwar Sadat's visit), as it was in Paris in July 1939 (41, my italics) – arises partly from his frustration at having to rely on memory alone and often being unable to turn it into knowledge; and partly because the later event allows access to the earlier one. Saul laments particularly the loss of his father; reading the books his father left behind merely emphasises the impossibility of recon-structing 'a sensibility that never revealed itself to me, whose only remaining trace is my uncertain memories, these books, and a few scattered letters' (56). Yet Saul's revenge on these inaccessible parents is to show that he knows better than they did, describing with belated disbelief the 'panic' that induced them to hide their son in France, in August 1942, in a children's home – a Jewish children's home (71).

Alongside Saul's efforts to retrieve the past, reconstruct his parents and their motives, and supply himself with a seamless identity, is the fact that his life before 1945 had 'disappeared' until he set about recalling it in Israel in 1977. The real force of the book's title is in reference to this effort at recall, and is perhaps best seen as an ironic comment on Meyrick's epigram: it is not that the arrival of memory confers knowledge, but that memory may suddenly flood the subject with something threatening and disruptive.[12] Saul claims that his childhood got 'lost': 'The first ten years of my life, the memories of my childhood, were to disappear, for there was no possible synthesis between the person I had been and the one I was to become' (80). The intermediary identity of Paul's new persona, both Catholic and French and agent of this willed forgetting, was baptised Paul-Henri-Marie Ferland at the Montluçon convent. Immediately after this renaming, Paul tried to retrieve himself by running away, back to his parents – much as Saul also tries to return to those lost figures – who were in hospital in town.

The scene of this temporary reunion is the book's centre, an imperfect memory around which the rest of the text revolves. Even its recall is imbued with forgetting. Saul cannot work out how he found his parents in the hospital: whether they were there recklessly under their own name, or if he had somehow known and remembered an assumed name – of which he now has no memory (85). He can only speculate how his parents felt as they prised his hands off the hospital bed-bars so that he could be sent away a second time (88). What Paul himself felt is 'lost forever' (80), although the child knew the separation's meaning because his father kissed him for the first – and last – time (79). Even when it is retrieved, memory loses its subjectivity and Saul only has access to a scene viewed from the outside, as if in the third person:

> of this heartbreak there remains only a vignette in my memory, the image of a child walking back down the rue de la Garde, in the opposite direction from the one taken shortly before, in a peaceful autumn light, between two nuns dressed in black. (88)

It is almost as if the original affect from this scene has been replaced with its opposite – serenity and obedience – and unease signalled only minutely in the ominously black-clad figures of the nuns.

Saul is impelled to use third-person narration to describe Paul-Henri, a child different from the Czech Paul. The effects of split identity actually permeate the text's language:

> I did not react at all, for instance, even when a faintly comic episode occurred in this context that to me was not at all comic. (97)

> Mademoiselle Madeleine, who supervised our walks, was sometimes surprised at the apathetic air of poor Paul-Henri, but did not pursue the matter. (99)

In the first instance, a temporal difference between Paul and Saul creates the contradiction here in which 'I' and 'me' are both Paul, but the person narrating this episode and describing it as 'comic' is Saul, who is not the subject of his own first-person utterance. In the second quotation, Saul describes his younger self in the third person to convey not only Madeleine's view of him as the French Catholic Paul-Henri, but also his own externalized view of himself *at the time* as a foreign being.[13] Both examples enact in miniature the patterns of the text as a whole and its 'deep clefts' (100), which exist not only diachronically, between times, but also synchronically, within the subject.

If Paul only became aware of his own Jewishness in 1938 when he was five, it could only be with belated knowledge that Saul would be able to look back and recognize signs of Jewishness in his family before the war. Indeed, his evidence that his father 'was not entirely indifferent to his origins' (6) is the Star of David on the *ex libris* plates pasted into books Saul looks at in the present. Past memory does not help: Saul knows only that Paul visited many churches in Prague but cannot recall the famous Altneuschul synagogue. Saul cannot remember himself as a Jewish child. The forgottenness of Judaism is another means of shedding affect in the memories Saul does retrieve. When describing the 'conversion' illness he underwent at the convent which allowed for his acceptance of Catholicism, Saul turns personal memory into a memory about Jewish history:

> Was this sick child really me? I imagine that if there were such a thing as a collective Jew, he might well ask himself the same question: am I the same today as the Jew of thirty-five years ago? (100)

Of course this comment is appropriate, as Saul's life and memoir are directly shaped by the two central events in modern Jewish history: the Holocaust and the founding of the state of Israel. Yet the comment also turns a personal memory, at its most subjective, into a public one. In the third person again, Saul describes his young self as, 'a child who saw one world founder and another reborn' (135). The child and the lost (Jewish) world can only be remembered, or forgotten, together: Saul's childhood 'appeared to be buried once and for all' as part of 'the world that had gone under with it' (102).

As the deliberate nature of Saul's affective 'forgetting' suggests – 'since I could not forget the facts, I made up my mind to view everything with indifference' (102) – the 'lost memory' which precedes the writing of *When Memory Comes* was only partial. The facts remained, but their affective meaning was repressed and they remained unrepresentable (Saul suffers 'paralysis' on trying to speak or write about his experiences (102)) until 1977 in Israel.[14] Because of this separation it is hard to tell whether Paul-Henri's decision to become a Jesuit priest is a belief or a performative act, even though Saul uses an unusually expressive verb to describe this decision: 'I soon *felt* a vocation: I wanted to become a priest' (110, my italics). The opposition recorded in *When Memory Comes* is one between memory and knowledge in the sense that the former suggests the recall of feeling, the latter the recall of fact. The way is laid open for viewing the past with 'the gaze of the historian', as Saul puts it (144), both as a means of seeing his past clearly and as a future vocation.[15]

Saul's escape from his destiny as Paul-Henri, the self-righteous would-be priest and teller of antisemitic stories (119), occurs almost because of a single question of totemic resonance, put to him by Father L. at the Sodality: ' "Didn't your parents die at Auschwitz?" ' (137). Learning the details of the extermination of the Jews, among whom were his parents, releases Paul-Henri not only to consider himself as Jewish, 'no longer despite myself or secretly, but through a sensation of absolute loyalty' (138), but in the same moment to start to remember his own past – his parents' is radically different from his. Saul claims that 'Had I been born of a "really" Jewish family, at least I would have had coherent memories' (139). It sounds as if Saul imagines both that the memories themselves would have been given logic through Jewishness itself; and that a more Jewish self would have resisted the metamorphosis into Paul-Henri Ferland, who 'had no remaining link to the Jews' (139). In fact it is Paul's age and circumstances rather than his upbringing which make him susceptible to another lifestyle.

Saul's memoir conveys the difficulty of remembering rather than its completion, and the same is true of his retrieval of Jewishness. Despite the final line of the memoir, which belatedly describes Saul's arrival – 'Out of the darkness there loomed up before us the land of Israel' (186) – Zionism does not represent Saul's homecoming either. He remains outside all his worlds as a 'spectator'.[16] *When Memory Comes* ends without resolution, apart from its own existence and the effort that it represents. Unlike Perec's *W*, it ends without abreaction either, to use the Freudian term for the emotional discharge of, and liberation from, the affect 'attached to the memory of a traumatic event'.[17] In *W* the adult Georges, the narrator, declares that 'writing is the memory of their [my parents'] death and the assertion of my life' (42); it does not matter that he can remember even less of his childhood or Jewish background than

Saul, and the text becomes the memorial or epitaph Georges' parents do not have. Part of the reason for the incompleteness of mourning[18] in *When Memory Comes* arises from the temporality of the present-day part of the text. As a diary it constructs an immediate present, suggesting a retrospective view only of the childhood memories, not of the moment of writing or what followed. Only Paul is scrutinized, not Saul.

'Only part of the truth survived' (2): Shlomo Breznitz, *Memory Fields*

The second temporally divided text I will consider is Shlomo Breznitz's *Memory Fields: The Legacy of a Wartime Childhood in Czechoslovakia*. Breznitz was born in Bratislava in 1936; he and his sister spent four years being sheltered in a convent orphanage by the Sisters of St Vincent in Zilina. Both Breznitz's parents were deported to Auschwitz and only his mother survived. The subtitle of Breznitz's first-person memoir appears revealingly misleading: *Memory Fields* is not so much about the 'legacy' of Shlomo's wartime childhood (except in so far as the text itself constitutes that legacy) as about the childhood itself. The past takes narrative precedence over the post-war present, which is narrated in irregular interjections often set within square brackets,[19] or set apart by spaces and ellipses. The moments from the present take in many periods from 1959 to the moment of writing.

   Memory Fields bears some superficial resemblances to *When Memory Comes*, due in part to the similar nature of the boys' experiences. The adult Shlomo tries to reconstruct his father from dimly remembered scenes, and the child (known as Juri at the convent) understands that a momentous separation is taking place when he sees his father cry for the first time (31). Like Saul in *When Memory Comes*, Shlomo, the adult narrator of *Memory Fields*, speculates on his father's unaccountable failure to rescue the family: 'Could it be that Hitler's conquest and systematic persecution of the Jews came to him as a surprise? [...] Can one gamble on one's family?' (66). The adult Shlomo writes in the present of January 1991 amid Iraqi attacks on Tel Aviv (65), just as Saul wrote at another moment of political uncertainty in Israel's history, during the time of Anwar Sadat's visit in 1977. But the most striking feature Breznitz's text shares with Friedländer's is the 'freezing of feelings'.[20] In *Memory Fields* this does not take the form of being unable to recall the emotional content of past scenes, as in *When Memory Comes*, but describing emotive scenes without affect in the present. While Friedländer's is a text concerned with a forgotten childhood and feeling, *Memory Fields* is about a photographic, 'eidetic' memory (83) which constitutes both the plot and narration.

This overlap of form and content in *Memory Fields* is clearest in the two striking episodes in which Juri transcends his hidden status due to his powers of memory – episodes about which the narrator is able to supply detail photographically. In the first, the commander of the local German garrison visits the convent at Christmas; Juri and his sister Judith are the only children among the orphans who can sing 'Silent Night' in German. As they sing, however, Juri realizes, as the pressure of the Mother Superior's hand on his increases, that the children are giving themselves away by their very success :

> In a flash I finally understood: Why was it that the two of us were the only ones to know the German version of this song? Where were the rest? There were no others because in this country only Jews (*Jews*) understood German. The person above the medals must have known this, too; after all, it was he who had trapped us. (80)

The commander signals his own understanding nobly, however, and reassures the children by telling them in German that their parents will return. Shlomo describes Juri and Judith sobbing at this message; the commander comforts Judith, while Judith tends to her brother. However, the narrator separates himself from this episode; he recognizes its dramatic irony and in doing so strips it of affect. Shlomo completes his narration of the scene with a distancing irony: 'Mother Superior tried to join in, but, realizing that all the major slots were filled, she abstained, and eventually she sat down.'

In the second such episode, to a local prelate Juri seems to fulfil a church tradition that a Jewish orphan would be a future Pope when he recites Latin liturgy from memory. Shlomo again reproduces in full the dialogue between the boy and the prelate, and recalls that Juri was transfixed by the hair growing out of the older man's ears (104) and by his need to go to the toilet. The narrator deliberately distances us from the prelate's questions by an adult analogy for the boy's confusion:

> So it was the indirect approach, like a fianchetto in the chess opening. The bishop (should be prelate) is developed sideways but sooner or later commands the long diagonal. (105)

As in the 'Silent Night' scene, the narrator recognizes schematic form rather than emotive meaning: while this form was the irony of a play in the former, in the second it is a game of chess. The irony in both cases depends on an absolute contrast between Jewish and Christian worlds during the Holocaust years – in two episodes where hidden children's Jewishness becomes explicit – symbolized by the child Juri's puzzlement at adult concerns. Although he and his sister quickly realize the implications of singing 'Silent Night' in German, Juri does not discover why the prelate was so interested in him until after the war. Affect is not missing from *Memory Fields*, but in both these episodes it is described and not reproduced.

Memory Fields is characterized by a disavowal rather than a forgetting of emotion, and as this takes place as an act of narration the reader is a witness to the act of suppression. In *Memory Fields* this suppression of affect takes several forms. Each chapter has an epigraph from writers as diverse and unexpected as T.S. Eliot, Coleridge and Ivy Compton-Burnett; the effect of this is to subsume the child Juri's experience back into common culture – as if such quotations can aptly sum up what he experiences. The same is true of the adult Shlomo's habit of distancing his memories by surrounding them with an everyday discourse, again in square brackets, of similar events, psychological speculations or other comparisons. For instance, one chapter is entitled 'Lessons in Cruelty' and prefaced by an epigraph from J.A. Froude's *Party Politics*: 'Fear is the parent of cruelty.' Shlomo describes how Juri's bread was stolen from him by another boy at the convent in the 'simplest type of cruelty' (50).

General 'lessons' are drawn from very specific events; and comparisons are made with less extraordinary ones. For instance, Shlomo follows up his description of the remarkable scene in which Juri is called upon to demonstrate his complete memory of the Latin liturgy to the prelate by observing, within square brackets, 'During my long years of university teaching, I have always been intrigued by the fright – indeed, the total panic – of most students taking oral examinations' (103). The reader may not agree that this is the most interesting question to arise from what Shlomo has just described; but it is a way for him to control the past, by implying that the present can cast helpful light on it. At the same time, this musing slows down the action, putting off the resolution of this part of the story, in a demonstration of narrative and affective control. Rather than representing the violence of the past as semiotic eruptions into the fiction of the present, in *Memory Fields* the story is told with rationality and calm even when what is told is the opposite. Indeed, such rationality is the effect of the text's split narration, and perhaps the force of the subtitle's use of the term 'legacy': Shlomo's comments on the past unite it with his present,[21] even though he admits that he sometimes cannot determine what really happened (63), and the text is full of the rhetorical questions of unknowability (66).

'I have no childhood memories' (6): Georges Perec, *W or the Memory of Childhood*

Georges Perec's novel *W or the Memory of Childhood* appears at first sight to be divided between two different narratives: one fictional, the other autobiographical. The fictional part consists of a detailed description of the island of W, which is devoted solely to state-regulated sporting competitions of great savagery. In the memory part of *W*, the older Georges tries to unearth and make sense of the 'scraps' (68) of childhood memory he possesses. The conjunction 'or' in the book's title seems to imply that the reader must choose between the two interleaved texts – the science-fiction, or 'utopian', fantasy about the island W, or Perec's childhood autobiography. However, like an alternative subtitle to an eighteenth-century novel, both refer to the same events.

On second sight, Perec's book is more complex than even this makes it sound. *W* is a novel, so what appears to be non-fictional autobiography is in fact fictionalized,[22] while the fictional part turns out to be allegorically about the historical reality of the camps. Each of the two narratives is itself divided into two. This is clearer in the fantasy portion, as has been noted by various commentators.[23] The novel begins with a realist pre-amble, in which a first-person narrator, an army deserter, is told of the search for a child named Gaspard Winckler whose name he has been given. The boat the child was on went down near Tierra del Fuego, and although everyone on board, including the boy's mother, was killed, Gaspard's body was never found. This is followed, after '*points de suspension*' or ellipses – the mark (***) on an otherwise blank page (61) – by a third-person account of the island of W, again somewhere off the coast of Tierra del Fuego. The autobiographical half of *W* is also divided into two, however, separated by the same ellipses. The second begins after Georges has recounted the deportation of his mother to Auschwitz.[24] Indeed, the single memory referred to with surprising literalness in the title of *W or the Memory of Childhood* is recounted in this initial section: 'The only surviving memory of my mother is of the day she took me to the Gare de Lyon, which is where I left for Villard-de-Lans in a Red Cross convoy' (26).

The two narrative modes – fictionalized autobiography and symbolic[25] fantasy – are linked, both by the 'threads' described by the narrator Georges, and also in a different way: as if one story were the lining of the other, invisible but essential to its construction. Despite appearances, both are about the child Georges. In the autobiographical sections of the text, set in plain type, the older Georges describes and dissects the 'pseudo-memories' (14) of his forgotten childhood; and in the fantasy parts, set in italics, about the authoritarian 'sports state' (72), a different narrator puts forward what we are told is a story Georges invented at the age of bar mitzvah, thirteen (6).

Indeed, despite the accurate observation by many critics that *W* is hard to read due to its bifurcated structure, and that it is hard to detect why these two stories are placed side by side,[26] Perec's own preface makes almost disappointingly clear the fact that the alternating tales are 'inextricable', and that it is precisely their 'overlapping' that constitutes the text's meaning (v; this statement appears on the back of the French edition in place of a blurb).[27]

At its simplest, the preface suggests that the genocidal mass murder of the Holocaust, which the child Georges lived through as a 'witness' (1) but did not experience, underlies and invisibly constitutes the childhood memories which appear free of it. Georges' knowledge of the war and his personal losses – the death of his father in combat, his mother at Auschwitz – reappear obliquely in his tale of a totalitarian Olympic state: this is true for the child, who cannot otherwise express his historical knowledge, as much as for the reader. The 'overlapping' takes place only in the act of reading, and at the brief moments in *W* when the textual rationale for the chilling 'sports state' tale is made suddenly clear. The first of these moments occurs at the beginning of *W*, where the two narratives start off in a mingled form. The narrator speaks figuratively of his efforts to find out about the Holocaust (a word he never uses) as a journey to W, in language which enlists the image of the sports-state dystopia:

> Gradually, I forgot the uncertain adventures of the voyage. But those ghost towns, those bloody contests (I believed I could still hear the shouting), those unfurled, wind-whipped banners came back to live in my dreams. [...] For years I sought out traces of my history, looking up maps and directories and piles of archives. I found nothing, and sometimes it seemed as though I had dreamt, that there had been only an unforgettable nightmare. (3)

Here the terms of the two stories are genuinely inextricable. The same words do double duty for the Nazi occupation of France and the deathly Olympic competitions on W ('bloody contests'). The elusiveness of remembering an event to which one was a 'witness' without being an 'actor' (4) in it simultaneously refers to the Holocaust and the improbably dark fantasy of W ('unforgettable nightmare'). Both terms of a metaphor are clearly present here. Despite the text's concern with reversibility, though, it does seem that the metaphorical structure is stable: the Holocaust is the signified in both narratives and only fleetingly or obliquely the signifier (it is mentioned as 'History with a capital H [...] the war, the camps' (6) which substitutes for Georges' childhood memories). In the rest of the text the signifier and signified are wrenched apart and represented separately – hence the alternating, parallel narratives.[28]

The island of W is in fact metonymic as much as metaphoric of Nazi genocide, as the associations it may spark off in the reader as s/he tries to decode *W*'s plot are actual links between Nazism and sport – the use of sports facilities such as the Vélodrome d'Hiver (a winter cycling-track) in Paris as centres for rounding up and deportation;[29] the 1936 Olympics; Nuremberg rallies; the cult of fitness; the transformation of humiliation and murder into 'games'.[30]

The two terms of the metaphor are restored to closeness at the end of *W*, where the Holocaust as the historical signified bursts through the fantastic signifier of W: '*[The Men] must get out of their compounds – Raus! Raus! – they must start running – Schnell! Schnell! – they must come into the Stadium in impeccable order!*' (155). The 'threads' of connection between the two narratives (v, 12, 55)[31] resolve into a twisted skein: the older Georges describes the 'Athletes' as if they are undisguisedly camp inmates dressed in 'striped gear', bald, emaciated and 'ashen-faced' (161). This gives way to an irruption of Holocaust signifiers out of the heart of W, as its impregnable Fortress[32] turns out to be the site of encrypted memory. The person who gains access at last to the Fortress will discover

the subterranean remnants of a world he will think he had forgotten: piles of gold teeth, rings and spectacles, thousands and thousands of clothes in heaps, dusty card indexes, and stocks of poor-quality soap. (162)

The final chapter of *W* belatedly reveals the text's origin in the combination of a twelve-year-old boy's drawings of 'stiff' and 'inhuman' sportsmen engaged in 'unending combats', with a passage from David Rousset's *L' Univers concentrationnaire* which obviously stuck in the narrator's mind during his researches into his own past. ' "Anything can be turned to sport" ', Rousset reports amid a sickening description of humiliations and punishments which ape gymnastics or competitive games (163).

As in Perec's preface, the interwovenness of the text's two narratives is emphasized, but unlike the extra-textual assertion of this fact at the novel's beginning, here the older Georges lays bare the devices of his text while remaining within it. The boy's lost and indirect memory of the war emerges in his drawings of sporting figures who are really soldiers; while the guards in charge of Rousset's 'punishment camps' are brutal sportsmasters who are really the SS.[33]

W represents a division between knowledge and affect in the way that *When Memory Comes* and *Memory Fields* do, but in reverse. Although the narrator claims that, 'like everyone else' (12), he has 'no childhood memories' (6),[34] it seems rather that, as in Friedländer's case, the disappearance or deliberate forgetting of Georges' private history is due to the overwhelming nature of public history (6). Georges recalls or reacts with affect, even if the 'idea' to which the affect was originally attached is lost. For instance, when a strange woman who turns out to be his aunt Berthe comes to visit the child Georges the narrator reports, 'I have an absolutely vivid memory not of the whole scene but of the sense of disbelief, hostility and mistrust which I felt' (105).

The older Georges admits that some of the events he recalls did not actually happen to him but were 'invented or borrowed' (135). The belated temporality which characterizes *W* is divided clearly between the fantasy and memory sections. This occurs most strikingly in a horrible detail about the death of Gaspard Winckler's family at sea in the region of W; his mother Caecilia had been crushed by a trunk during a storm, and although dead when rescue came had clearly spent a long time trying to free herself: 'her fingernails had made deep scratches in the oak door' (58). This death seems to be an obvious 'thread' between W and the Holocaust, partly because it reproduces the death of Georges's mother at Auschwitz, and because it may remind the reader of a striking detail from Alain Resnais' 1955 documentary film *Night and Fog*: a gas chamber at Auschwitz is shown, in which the only literal trace of its past is the finger-nail scratches in the ceiling. Later the older Georges appears to provide a source for the detail of Caecilia's death in recalling a concentration camp exhibition he saw after the war, including 'photographs of the walls of the gas chambers showing scratchmarks made by the victims' fingernails' (158). The placing of these details shows a reverse temporal logic: the fictional account of Caecilia precedes the account of the biographical incident that inspired it. I would argue that both are fictional, and that Resnais' film is a much more likely source for this detail than a photograph in an exhibition.[35] What *W* shows is that childhood memories from the Holocaust era may not be what we expect. They may effectively conceal their subject (as in the science-fiction sections of the text), represent it tangentially (as in Georges' conjecture that his memory of having a medal ripped off actually represented a star being pinned on) or so obliquely it is barely present (Georges' one memory of his father is of his giving the child a gold key or coin, he is not sure).

'All the threads were broken' (*W or the Memory of Childhood*, 55): Conclusion

Finally, I will consider the 'threads' which connect the different parts of each of these narratives. In Friedländer's *When Memory Comes* and Breznitz's *Memory Fields*, the non-fiction genre means that the connections between past and present can be made explicitly (for instance, Shlomo's association of the smell of baked mud with his father: 'To this day such a smell brings out in me a mysterious feeling of excitement. Here is one such occasion' from 1959 (10) – a link which omits the Holocaust years) if not always expected (for instance, the comparison made in *When Memory Comes* between Israel in 1977 and France in 1939). For both narrators, the threads are valued as a means of access to an otherwise vanished past. However, Shlomo's effort to reach fullness of memory is more successful than Saul's; what he says of an incident explained to him after the war is generally true of his memoir: 'Suddenly, certain things that I had not comprehended when they happened made more sense' (109).

In Perec's *W* such threads of connection are implicitly denied. Yet its fictional nature means that the different sections of each are in fact closely 'stitched' together in various ways.[36] The division of *W* into two halves does not ostensibly follow a temporal pattern and the threads are not as clearly diachronic links between past and present as they are in Friedländer's and Breznitz's texts. Rather, fictionalized autobiography in *W* is synchronically interleaved with science fiction, a generic opposition which resolves itself in the common image of the camps. That is, the camps themselves are the central thread linking the two halves of *W*. Georges claims that he does not know the location of the 'break' in the 'threads' attaching him to childhood (12). It seems plausible that such a rupture could have occurred after his mother saw him off at the Gare de Lyon, before the 'points de suspension' dividing parts one and two of both narratives.[37] However, it is not the links that alter after the ellipses, it is the text itself which changes: Gaspard Winckler no longer tells the tale of W and his place is taken by an impersonal narrator. Indeed, for all three texts the threads are not simply a device but the very subject of representation, either as a connection between past and present; or the bar beneath a particular signifier which both demands and denies access to the suppressed signified of fact, or to another signifier of memory.

2
Choral Narration

This unusual way of narrating what happened to large groups of children consists of anthologies of the voices of children, whose oral or written experiences have been collated.[1] 'Choral' works do not distinguish narrators or characters in the usual way, as no individual details of names, ages or – in some cases – gender are given, so the children whose voices we read are anonymous. Such anonymity contrasts with other examples in this study, which are all by individuals whose experiences and suffering were extremely particular and often undergone alone.

Choral narration is especially unusual in contrast to the habitual emphasis in Holocaust memory on naming and the retrieval of individual identity. This unsettling form of narration is well suited to representing children's experiences. Especially if the children are from similar backgrounds, what they undergo and the details they remember are often very alike; paradoxically this similarity increases rather than reduces the reader's sense of calamity. Claudine Vegh's 'choral' work *I Didn't Say Goodbye* recounts the memories, thirty-five years on, of French children whose parents were deported during the war; her interviewees are given first names only. The title of the collection itself refers to a refrain heard throughout the interviews. One of the interviewees, Paulette, draws attention to the paradoxical transformation of individual into general trauma in these 'choral' accounts: 'It's the same as for everybody else: I was in hiding, my father was deported, and he didn't come back, my mother found a replacement. That's all, I've told you everything.'[2]

In this chapter, I will discuss Clara Asscher-Pinkhof's fictional short stories in *Star Children*, Henryk Grynberg's edited collection of testimonies, *Children of Zion*, and Karen Gershon's 'collective autobiography', *We Came as Children*. In all these cases, and in Vegh's work, choral narration has been chosen to represent the experience of children who were Holocaust 'evaders'. Although Asscher-Pinkhof describes the internment of Dutch children in Bergen-Belsen and Grynberg the slave labour undergone by Polish children in the Soviet Union, those whose stories or voices we read escaped and survived: *Star Children* and *Children of Zion* are narratives of Zionist escape, while *We Came as Children* concerns the assimilation of refugee children in Britain.

Stories of redemption: Clara Asscher-Pinkhof, *Star Children*

The Dutch author Clara Asscher-Pinkhof began writing about the 'star children' – her term for Jewish children in Holland, made to wear stars on their clothing from May 1942 onwards – during the war, and completed her book *Star Children*[3] in 1946. She had been liberated from Bergen-Belsen in July 1944 and sent to Palestine as part of a group exchanged for German prisoners of war.[4] Asscher-Pinkhof was a children's writer before the war, and although *Star Children* is published as a young adult's book in Germany and Holland, in the USA – where the English translation was published – it is presented as a book for adults.[5] *Star Children* consists of short chapters, each about a single child, arranged according to what Hans Keilson calls the phases or 'sequences of persecution or traumatization'.[6] The text's chapter-headings follow the trajectory of Jews under Nazi rule in Holland. This descent begins in 'Star City', then moves to the internment centre 'Star House', from where people are deported to 'Star Desert', and finally to a concentration camp outside Holland, 'Star Hell'. Although the locations are referred to throughout *Star Children* by their fictional and not by their actual names, each has a clear historical referent: 'Star City' is Amsterdam, 'Star House' is the Joodse Schouwburg Theatre where Jews were interned before deportation to Westerbork ('Star Desert'), a staging post for Bergen-Belsen ('Star Hell'). These fictional names have more than an allegorical irony, as they depend on the name actually given to Belsen's barracks for Dutch exchange Jews, which was 'Star Camp'.[7] Asscher-Pinkhof's symbolic use of 'star' both draws upon and ironizes this odd nomenclature, which she reads backwards into the stages of Dutch Jewish life preceding imprisonment in the camp.

The structure of the text, as a descent into increasingly persecutory measures, clearly unites temporal and spatial markers to create its meaning. In this way *Star Children* relies upon what Mikhail Bakhtin calls 'the chronotope': the means by which a particular text unites images of time and space.[8] In *Star Children* geographical locations are used to convey the passage of historical and personal time. We know that time is passing because locations change and conditions get worse – the stories move from privation in 'Star City' to camp existence in 'Star Hell'. The choral format becomes another chronotopic indicator as we do not follow the fate of a single person, nor do we read more than one story about any character.[9] We are not in the realm of biographical time, but historical time; we understand what is happening and when because of this broad view, not because details are provided. If locations chart the passage of time in *Star Children*, then time itself is multiply constructed. We are given no dates, and the specific temporal markers mentioned are cyclical ones. Because we learn that deportations from Star House take place on Tuesdays, we read stories concerning successive Tuesdays; in Star Desert and Star Hell there are stories set on Jewish festivals (Hanukkah (173), Purim (226), Passover (227), Shavuot (234)). The text's chronotope appears to represent the viewpoint of a Jewish child, but it also makes the text appear more mythic than actual.

Yet the 'choral chronotope' of *Star Children* does a double duty because, underlying the mythic, cyclical temporal mode, is the representation of a specific historical episode, the internment in Belsen of a group of Dutch Jews to be exchanged for German prisoners.[10] This episode is never explicitly described, but it is indicated by small signs, most strikingly Asscher-Pinkhof's decision to name the text's locations after the Belsen barracks, 'Star Camp'. There are other specific historical indicators: in 'French' a young girl reads some graffiti apparently referring to the Warsaw Ghetto Uprising, implicitly dating this episode from 'Star Hell' to some time after mid-May 1943. Immediately afterwards we learn that at the time of Shavuot the children have been in the camp for six months (235), locating the action in the summer of 1944. The exchange itself took place in July 1944. The children's ignorance of dates and events is echoed by the text, which reproduces only the kinds of temporal sign a child might notice; and this fidelity to restricted viewpoint coalesces with the text's mythic leanings.

Star Children is narrated from the viewpoint of an adult observing children – and also addressing them, if we read the book as one for young adults – using the mingling of narratorial and character's discourse typical of free indirect discourse. The translators observe that 'the sketches were written from a child's point of view' and that this accounts for 'the simple word choice, the straightforward style, and the references to horrors in naïve and innocent terms' (16), and indeed this seems to be the case at first. For instance, the German 'Green Police' are never described or fully named, but referred to as 'the men in green'

(26 and passim);[11] the commandant of 'Star City' is called 'the mightiest power' (91, 108); righteous gentiles are 'aunts without stars' (168); even the phrase 'star children' sounds like the word of a child. But the narrative voice in *Star Children* is always that of an adult, not only in those stories which are about children so young that their voice cannot feature at all (for instance 'A Laundry Basket Full', 77–80), or in the development of a performative metaphor to describe the bathetic use of the theatre as a holding-station (120–1).

Use of free indirect discourse[12] allows the adult voice to disguise itself by taking on some features of children's language rather than genuinely mingling the registers on an equal footing: childlike discourse is the pretext for what turns out to be a myth of salvation. It is often clear that the stories' viewpoint is that of an adult, for instance in this sentence: '[The men in green] shout everything they have to say; they cannot do otherwise' (128). The first clause could be a child's discourse; the second can only be that of an adult seeing the scene without a child's local view. In the story 'See Again' an adult's voice is only thinly cloaked in childish accents when discussing those who sheltered 'star children': 'It was not permitted, was it, to hide star children and take care of them and be good to them, you go to prison for doing that, if it is noticed' (168). In the same sketch again it seems that the narrator has got into the habit of using a child's discourse for straightforward narration: 'There are penal barracks where grown-ups go if they had hidden and then were found. They must work very long hours and wear strange blue overalls with red shoulders' (170).

It seems that the agenda of *Star Children* is near to the surface in these examples – the childlike discourse is used as a method of emphasizing the absurdity of the Nazis' policies, most particularly when these were directed against children. This is a polemical defamiliarization which both acts on behalf of the 'star children' and uses them as a symbol. Again, the text's choral construction forms a central part of this project. In 'They Put Their Heads Together' the narrator describes educational activities in 'Star Hell', such as Hebrew lessons: 'You can understand only the few boys who know a mouthful of Hebrew – if you yourself know Hebrew, that is!' (223). Within a single sentence the object of the narrator's free indirect discourse shifts from one child to another – from the one who can recognize Hebrew to one who cannot. This reveals, or, rather, emphasizes the fact that at no point is an individual child's voice being cited; the text is impressionistic rather than realist; and the narrator's viewpoint takes precedence, rather undemocratically, over the voices of the generalized characters.

Elsewhere, straightforward omniscience takes over: in 'Packages' only the narrator knows how a boy's neighbours sent him his atlas from home: 'He will never know how they found it' (144). An apocalyptic version of omniscience is even more striking: 'Their [the children's] might reaches to the end of the world – to eternity' (156). This religious discourse is an extreme version of adult omniscience, uttered over the heads of the children it is about: 'The broken heart will be saved, that will remain – remain – together with all the other broken little hearts – until the end of days' (162). The notion of a child addressee makes most sense here, as the kind of reader who needs to be reassured that the star children's story is not – despite its context – one with 'an unhappy ending' (229). Within the text's narrative of the group of Jewish prisoners exchanged for German prisoners in 1944, this is true: there was a happy ending for them, and, like Thomas Keneally's *Schindler's List*, this is an unrepresentative Holocaust story.[13] Even the text's effort to commemorate the deaths of the majority is redemptive: the narrator notes that we have just read about 'a handful of star children chosen by chance from the crowds' of those other 'star children who did not live long and happily, whose stars were torn off by God Himself and placed among the other stars in the heavens, as eternal evidence' (255).

The other effect of the narrator of *Star Children* adopting the discourse of children is that of pathetic irony: that is, the adult narrator makes the reader aware of the pathos of the child's situation, to which the child is oblivious, without explicit comment to that effect. The sketch 'Merry Child' concerns a child who is delighted that at six she is old enough to wear a star, 'something marvelous and new', but regrets that as everyone else at school is also six she will not be the only one (28). The story's apparent epiphany is the child's realization that ' "it's not entirely nice, that star" ' (29). However, the story's actual epiphany[14] is reserved for the (adult) reader, who sees both that the star should be a source of pride, and that only someone of great innocence could continue to believe this notion. The same is true of another story, 'Must', in which a child cannot understand what her grandfather means when he says he was deported 'voluntarily' along with the rest of his family. The little girl's idea of obligation and necessity clashes with that of the Nazis: her grandfather says he did not ' "have to go" ' and therefore has ' "gone voluntarily" '; she disputes this, saying that indeed ' "you *had* to, Grandfather" ' since otherwise he would have been left alone. As in 'Merry Child', the child in 'Must' speaks the truth even as she gets it hopelessly wrong, and that is the sense we are left with as the grandfather adopts her way of using the verb 'must': he agrees with a confusing paradox, ' "That's why I had to go voluntarily" ' (100). The pathetic irony of this situation is that the little girl may be instinctively right, but the Nazis' sense of 'must' has the upper hand.

The gentle, morally stable device of pathetic irony in *Star Children* fits well with its focus on a particular and unusual episode in the history of Belsen. Indeed, the phrase 'star children' comes to have its own redemptively ironic meaning: all the children we read about are in the end saved as part of the exchange; none dies; the 'star' stops signalling malign difference and instead marks the children out for life. The children's viewpoint is vindicated: the little girl in 'Merry Child' was justified in being pleased with her star, the boy in 'After Eight' right to be glad his parents were forced to stay at home more often (50).

A 'documentary tale': Henryk Grynberg, *Children of Zion*

Henryk Grynberg's text *Children of Zion* is unusual and initially difficult to read, an effect which is the result of particular editorial strategies. By the end, however, the reader will feel that Grynberg has successfully structured his text to mirror its 'difficult' content. In *Children of Zion*, Grynberg has taken material from an archive of interviews gathered in Palestine in 1943 by the Polish Eastern Center for Information; he describes his role as one of 'selecting and arranging' this material (xi). The interviewees were the 'Tehran Children': young, often orphaned Polish Jews who were allowed to leave the Soviet Union for Palestine through Iran under the 1941 Sikorski–Stalin agreement between the Polish-government-in-exile and the Soviet government.[15] Grynberg has placed his chosen 'fragments' (ix) from these interviews in short, chronologically arranged paragraphs. Each new paragraph represents a different voice, so that the same event is narrated several times by different voices, for instance on the forced deportation of Polish exiles to Siberia in 1940:

> On Friday evening the NKVD surrounded the streets and told us to pack our things.
> On Friday evening the NKVD men appeared. [...]
> On Friday, in the night, NKVD men made a thorough search of our house, then took us to the station. (74)

This almost liturgical repetition is partly due to the questionnaire format of the original testimonies, which has produced responses that are uncannily alike. It is also the result of Grynberg's editorial decisions, which have constructed a text with a strongly Jewish form, as the extract above suggests: the reader is reminded that it is usually something rather different – the Sabbath – that begins on Friday evening.

By these means the events of August 1939 to late 1943 are narrated: many Jews living in the border area of Poland when it was divided between Germany and the Soviet Union elected to go to Russia, but were resettled – along with many non-Jewish Poles – in camps near the Arctic circle and in the central Asian republics of Kazakhstan and Uzbekistan for forced labour in very harsh conditions.[16] Poles in the Soviet Union were granted an amnesty after the Nazi invasion of Russia in 1941, but the conditions in which they travelled away from Siberia were felt by many to be worse than those endured in exile (132). By March 1942, 871 Jewish children had arrived in Tehran (x),[17] most of whom departed for Palestine around a year later.

Yet it is not just the narration of these events, remarkable though they are, with which *Children of Zion* is most concerned; nor is it the individual children, who remain anonymous within the body of the text.[18] It is precisely the 'recasting' (x) of the original interview material which is significant, and which slows down and defamiliarizes not only the process of reading but our view of the events themselves. The importance of Grynberg's editorial structure is even clearer when his text is compared with two other compilations of testimonies by the 'Tehran Children'. First, Irena Wasilewska's *Suffer Little Children* was published in 1946, before the fate of the children was resolved. Wasilewska was herself deported to a penal labour-camp in the far north of the Soviet Union, and after the amnesty of 1941 became a social worker for children; the material in her 'documentary' text is composed from 'letters, reminiscences and tales' sent to her by children she knew.[19] Wasilewska claims that it is not she but the Polish children[20] who are the book's authors, and that although she has divided the testimonies into chapters and only left out 'unimportant' or potentially harmful material, she has 'added nothing and omitted nothing'.[21] But reading Wasilewska's text alongside Grynberg's emphasizes how much she has added – a narrative voice; and what she has left out – an interventionist editorial strategy. The following quotation reveals that, understandably, given her close involvement in and temporal proximity to the events, Wasilewska did not quite see the potential in her material for a new kind of presentation. Instead, she adheres to a rather conventional mixture of quotation and narration:

'My daddy was a butcher in Kovel' – 'Mine was a weaver in Bialystok', I read. 'My papa was a *soltys* [village elder], and every single person in our village was deported' – My daddy was a pastry-cook in Lvov' – 'Mine was a professor in Vilno'. [...] And now they were travelling together, men, women, and children, who were suddenly and precociously mature. The congestion was indescribable.[22]

Grynberg's *Children of Zion* begins in a strikingly similar way,[23] but he refrains from narratorial comment. This section, entitled 'We Lived Pretty Well', lasts for much longer (3–5) than Wasilewska's few lines:

My father made leather goods. He ran a workshop with several workers, and we lived pretty well.
My father was a hat-maker, and we lived pretty well. [...]
My father manufactured brushes. We were never rich. (5)

Grynberg's editorial hand is perceptible in all of this apparently autonomous material; it is arranged in patterns of father's profession and the great similarity of expression is maximized.

Irena Grudzinska-Gross and Jan Tomasz Gross's 1981 compilation *War Through Children's Eyes* draws on the same archive of children's questionnaires and compositions as Grynberg's *Children of Zion*. Grudzinka-Gross and Gross have followed the form of the documentation itself, arranging the testimonies according to the children's original area of residence in eastern Poland; each deposition is by a child identified by first name and initial, and each is a self-contained statement. Thus although there is progression within each testimony, the text as a whole does not move towards a goal – 'Zion' – in the way *Children of Zion* does. As Grudzinska-Gross and Gross's *War Through Children's Eyes* is one of a series entitled 'Hoover Archival Documentaries' this documentary imperative makes sense, in contrast to Grynberg's much more interventionist approach in a text which belongs to the series 'Jewish Lives'. However, these differing approaches are also the result of the different ethnic histories of which each forms part, even though both texts narrate the same occurrences. *War Through Children's Eyes* concerns a period of great hardship in Polish wartime history, while *Children of Zion* concerns an event which took place on the periphery of the Holocaust. There are some differences between these two events: many Jews initially welcomed the Soviet occupation in preference to the Nazi occupation; they were punished by the Soviets for practising their religion (but so were Catholic Poles); Jewish children describe antisemitic bullying in orphanages after the amnesty and discrimination against them as they tried to leave for Tehran; finally, most of the Jewish children remained in Palestine after the war. Yet the basic similarities in the events recounted, alongside the different ethnic origin of the children whose accounts are used, emphasizes the fact that Grynberg has placed a specifically Jewish, epic cast upon his compilation. Indeed, *Children of Zion* is in part a polemical response to *War Through Children's Eyes*, since Grynberg makes clear in the Preface that he is redressing the 'disproportion' in Grudzinska-Gross and Gross's text, which includes only four out of 120 (130 in the Polish version) testimonies by Jewish children (x).[24]

Children of Zion makes the reader question the relation between historical events and the individuals who experience them in an even starker way than other Holocaust writings.[25] It appears that individuality in Grynberg's text has become so suffused with history that it all but vanishes, as in this description of the arrival in the penal colonies (*'posiolki'*) of the Soviet far east:

> Our *posiolok* was in the Vologda *oblast*.
> Our *posiolok* was in Novosibirsk *oblast*, Seroi region.
> Our *posiolok* was in the Krasnodar *oblast*. (87)

As Michael Bernard-Donals puts it in a discussion of the 'rhetoric of disaster', such repetition (of structure, if not detail) has a profoundly alienating effect on the reader: form and content are matched in this way. Bernard-Donals cites the detail which characterizes Abraham Lewin's chronicle of the Warsaw Ghetto in *A Cup of Tears*: the 'repetitive language of metonym here, in which street names and family names are run together as a litany of destruction, seem[s] alien to both the writer and the reader'. The events 'as they are written – dissolve as experiences'.[26]

Even when one voice is quoted at length in *Children of Zion*, the unemotive narration of horrifying events still makes the utterance appear depersonalized, as in this account of surviving a mass-killing in Wyszków, September 1939:

> I turned my head and saw Mr Stanski. He helped me up and dragged me to the forest. He told me that as soon as he'd heard the shots he'd dropped to the ground and pretended to be dead. [...] The night was so dark we could not see each other, and I lost Mr Stanski in the forest. (22)

This apparent depersonalization is also the effect of what Grynberg calls 'that rare synthesis of child's narration and official report' (x) which he has tried to preserve in his selections, a synthesis which makes *Children of Zion* both difficult to read and particularly effective as a child's-eye-view Holocaust representation. The voices which narrate events in this text do not manifest their children's-eye view by being unknowing or innocent; their childlikeness resides in the description of events rather than emotions, and in their uncluttered clarity of recall.[27] Depersonalization results not only from a necessary suppression of affect, but also from the way this material was gathered. However, the effect on the reader is one of 'intransitivity'; the absence of affective content and description denies her or him the illusion of thinking ' "I know this." '[28]

Although the children's names, ages and gender are not given in *Children of Zion*, their testimonies are full of the kind of detail which usually individualizes accounts of catastrophe. However, in this context such details are so widely shared that they continue the sense of dissipation. This is especially true of accounts of religious observance at this troubled time. During the deportation to Siberia several children note the problems raised by having access only to non-kosher ('*treyf*') food on the journey to Siberia:

> Even though we were famished, my father would not allow us to eat *treyf* soup [...]
> We received four hundred grams of bread daily, and soup – which we did not eat because it was *treyf.*
> My father would not eat the soup because it was *treyf* [...] (79)

Rather than being the distinctive, individual feature that religious observance often is in other Holocaust writing (Eliezer refuses to fast on Yom Kippur in *Night*; a rabbi at Auschwitz gives Vladek in *Maus* hope by reading his tattoo numerologically[29]), the same response repeated in this way in *Children of Zion* has a rote effect, emphasizing the communal and 'choral' aspect of the children's experience. Just at the moment when the communal meaning of the children's tradition is being effaced,[30] it reappears in this textual form. The text's way of charting time often involves reference to the calendar of Jewish festivals, so that Jewish time in *Children of Zion*, as in *Star Children*, is the same as child-time.

Children of Zion has a title which sounds biblical but is actually political. On the one hand the phrase 'children of Zion' is simply a synonym for 'the Jewish people', and thus draws ironic attention to the reason for the events described: being 'children of Zion' once meant divine chosenness, but now means being singled out for mass murder; while on the other hand it refers specifically to the 'Tehran Children' who eventually settled in Palestine as young people fulfilling the Zionist dream. Such a duality is related to the fact that the fate of children is being discussed, as it clearly reveals an adult hand at work. This work is editorial in Grynberg's case; in the case of the similarly mythico-historical *Star Children*, it is narratorial – the latter's quality is partly an extension of Asscher-Pinkhof's role as carer to the children whose stories she narrates.[31]

It may seem at first that the unusual construction of *Children of Zion* has partially thrown off conventional linear historicity. Because of the multiply-voiced and thematic format Grynberg has chosen for the children's testimonies, a new paragraph marks not narrative progression but narrative repetition. For instance, the German occupation of Polish towns in 1939 is told not in one but in seventeen different voices/ paragraphs, culminating in one which describes the fall of Warsaw (19–27). The narrative's habit of progressing only within a single paragraph undoes the usual experience of reading: here, when we reach the end of a paragraph we are thrown back to another which describes almost identical events, or which is another account by a different child of the same town's fate:

> When the Germans entered Dlugosiodlo they shot the first Jew they saw on the street. I do not remember his name, but he was the brother-in-law of our friend Paskowicz. Soon thousands of Jews who had been driven out of Wyszków arrived, nearly naked and barefoot. Poor, tiny Dlugosiodlo had no room for so many people. A communal kitchen was set up, but money was lacking for everything.
> When we got to Dlugosiodlo the town was overflowing with refugees, and we spent the night in a stable. [. . .] (26).

This device of sickeningly circling around the same event without any resolution replaces a conventional linear construction. It has a temporal and narrative radicalism comparable to experiments with narrative and historical time in Holocaust fiction.

However, running apparently counter to the stalled, repetitive narration in *Children of Zion* is a strongly teleological thread, which is the children's destination and our knowledge that they will reach Palestine. Despite the terrible loss of life which takes place during our reading of this text, we know from the outset the provenance of the material quoted and that this is a narrative of survival. In fact, much of the children's experience takes place outside Nazi-occupied Europe, where they would have faced more certain death from the Einsatzgruppen and deportation to death camps, making theirs a story of evading as much as surviving the Holocaust.

Finally, it is significant that Grynberg calls *Children of Zion* an 'epic' (xi), and I would argue that the text we read is a specifically Jewish epic. According to Mikhail Bakhtin epic is characterized by three features:

> (1) a national epic past [...] serves as the subject for the epic; (2) national tradition (not personal experience [...]) serves as the source for the epic; (3) an absolute epic distance separates the epic from contemporary reality, that is, from the time in which the singer (the author and his audience) lives.[32]

If *Children of Zion* is an epic, it is one that is profoundly ironized. The Jews of Poland could not really be said to have had 'a *national* epic past', although they had lived as members of the Polish nation for over a thousand years. Nor is '*national* tradition' exactly the 'source' of this epic; rather, religious and cultural tradition is drawn upon at exactly the moment of its destruction – at least, in this context (as we have seen, the significance of the children's voices in *Children of Zion* is that they speak from Palestine). The 'absolute epic distance' between 'the author and his audience' is partially present here,[33] as the book was edited by a writer living in the US (although Grynberg is himself a child survivor of the Holocaust), and most of the readers of the English edition of the book will indeed be 'distant' from the events recounted. This is in contrast to the adult survivors themselves, one of whom is quoted in Israel Gutman's 'Afterword' as saying, ' "We will always remain the 'Tehran children' " ' (178): for them the past is apparently always present.

Despite this ironic attitude to the epic, *Children of Zion* does possess enough of its features to appear as a 'dark' or 'reversed' epic.[34] The past is closed off in the sense that we witness the end of Jewish life in Poland, and this text is its 'memorial';[35] the individual is not the text's focus: *Children of Zion* relies instead on 'impersonal and sacrosanct tradition' since 'Individual life-sequences are present in the epic as mere bas-reliefs on the all-embracing, powerful foundation of collective life.'[36] As an epic, *Children of Zion* is one which recounts not the foundation – which Bakhtin is concerned with – but the destruction of a community. Although the text concerns the past, as befits an epic, it is the future that it points towards: a future subtended elsewhere, in a different country and outside the text. This goes against Bakhtin's observation about the epic's emphasis on the past as the '*only*' source of anything good; in *Children of Zion* this is all in the future. The way Bakhtin's observation could apply to Grynberg's text is in the implicit Biblical reference of the title: the epic recalled is not the past itself but another text, and *Children of Zion* is a new Exodus.

'Our rescue was quite impersonal':[37] Karen Gershon, *We Came As Children*

Gershon's 'collective autobiography' was published in 1966, composed of the comments of 234 former child refugees to Britain who arrived on the *Kindertransport* trains during 1938 and 1939.[38] In her foreword, Gershon notes that the text was compiled 'in gratitude and as an explanation' (iv): gratitude for the haven offered to over ten thousand children who came to Britain before the war on children's transports,[39] and an explanation both of why many of the children chose to stay at the war's end,[40] and of their adult lives in Britain. As with Henryk Grynberg's compilation *Children of Zion*, the choral format seems to have been chosen as most fitting for an account of escape and survival; although many of the children recount the loss of their families in the Holocaust years, they left their native countries before war broke out. The very notion of the children's voices as a chorus implies that they are not the central figures in the action, but a part of its background. Anonymity is also fitting in such a context; one former child refugee notes of the last moments in Germany, 'It occurred to me there [at the station] that our grief was no longer a personal one' (26). Although the way of representing the *Kindertransport* experience in *We Came as Children* is an individualized one, it is indeed not personal. It contrasts most clearly with conventionally structured memoirs by individual *Kinder*, in which the concern is to name and remember a home-town, lost parents, kind foster-parents and other details, and to present a version of a *Bildungsroman*: the child concerned passes through various stages to emerge as a naturalized subject in an 'adopted land', as the subtitle of Vera Gissing's memoir has it.[41] The contrasting lack of easy adoption emphasized in Gershon's text is matched by its choppy, multiple form.

Gershon, like Grynberg, has arranged her material in short paragraphs, each of which – marked with ¶ – represents a new and unnamed voice. Contributions from those who were not child refugees appear in italics. Gershon's aim, stated in an Editorial Note, is 'that the combination of different voices will have the same effect as a conversation' (vi) – an interesting alternative metaphor to 'chorus', although perhaps less appropriate, as 'conversation' implies an exchange rather than just a presentation of perspectives. Gershon's juxtapositions often appear to emulate a conversational effect: one child relates how at the last minute arrangements to send her or him to Holland were changed and s/he went instead to Britain; the next voice 'answers', 'Some of the children I knew who went to Holland were later returned to Germany and used for medical experiments' (21).

The metaphor of conversation emphasizes the fact that, like Grynberg's, Gershon's role is editorial rather than narratorial; the difference between these two strategies is highlighted by the appearance of what is clearly the same interviewee, using almost identical phrasing, in her text and in another text of a very different kind. In *We Came as Children*, an anonymous former child refugee describes the 'discrimination' he suffered as a boy of sixteen in a foster home, including being given less to eat than anyone else: 'My position was somewhere between that of a poor relative and a domestic servant, without the privileges of the one or the rights of the other' (63). In Marion Berghahn's *Continental Britons: German-Jewish Refugees from Nazi Germany* what appears to be the same interviewee is afforded the partial anonymity of a sociological study ('Mr I'). His plight is narrated – '[The foster-parents] were particularly angered by the *naturally good* appetite of the 16-year-old boy' (my italics) – and Mr I's observation, ' "I was a mixture of servant and poor relation in their house without the rights of either of them" ', is cited to support Berghahn's statement that, 'The majority of the respondents, however, were unhappy'.[42] The democratic juxtapositions of Gershon's non-fictional yet literary text, which draw in the reader as part of the unnarrated 'conversation', contrast with Berghahn's direct sociological commentary.

The fact that Gershon's textual stance is editorial rather than narrational is surprising as she is one of the *Kinder* herself; unlike Gerhard Durlacher, however, who is both character and narrator in his *The Search*, Gershon deliberately withdraws from *We Came as Children*. Her 'sequel', *Postscript: A Collective Account of the Lives of Jews in West Germany since the Second World War*, sets itself up as choral in the same way as *We Came as Children*. In the 'Editorial Note' Gershon repeats the same phrase: 'I hope that the combination of different voices will have the same effect as a conversation',[43] and describes the system used to differentiate the various voices. However, the same format is not as successful when used in this different context. *Postscript* as a whole is distanced from its subject, partly for reasons suggested by its title: this is an aftermath, not the threshold of a future.

We Came as Children is structurally different from other compilations of statements from the *Kinder*, including Bertha Leverton and Shmuel Lowensohn's anthology of former child refugee statements, *I Came Alone: The Stories of the Kindertransports*. This text, especially in contrast with Gershon's, appears barely edited. The former child refugees' statements are arranged alphabetically by surname, and each is given apparently in its entirety; each respondent is fully identified, by current and previous name and home town. Mark Jonathan Harris and Deborah Oppenheimer's *Into the Arms of Strangers: Stories of the Kindertransport*,[44] based on the 1999 documentary film of the same title, resembles *I Came Alone* in giving precisely the information withheld by *We Came as Children*: not only is each 'witness' identified throughout, but a biography is supplied for each at the book's end. Unlike *I Came Alone*, Harris and Oppenheimer's text focuses on the same thirteen *Kinder* whose stories are interleaved throughout in chronological order. The text is both subjective and highly personalized. The editorial strategies of *Into the Arms of Strangers* were clearly strict, including the choice of interviewees, and result in the text's narrative seamlessness despite its several contributors.[45] Both *I Came Alone* and *Into the Arms of Strangers* by their conventionality emphasize the formal importance and innovation of *We Came as Children*.[46]

If *We Came as Children* is a 'thank-offering to Britain' it is an ambivalent one,[47] although it does have a great deal to say about the construct of Englishness. The generosity of Britain and the World Movement for the Care of Children from Germany is a given, since all Gershon's respondents survived the war and then remained in Britain, but their stories cover a huge spectrum of emotional, aspirational and educational experience (although of course the hardships some child refugees underwent is of a different order from the forced labour described in *Children of Zion*).

While Henryk Grynberg's *Children of Zion* presupposes the eventual arrival of children in Palestine, the role of promised land is assumed ironically in *We Came as Children* by Britain.[48] Gershon's 'collective autobiography' is a tale of varieties of assimilation and their triumph when the process begins at an early age and in particular circumstances. Indeed, it is not Britain as a political entity (one naturalized refugee speaks in this sense of her 'beautiful blue British passport' (145)) but England, a mythic location, which takes on the role of promised land in Gershon's text. Although several of Gershon's respondents were placed in Scotland (62, 78, 82), it is always 'Englishness' that is aspired to. The respondents recognize, through living it out, the discrepancy between the formal citizenship offered by Britishness and the informal cultural identity of Englishness, which is even harder to accede to: 'I am no different now to the "bloody foreigner" I was before [naturalization] – I still have my accent' (129); 'I am British though I shall never be English'

(168); 'I am very proud to be British and that our children will be English (that oh-so-subtle distinction)' (163).

The process of assimilation is traced retrospectively in *We Came as Children*, and this retrospection characterizes Gershon's text throughout in both form and content. While the interviews Grynberg used were collected the same year the 'Tehran Children' arrived in Palestine, in Gershon's a quarter century's difference means that adults are recalling distant childhood selves. At the end of Gershon's text the choral effect is at its most pronounced and narrative all but vanishes, precisely because of retrospection – and therefore in a manner unavailable to Grynberg:

¶ I am still a refugee because the scars inside me are too deep.
¶ I am still a refugee because I still feel different
[...]
¶ Home is where one can live with a feeling of permanency.
¶ Home is with my children. (160)

At the beginning of *We Came as Children* the respondents describe the details that summed up the foreignness of Englishness to newly arrived European children, but this is a humorous and affirmative defamiliarization for both British readers and the former child refugees themselves. They mention the difficult pronounciation of 'Harwich' (31), milky tea (36, 97), hard, shiny toilet paper (46), open fires (63), pantomimes (37), and the gradual shedding of 'Germanness' by being forbidden to 'talk German loudly in public; better still not to talk loudly at all' (38). One foster-parent describes such early experiences as a threshold intiating her foster-child into Englishness: '*by the time we arrived home, prolonging the journey by a tour of the Essex countryside and tea at an Old World Cottage, she was one of us*' (48).

In contrast to Grynberg's Jewish epic, Gershon's non-Zionist chronicle of assimilation reveals that the rejection of European origins in Britain also entailed a rejection of Jewish identity.[49] One respondent says: 'To be reminded that I was Austrian, or worse still Jewish, and a refugee child, was an insult' (88). This notion that having Jewish origins disqualifies one from Englishness even more thoroughly than having 'Continental'[50] origins is echoed by others: 'I learned very quickly to omit any reference to my nationality when being introduced to people, and adopted the same attitude to my religion', so as to pretend 'to be as average and English as possible' (89); 'I don't particularly explain that I am Jewish – before the war is such a long time ago that it doesn't matter now' (162), suggesting that Jewishness was a temporal and geographical effect to be left behind. Indeed, Jewishness is shed along with childhood.

The emphasis in *We Came as Children* on assimilation and differences between the European and Anglo-Jewish communities marks a further link between its unusual form and often uncomfortable material. What it narrates is the trauma of transplantation rather than the success of rescue. This is partly due to the self-selecting nature of the voices quoted: even those respondents who remained in Britain in *I Came Alone* are more religiously observant than Gershon's; while histories of the refugee movement often describe it in a far more positive way as the continuation of British Jewry's habit of welcoming other Jews in trouble.[51] However, once more the form of *We Came as Children* offers a clue to these apparent contradictions. It is not just that its chorality and absence of personal detail make it as much a mythic text – and again one with overwhelming historical origins – as Asscher-Pinkhof's and Grynberg's. It is also that the effects of all three texts are *literary*, not sociological or historical. The reader cannot look for accuracy or authenticity in these texts despite the fact that their basis lies, in the case of Grynberg and Gershon, in testimonial material. In his study of the fate of Jewish war-orphans in the Netherlands, *The Sequential Traumatization of Children*, Hans Keilson makes an observation which applies usefully to *Children of Zion* and *We Came as Children*, although it has a different meaning in the context of Keilson's clinical case study:

> In contrast to other artifically created groups [these] Jewish children had a common biography. This factor is important in the conception of the present study. The individual biographies of the Jewish children must be seen against the background of the biography of the group as a whole.[52]

The facts that the Jewish *Kindertransport* children arrived in Britain 'alone' at a young age, often from already assimilated German and Austrian families,[53] just before Britain declared war on their native country, predisposed many of them to try to blend in as effectively as possible. Any description of the child refugees represented in Gershon's text as 'the saved Jewish remnant of the twentieth century'[54] is therefore inaccurate: the children in *We Came as Children* were saved, but not as a specifically Jewish remnant. Similar use of individual yet impersonal choral narration in Grynberg's and Gershon's texts thus has quite different effects. While Grynberg's children live on as Jews – hence his use of an epic form – Gershon's adopt the Englishness which means a 'drift and defection'[55] away from Jewish life.

Conclusion: why choral narration?

The three texts in this chapter are ostensibly of very different genres: *Star Children* is fiction, *Children of Zion* biography, *We Came as Children* autobiography. However, they are drawn together by their concern to represent a body of children's voices. The impetus behind 'choral narration' is partly that it conveys to the reader something of the large-scale cost of the Holocaust, even though in each case it is a 'rescue' that is recounted. The other reason is even more telling, and unites the children's perspective in all the texts with their Holocaust content: since the Jews as a group were the target of persecution, the narrative of Dutch exchange children in Belsen, 'Tehran children' and *Kindertransport* children can only be narrated from the perspective of that group.[56]

The reader of a choral text might expect its structure to allow the voices of the children themselves to be clearly heard, in contrast to novels and testimonies in which the child's voice is subsumed by that of an adult's retrospective narration. In other words, Bakhtin's notion of polyphony, in which the voices of fictional characters are on an equal footing with that of the narrator, might usefully apply to these texts. However, its applicability is different in all three cases. I would say that the narrator of *Star Children* does not credit her fictional subjects with such autonomy; their voices are subordinated to an adult pattern, much as the text's author looked after the real-life children. However, the editorial strategies of Grynberg and Gershon, perhaps unexpectedly, given Bakhtin's preference for fiction as a democratic genre, allow their children's voices greater freedom than this. Although both editors arrange, juxtapose and omit, their adult voices are not heard within the body of their respective texts: we read only those of the Kindertransport and Tehran children.

Further, the children were responding to questionnaires in both cases. Grynberg states this explicitly, and while Gershon does not, the absent questions are still very clear to the reader. For instance, Gershon must have asked her respondents to comment specifically on, for instance, their attitude to Germans (134–7) and to reparations payments (137–8). This technique could be described in various ways. In omitting the original questions which she posed, Gershon the editor appears to have suppressed, but has in fact freed up, a polyphonic potential among her respondents. Their statements are not just part of a formal question-and-answer dialogue, but actually dialogic; meaning is generated by clashes between and within the voices. Unlike a chorus, these voices in the three texts I have discussed comment upon each other in a distinctive representation of the fate of large groups of children.

3
Lost Memories

In this chapter I will discuss three texts – Ingrid Kisliuk's memoir *Unveiled Shadows: The Witness of a Child*, Claude Morhange-Begué's memoir *Chamberet: Recollections from an Ordinary Childhood* and Raymond Federman's novel *The Voice in the Closet* – each of which tries to reproduce the trauma of a Holocaust childhood, and the impossibility of its recollection, by the use of experimental narration. In each case, the figure of the child in the past has not been reconciled with the adult subject in the present, and this disjuncture is reproduced in narrative terms. This is fitting as the adult subject who tries to recall is also the one who writes, and the two acts are, in each case, either interwoven (in Kisliuk's *Unveiled Shadows*) or at odds with each other (in Federman's *The Voice in the Closet*). The child's experience remains unattainable, and the child him- or herself is a figure for lost or impossible knowledge.

In Morhange-Begué's *Chamberet* and Federman's *The Voice in the Closet* in particular, great emphasis is placed on the spatial and geographical location of the originary trauma: respectively, a village in France, and a cupboard in a block of Parisian apartments. Like the child's foreclosed memory, the space of childhood is reproduced narratively, and I have used Mikhail Bakhtin's notion of the chronotope – that figure which unites temporal and spatial markers in a text – to analyse its effects.

Ingrid Kisliuk, *Unveiled Shadows*

Ingrid Kisliuk's memoir *Unveiled Shadows: The Witness of a Child*[1] concerns the effort of memory, emphasized in the narrator's description of this text as the 'account of an adult, unveiling the experiences of a child' (x): the two personas have not been united. The child Inge Scheer[2] left Vienna with her family in 1938, when she was eight, for Belgium; they lived under assumed non-Jewish, non-Austrian identities – Inge became Irène – in occupied Brussels. Ingrid, the adult narrator, describes how she and her parents survived, although her elder sister Herta and other relations were deported to Auschwitz where they died.

Unveiled Shadows represents the act of writing as simultaneous with that of memory; indeed, writing both encodes and provokes memory. Memory is preserved in written documents reprinted in the text – these include letters written by Herta from the Belgian deportation camp Malines, or thrown from a train bound for Auschwitz; and Serge Klarsfeld's listing of all Belgians who died in Nazi camps, *Mémorial de la Déportation des Juifs de Belgique*.[3] Although letters which no longer physically exist are also quoted, it is those kept locked in 'the dreaded "box" ' (xiii) which symbolize the possibility of memory corroborated beyond its own unreliable powers ('Could I honestly say that I recall these events?' (xii)). Memory is provoked in the act of writing itself – 'I never considered that possibility before writing this' (42), Ingrid notes of a detail about a dead relation[4] – and also by the division of the narrative voice into two: that of the adult Ingrid and a second, questioning voice, which often appears in the text in italics. For instance, Ingrid relates how she was searched at the former Austrian border as the family fled towards Belgium, and when money was found in the seam of her coat she sobbed hysterically, unrestrained by her mother:

> *Did she purposely not say anything to you, thinking that your sobbing might dim [the SS man's] anger?*
> Until now, I never considered that a possibility. (25)

This technique resembles the larger-scale narrative splitting in texts by Perec, Friedländer and Breznitz (see Chapter 1). It also resembles the high Modernist experimentation with narrative voice in James Joyce's *Ulysses*, in particular the 'catechism (impersonal)' in the episode 'Ithaca', in which Leopold Bloom and Stephen Dedalus talk late at night, but in which conventional narration has been abandoned in favour of long, digressive questions and answers from a source it is hard to locate. However, the Holocaust memoir form of Kisliuk's text disrupts such a comparison. In *Unveiled Shadows* the splitting of a first-person narrative voice into two takes the form of an intermittent dialogue between Ingrid's narrating self, and a second voice which is sceptical about the precision and accuracy of Ingrid's memory. It is a voice which arises from the process of writing, as Ingrid has to consider placing her memories in narrative order:

> *How strange that you remember what now seem such trivial incidents, whereas you forgot others, much more important episodes of that time. (17)*

The second voice says this in response to Ingrid's memory of family arguments and being bullied by her cousin in the midst of Anschluss Austria; but, as we have seen, this is exactly the oblique yet detailed form taken by children's Holocaust memories. The second voice thus speaks on behalf of a sceptical or bemused reader as well as Ingrid's adult self.

It is often clear that the second voice is a transcription of Ingrid's internal polemic, as Mikhail Bakhtin calls it, and forms a part of the dialogic process of recall. Indeed, it is as if a habit of self-scrutiny in the effort not only to remember but to align different identities has produced this literal double-voicedness, which is often cast in the form of a question demanding a response. For instance, the second voice asks why Ingrid says she was brought up trilingual when in fact she knew four languages: 'You didn't include Yiddish in your inner enumeration of languages. Has your arrogance prevailed through the years?' and retorts to Ingrid's apparently innocent observation that she has nothing left from her time as a child actor in Yiddish theatre, '*Have we here another example of your efforts to eradicate from your mind undertakings of Jewish content in your childhood?*' (50). The second voice appears to be more attuned to the Jewish aspects of Ingrid's memory than the narrator herself; as with Saul's efforts to remember in *When Memory Comes*, to elide the Jewish content of the past is to lose it altogether.

Ingrid remembers her father describing the pre-war death of her grandfather as a reunion with his wife, Ingrid's grandmother, a memory which makes the second voice prompt Ingrid to recall her sister Herta's coded way of describing existence in Auschwitz's universe of death:

> But wait! Didn't Herta use similar words, four years later, in her postcard from Auschwitz?
>
> Yes! That's right, it occurred to me just now! [...] She wrote an enigmatic postcard, addressing my parents by their first names as though they were her friends, and said [...], Contrary to all my expectations I met your mother here. (11)[5]

Yet the second voice is not consistently a force for Jewish memory; rather, it is a self-conscious voice which insists on raising any 'painful' issue

Ingrid would rather forget, such as the lack of foresight among civilians fleeing from Austria in 1938 (68), and the naïvety of Ingrid's parents in returning to their apartment in Brussels from a hiding-place (96). By its very nature the second voice is a backshadowing one, in Michael André Bernstein's phrase, not averse to apportioning responsibility for calamity to its victims; while Ingrid's view is the more sideshadowing one that the past is not fixed in the sense that new interpretations and facts can be retrieved in the present.

The second voice challenges Ingrid to verify the detail of what she reports and questions assumptions about her memories: 'Why on foot, were there no trains?' (66); 'How can you be sure of this event if you cannot actually remember it?' (79). The result of this questioning is not of course increased accuracy, but greater insight into the process of retrieving 'old, painful memories' (x). Indeed, the same could be said of Ingrid's episodes of recall at the moment of writing; this present-time memory is a trope for, rather than an accurate record of, the process of memory. The possibility of healing an internal breach[6] is indicated when Ingrid integrates a question about memory into her first-person narration in describing the liberation of Brussels: 'How did I get to that intersection to watch that marvelous sight of the incoming liberators?' (147); and those parts of the text describing Ingrid's attendance at a Hidden Children's conference and visit to Belgium are narrated in a single first-person voice (169ff.).

In Miriam Winter's memoir *Trains* the same dialogic process of remembering takes a slightly different form. Questions are posed to the adult Miriam by schoolchildren in the present (about why she did not search for her family (22), and why her rescuer Maryla took her in (175)); and Miriam asks herself questions about the young Marysia she once was: 'Did I really understand that my life was at stake?' (74). Miriam answers this question as an adult – 'I knew that I had to hide, but I was only a child and my task was too hard for me' – in the effort not just to remember facts (her father's name, 36–7) but her own internal state. In the present Miriam rereads a diary she began in 1946 at the age of thirteen, but finds her younger self Marysia still opaque:

> I didn't make any entry, not even a camouflaged one, about my Jewishness, nor about my real family. Maryla figures there as Mamusia (Mother) and Rysiu as *Tatus* (Father). After our parting in 1948 I put quotation marks around those words. In revenge or as an editorial comment? Symbolic mutilation? (136)

As in Friedländer's *When Memory Comes* and Breznitz's *Memory Fields*, idea and emotion are separated in *Trains*. Even with the evidence written by her younger self, Miriam cannot reconstruct the emotional or subjective existence of Marysia – partly as a result of the younger girl's 'frozen' (106) interiority.

The title of Kisliuk's memoir *Unveiled Shadows*, with its suggestion of the revelation and reclamation of suppressed and forgotten material, shows in what sense Inge Scheer had a 'hidden' childhood. The young Irène and her family lived in the open but under false identities; they hid aspects of themselves, relying on their daughter as a Belgian spokesperson to cover up the poor language skills and Austrian accents of the parents. Irène herself, Ingrid relates, experienced this as a claustrophobic burden as if she were physically in hiding: 'What to say next to cover the lie became a challenge, until I was totally entangled in a fictitious existence, so much so that since I wished to be that person so badly, I came to feel that I was in some way that other me who kept gaining strength over my true identity.' This is an 'imprisonment in deception' (111).

'I come within an ace of witnessing' (43): Claude Morhange-Bégué, *Chamberet*

Claude Morhange-Bégué's *Chamberet: Recollections from an Ordinary Childhood* resembles Georges Perec's *W or the Memory of Childhood* in its concern with the continuing absence of memory rather than its successful retrieval.[7] Indeed, like memoirs by Patrick Modiano, Miriam Akavia and Pierre Pachet, *Chamberet* is partly a projected or imagined autobiography of someone else.[8] *Chamberet* is about Claude's mother's arrest, her time in Auschwitz and her return to France. It concerns the betrayal and deportation of Claude's mother to Auschwitz on 8 April 1944 when Claude was eight. *Chamberet* is also the account of Claude being saved from the threat of deportation just as her mother was arrested; these two narratives conflict throughout the text. *Chamberet* circles around the precise details of its two primal scenes – the reconstructed arrest of the mother, and the imperfectly recalled rescue of the daughter. The latter is described in terms of its elusiveness:

That silence: I write it and write it again, wanting the words which recreate it and its reality, wanting also a sure idea of the exact order of events, the hands that took me by the shoulders and gently, firmly turned me around toward the door I had just entered by, and through which I must now go back out, this instant, but calmly, without a fuss; wanting a recollection of the words that must have been spoken to me – and spoken to me by who else but the teacher? – giving me instructions to go, to clear out at once, to escape. (4)

The words the adult narrator Claude 'wants' are both those which evade her at the moment of writing in the present,[9] and those which were not uttered at the time; but her re-creation itself includes snatches of the kind of phrase that might have been used: 'this instant', 'clear out at once'. As in the case of Freud's Wolf Man, it is only with the different kind of knowledge of adulthood that this scene makes sense to Claude: 'For *today*, years later, I realize that it was by the skin of my teeth I got away *then*, with my mother in the classroom across the hall, already under arrest and lying with might and main to try to save her only off-spring' (4, my italics). At the time, the child Claude neither saw her mother's arrest nor understood the danger she and her mother were in.

This scene is redescribed many times during the course of *Chamberet* as Claude tries to 'fill in the gaps' from the viewpoint not of increased factual knowledge, but of adult 'imagination' (7). It is a scene of some-thing failing to happen – Claude is not arrested, she does not witness her mother's arrest, nor does she understand until she is older the danger facing her mother, or that she might have been taken too. Indeed the prose Claude uses in the present – with its long, poetic sentences, abstract accounts of the effort of memory (16) and descriptions of the child's world more generally (the garden, 14, her bedroom, 22) – is an effort to substitute for the words and events she cannot remember. Chamberet itself constitutes an ambivalent temporal, rather than geographical, location as the text's eponymous site of the inability to reconstitute or return; Claude notes that the garden and barn at Chamberet no longer exist 'except in my mind' (39). Claude frequently comments on the failure of memory, its devolution into imagination or reconstruction, how it must be supplemented with adult knowledge: 'I do not remember any words being addressed to me; I can't say now whether anything was said at all'; 'there does indeed arise one sentence, be it actual memory or phantasm: *Your mother has been arrested*'; '*I'm going to drop the little one off and I'll rejoin you*, my mother must have told them, but those are my words and I have no idea what hers were' (7); 'To [my grandmother] I want to ascribe some of the words she was to pronounce later on: *Something awful has befallen us*'; 'I no longer know what was said to me'; 'whether I have imagined it, I do not know' (11); 'ah, what might she have said, exactly?' (31).

Claude's uncertainty about utterance marks this text off from the fictive nature of other Holocaust texts which reconstruct dialogue. The words are only approximations, for instance of Claude's mother's promise to the people who took in the little girl: 'And there is no danger in it for you' (19). Such a technique allows the adult narrator to construct her text out of words which are precisely *not* those that were said, but which represent both the misunderstanding of the child and the adult's lost memory. Claude describes 'the language being employed by adults', which she cannot reproduce, as the parentheses show: 'Your mother has been arrested but (you mustn't worry), *but* (she'll come back soon), *but* (you've got to be brave)' (20).

Chamberet represents the effort to reconstruct an event and its meaning from the slightest of memories; indeed, the child Claude did not even witness much of what the older Claude would like to remember. The text's circling and repetitive form goes obsessively over what is in effect a single memory: Claude being silently pushed out of the classroom at the moment when her mother was being interrogated by the Gestapo elsewhere in the school building. It is true that each time Claude retells the memory, reconstructed details are added. But the narrative form of this memory of her mother is quite different from the way in which Claude represents the death of her father, which took place before the period with which the text is concerned. The details emerge only gradually, in the manner of a traumatic memory, although the 'far from clear' (35) facts of Claude's father's death have become no clearer in retrospect. The father was killed in his car, which might have been forced off the road by another driver. This death is reported at the text's outset (4), although the eight-year-old Claude does not understand where her father is (16), as she 'refuses' to accept his 'ugly death' (37) despite having seen his dead body (56). The details of her father's death are only given belated chronological form (97–105).

Part of the reason for the different shape of Claude's memory of her father's death is that it is outside the child's frame of reference – the reasons for the fatal car-crash are unknown – whereas the stories of mother and daughter overlap, appearing to give Claude access to her mother's experience. Claude sees her mother's arrest as the moment which ended the daughter's faith in maternal omnipotence (32), and feels she has 'betrayed' her mother through not being arrested but entering into a 'hateful bargain', as the adult narrator puts it: '*Her yes but not me [. . .] Do it to her, not to me*' (21). Claude also describes her resentment at having to hear – and now to tell – her mother's experiences in Auschwitz, which persist within in 'encysted' (24) form as a 'malignant' (45) memory.

The projected autobiography that Claude must relate – as she has only an 'ordinary' memory to tell – causes resentment, shown by her insistence in the present that her fate was parallel to that of her mother: 'Our paths diverged [...] and yet we underwent a simultaneous experience, our experience of the war' (63). Even as she struggles to relate her memory, Claude attempts to tell the story of an abandoned child rather than the deported mother – *me yes but not her.*

Chamberet's battle over memory is chronotopically constructed. Claude's mother was arrested and the daughter was saved at the same moment; yet they were geographically separated. It is the opposite of Bakhtin's chronotope of meeting, where time and place are united.[10] The book's title suggests that as readers we are part of the daughter's chronotope – the memoir is defiantly not named after the camps in which the mother was imprisoned. Claude describes a pre-arrest chronotope which was characterized by the collision of two worlds, the 'irruption' (80) of one into the other: during the schoolday she might come across her mother, who was the doctor employed to vaccinate the schoolchildren, just as she would suddenly realize that 'the outside world went on existing even when I wasn't there' (80). This chronotope of meeting vanishes at the moment Claude's mother is interrogated in a classroom while her daughter is propelled out of a room across the hall: 'Had I, at that moment, realized she was there, so very near, I would probably have rushed toward her unthinkingly' (80). The text describes the replacement of this chronotope with one in which there is no 'irruption' between worlds, and 'time has frozen' (21): 'I am at a loss. I cannot imagine where [my mother] is, what she is doing' (51) on the first night of her arrest. In this way *Chamberet* is a paradigmatic narrative; child and reader share the same chronotope, symbolized by the name of a French provincial village. Neither child nor reader can follow the mother's experience beyond her arrest, and may experience both the guilt and envy of this missed meeting.

Raymond Federman, *The Voice in the Closet*

Raymond Federman's novella *The Voice in the Closet*[11] has been analysed as a postmodern, Beckettian meditation on identity and fiction,[12] and as an eccentric form of autobiography. It has not, however, been read as a work of Holocaust fiction, one which concerns the experience of a child and tries to reproduce the child's voice. I would argue that these are not incompatible readings, but that the Holocaust underlies, and is even responsible for, the other two. It is the extreme nature of a paradoxically brief wartime event which sparks off *The Voice*'s existential and meta-fictional concerns; the autobiographical aspect of *The Voice* is also metafictional, as it concerns the youth of a writer, but is also impossible to understand outside a Holocaust context.

Raymond Federman was born in France in 1928 into a Jewish family. On 14 July 1942, the day of the great round-up in Paris, 'soldiers' came to arrest the thirteen-year-old Raymond, his parents and two sisters. Raymond was thrust into a cupboard on the landing outside their third-floor apartment by his mother, where he stayed all day, while the rest of his family were deported to Auschwitz and killed there. As he put it in an interview, Federman

> was in my underwear, and I had no idea what was happening to me. I just sat there, in the dark, and waited, for almost twenty-four hours, before I dared sneak out [. . .] Later, years later, and still today when I reflect on that closet and see that figure, that boy sitting in there on a pile of newspapers, it sounds, feels like a game. But I cannot tell how I felt then. Except that I was scared. And on top of that, in the middle of the afternoon I had to take a crap. And why not? So I unfolded one of the newspapers and took a shit on it. Made a neat package of it and later, when I left the closet, I placed the package on the roof.[13]

Although it was obviously a necessary but not sufficient moment of evasion, Federman's day in the cupboard saved his life – he sub-sequently fled to the south of France, and emigrated to the USA in 1947. The language Federman uses in this interview contrasts sharply with that in the fictive *The Voice*, but the concerns are shared ones. In the novel, the older writer teases out what he sees as the symbolic implications of the boy's 'naked' state in the closet, and the package of excrement that he leaves on the roof. The simple comments Federman makes above in the interview – 'when I [. . .] see that figure', 'I cannot tell how I felt then' – are a prosaic way of posing the very questions of memory, distance from one's own experience, and the impossibility of true retrieval, which are enacted fictively in *The Voice*.

In *The Voice*, the boy's incarceration in the cupboard in 1942 is replayed in slightly different forms many times throughout the text. However, in *The Voice* it is not the case, as it is in most other child's-eye views of the Holocaust, that an older narrator tells the story of, or meditates upon, his or her childhood self. Instead, the opposite is true. It is the child-hood self in *The Voice* who meditates upon and berates his older self ('roles reversed', says the boy (27)). The boy comments constantly on the writer's efforts to remember and represent the past, and impatiently decodes the older self's urge to make symbolic mileage out of the child-hood experience. The style of the following quotation, and that of *The Voice* as a whole, represents the superimposition of two voices and two timescales; here, it seems that 'he' is the older writer, while 'I' is the young boy: 'the fiasco of his fabrication failed account of my survival abandoned in the dark with nothing but my own excrement to play with now neatly packaged on the roof to become the symbol of my origin in the wordshit of his fabulation' (40).[14] Instead of the writer's 'fabulation', the boy demands that the writer pay attention to the concrete details of the day in the closet.

However, it is often hard to tell apart the two voices of child and writer, especially since the boy can only berate the writer as the latter writes him. Instead of separating the voices of child and adult into alter-nating narration, both speak together. In this way, a split narrative in the mode of Saul Friedländer's *When Memory Comes* or Saul Breznitz's *Memory Fields* has been transformed into a single utterance.[15] Through-out, the narration of *The Voice* shifts origin and pronoun, so that it is often hard to tell whether boy or adult is speaking, as the opening lines show:

> here now again selectricstud makes me speak with its balls all balls foutaise sam says in his closet upstairs but this time it's going to be serious no more masturbating on the third floor [...] yesterday a rock flew through the windowpane [...] nearly hit him in the face scared the hell out of him as he waits for me to unfold upstairs (27)

It appears here that the boy is being 'made' to speak. He is wearily lamenting the fact that his adult self is trying 'here now again' to achieve the impossible and write about a moment lost in time (it took place over thirty years previously) and in history (it was an event understood only later to be traumatic). The boy accuses his older self, who is writing in his own 'closet upstairs...on the third floor', of false paternity and a manliness based only on writing. The writer is dependent on 'machines' (28) – in this case, a Selectric golfball typewriter with fonts for different languages on changeable balls, which produces only rubbish ('all balls'). The boy repeats, mockingly, the writer's avocation that 'this time' the attempt to tell the story is 'going to be serious', not a self-indulgent expenditure ('masturbating'). Because the boy is speaking, it sounds as if 'yesterday' refers to his time-scale, the 'flying' rock to some antisemitic outrage in occupied Paris, but in fact he is talking about the writer's 'yesterday' and the window of his study in 1970s USA.[16] The tenses here are typically puzzling, as the writer was 'scared' in the past tense, but in the present still 'waits' for the boy's story to 'unfold' – 'upstairs' where the writer sits, and 'upstairs' where the Parisian closet was.

These unclear personal pronouns and tenses both separate and blur the child and the adult who writes about him. The whole novella consists of a single, unpunctuated sentence, full of indistinct internal clauses, so that different voices move in and out of each other. By the end (41–6), even the semblance of individual voices vanishes, and all the reader has is depersonalized fragments of the story uttered again out of order. It would be possible to see *The Voice* as uniting experimental form with metafictional content, as it shows that although – and because – the past is only retrievable through writing, the effort to recapture it is always doomed to fail. However, I would argue that the barrier between past and present in *The Voice* is not so much a postmodern representational paradox as the barrier of the Holocaust itself. The child is inaccessible to the adult because of what happened on 14 July 1942 and since that date. The boy was saved from genocide without knowing why he was in the cupboard, what would happen to his family, or what he had escaped; the adult knows all these things, and cannot return to the boy's state of ignorance. This is why Federman says, 'I cannot tell how I felt then': not just because he has forgotten, but because it is impossible to recreate such a state of mind.

The gap of pre- and post-Holocaust knowledge is not the only division between boy and writer. While the childhood voice speaks about a single, brief, but crucial day, the older self represents decades of history and knowledge. Yet boy and writer share one fate, as well as one voice: they are both locked in a closet. These closets are clearly different. The boy's is a cupboard outside his parents' third-floor Parisian apartment in 1942, while the writer's is partly his study, but also the prison-house of language in which he has immured himself, ever since he emerged from the closet, and specifically during a period of composition in the mid-1970s.[17]

The closets are the same in the sense that both boy and writer inhabit an enclosed space. The boy is in a junkroom 'where they kept old wrinkled clothes empty skins dusty hats and behind the newspapers stolen bags of sugar cubes' (30). The contents of the closet described here, particularly the clothes and newspapers, suggest *The Voice*'s double theme.[18] The newspapers portend the boy's future as a writer. The discarded garments are described as if apprehended by someone 'in the dark' (37) who cannot see, and indeed, like the child Claude in *Chamberet*, the boy does not witness – neither sees nor understands – his family's deportation. The clothes in the closet also foreshadow both plundered clothing and mass murder in the death-camps. As the reader would expect of a consciousness dating from 1942, the boy gives a sceptical definition of foreshadowing – 'the present feeds upon the coming future of this escapee' (39).[19] It is partly the moment from which the boy speaks that explains the absence of 'such words as Jews, Camps etc'.[20] from *The Voice*. This omission is also the result of the boy's youth. He sees his experience more in terms of the loss of his mother, and his last memory of her 'crying softly' (30, 36), than in broader terms. This means it must be the writer's voice which amplifies one of these images when speaking of the moment of release from the closet: by the time the boy emerged, 'the empty skins [were] already made into lampshades' (36). Indeed, the whole universe of *The Voice* is so saturated with its Holocaust context that it does not need to be named as such.

The older self, on the other hand, is in a different, less easily locatable closet. He has spent 'twenty years banging his head against the wall [. . .] writing himself into a corner inside where they kept old newspapers' (28) – this is not just the wall and corner of the Parisian junkroom, but also of the imaginary closet ('a metaphor I suppose') of the writer's inability to write his childhood story ('what's the use', 28). But this conceit of a shared closet cannot heal the gap between boy and writer. The antagonism the boy feels for the writer is clear from the beginning of *The Voice*. This is not just a temporal means of showing the adult writer's resentment at his own inability to conjure up his own past. It also conveys two different ways of representing a child's experience of the Holocaust: the child himself calls for unadorned language, while the adult writer turns experiential reality into metaphor. The boy makes a plea for the writer to record 'what really happened' (31), and to remember the context of the day in the closet rather than being simply 'obsessed by fake images' (33). Indeed, the boy sees the effort of memory and the act of writing as actually anti-memorial. He accuses the writer of 'displacing the object he wants to apprehend with fake metaphors which bring together on the same level the incongruous the incompatible' (37), and claims that it is the writer's disabused attitude which 'makes me forget my mother's face her dark eyes' (38).

It is no coincidence that the day in 1942, the 'primordial closet moment' (34), is the formative event Federman's work has kept returning to,[21] and which *The Voice* focuses on exclusively. The phrase 'closet moment' unites perfectly the space and time indicators that Bakhtin says constitute the chronotope, in the charged form that characterizes 'crisis events'. Bakhtin describes the liminal spaces in Dostoevsky's novels as chronotopes of 'crisis events', 'the falls, resurrections, renewals, epiphanies, decisions that determine the whole life of a man', set in a narrative time that 'has no duration and falls out of the normal course of biographical time'. Alongside the image of the threshold, Dostoevsky was interested in the 'related chronotopes' of 'the staircase, the front hall and corridor'.[22] As we have seen, the boy's experience in *The Voice* also revolves around liminal and constricting spaces: the cupboard where the boy spent a day on 14 July 1942 was on the landing outside his parents' apartment; eventually he ventured out onto the roof, then down the stairs. The soldiers are 'downstairs' (28) and in the 'courtyard' (27), while the boy and the writer are 'upstairs' (27) in 'two closets on the third floor' (33). These relative components combine in an impossible spatial meaning, so that when 'my father mother sisters too' are led 'down the staircase with their bundles moaning yellow stars to the furnace' they do not end up in the street but go straight to the hellish 'furnace' of a death-camp.

The 'closet moment' in *The Voice* is a chronotope which acts, literally and metaphorically, as a 'threshold' event, a word the boy uses – 'I stood on the threshold' (32). In this case, neither the boy nor his family could return from such a threshold to the time before he entered the cupboard. Once more, the threshold is a specifically Holocaust-related image in *The Voice*, as it represents the moment when the boy not only emerged from the closet but also left behind his innocence. The closet, as a historically infused chronotope, could only have the meaning it does in Paris on 14 July 1942 – without this Holocaust element, spending a day in it could not have been a 'primordial' moment. The chronotope of the closet keeps appearing to shade, however, into a metafictional one. When the boy declares his intention to 'step into the light' or 'emerge alone down the corridor out into the sun', he is not just getting out of the closet, and into the 'light' of Holocaust knowledge, but also out of the clutches of the writer – 'I will abolish his sustaining paradox expose the implausibility of his fiction' (40–1). Bakhtin summarizes a temporal paradox of the kind that constructs *The Voice*:

> before us are two events – the event that is narrated in the work and the event of narration itself [...] these events take place in different times (which are marked by different durations as well) and in different places, but at the same time these two events are indissolubly united in a single but complex event that we might call the work.[23]

In *The Voice*, the two events are even more entwined than Bakhtin suggests is usually the case. In Federman's novella, the event narrated symbolizes the act of narration. The boy says of the adult, 'his doodling words mimicry of my condition' (39): the writer's words 'mimic' by trying both to represent and to symbolize the boy's 'condition' of innocence. As it is impossible to return to or even retrieve the time of the originary event, the two 'different times' really are one: they both exist only in the post-Holocaust present.

The day in 1942 the boy spent in the closet is a formative moment not only in vocational and intellectual terms – the older self in *The Voice* sees it as the moment he became what he is today, especially a writer – but also the moment during which the boy's life was saved and his family lost. That is, a Holocaust meaning is crucial to the text's metafictional and autobiographical ones. This is made clearer if we compare *The Voice* to one of its intertexts, James Joyce's *Portrait of the Artist as a Young Man*. Despite their similarities, it is the differences between Joyce's *Portrait* and *The Voice* that reveal the role of the Holocaust in Federman's novella.[24] Although the *Portrait* and *The Voice* share a narrative about a young man escaping from social and historical constraints into artistic freedom, centring on the image of the 'artificer' (43) Daedalus escaping a maze while risking being 'burnt' (32) by the sun in the process, the meaning of the confines and of the myth itself is different in each case. The boy's literal 'sequestration' (34) in the closet, loss of his family and repudiation of his homeland, is not equivalent temporally or historically to Stephen's confinement by Irish tradition and religion, and his voluntary exile from land and family. Indeed, the very citation in *The Voice* of Joyce's use of Daedalus imagery makes clear the difference between the two contexts. Emphasis in *The Voice* on the boy's Daedalian surname ('Federman' means 'featherman' in German; the writer is thus an 'homme de plume' (32)) starts with the very moment when the arresting soldiers shout it out: 'it begins downstairs soldiers calling our names his too federman' (28). The boy is unimpressed at his older self's efforts to develop his Daedalian posture:

> watch him search in the dictionary callow unfledged youth almost hit him in the face federman featherless little boy [. . .] his fingers on the machine make me book of flights speak traps evasions (28)

The boy sees the writer choose from 'the dictionary' the phrase 'callow *unfledged* youth' to describe him; the writer has tried to follow 'the vocation of his name' by flying to safety in a way the '*featherless* little boy' could not – at least until his emergence from the closet. The boy mockingly recalls the rock that 'flew' through the writer's window and 'almost hit him in the face', as if that brute event is the closest the writer himself will ever get to flying.

Beneath the boy's anger lies the paradox that it is only by means of the writer's typing 'fingers' that the boy can 'speak' at all. The past, particularly a traumatic one, cannot be recaptured or returned to except through the present. Indeed, the act of putting the boy into the cupboard is repeated in the present by the writer – 'don't let him escape no not this time must save the boy full circle from his fingers into my voice back to him on the machine' (28). The boy sees and dislikes this analogy as he speaks of how the writer '*shoves me* into his stories' (29, my italics) just as his parents 'pushed me' into the closet (27). A parallel is drawn between literal and literary imprisonment. The writer's imperative – 'don't let him escape' – echoes the soldiers' shouts, but his utterance has the force that the boy must not be allowed *fictively* to slip through his fingers 'this time'. Instead, the writer must – now echoing the mother's voice – 'save' the boy, by putting him into print. Once more the boy contests this imagery and says the writer is 'pretending to set me free at last' (39); instead, the boy will do what the young Federman did, using the vocabulary of a Holocaust survivor: 'I will step into the light emerge run to some other refuge survive work tell the truth I give you my word' (40). As with its metafictional stance in general, here *The Voice* appears to be concerned with the simple impossibility of return to the past, and the affront the effort to do so may constitute. But because of its Holocaust context more than this is implied here. It is almost as if Holocaust representation itself constitutes a repetition of Holocaust brutality; only the indirect, self-conscious writing of a text like *The Voice* itself can avoid this.

Federman's novel *The Voice in the Closet*, like the texts by Kisliuk and Morhange-Begué that I have discussed, deploys the trope of incomprehension – not just that of inexperience, but a specifically Holocaust-related, temporal incomprehension. The boy did not understand his experience at the time, and in the present the writer cannot recreate that moment. Like *Unveiled Shadows* and *Chamberet*, *The Voice* is thus concerned with the gap between experience and memory, and the impossibility of representing a trauma which was not understood when it took place. The adult writer cannot make good such missing memory, and these three texts represent that failure.

4
Hidden Children

In this chapter I will consider texts about 'hidden children' in the Holocaust years. As Gunnar Paulsson notes in his study of life in hiding in occupied Warsaw, Holocaust 'evaders' – of which hidden children are a central category – have not been widely studied; however, many of the texts discussed in this study constitute just such accounts of 'evasion... as a Jewish response to the Holocaust'.[1]

Nechama Tec argues that all child survivors must have been hidden children given the difficulty of surviving as a child,[2] but the term as I use it here has a specific meaning. It is usually argued that there were two kinds of hiding during this time, for adults as well as children: either living under an assumed, gentile identity (Deborah Dwork calls this 'living "in hiding" ', while Eva Fogelman terms it ' "active hiding" ', Lawrence Langer ' "internal" ' hiding, Paulsson hiding 'on the surface'[3]), or literally living hidden away from the outside world in a confined space (Dwork calls this simply 'living in hiding', Paulsson hiding 'under the surface'). The striking feature of children's experience is that these categories become blurred. Rather than remaining an external masquerade, the camouflaging identity could become internalized and supplant the child's 'real', Jewish identity. Several texts, some of which I discuss in Chapter 5, represent the experience of children taking refuge in convents; this experience, although categorized by Fogelman as being 'visible',[4] overlaps with that of being hidden away – children were confined to particular places and their existence camouflaged by the presence of other children. Both options were relatively easier for children to take up than for adults, although were usually not chosen by them. Dwork mentions the rare phenomenon of children making their own decision to 'hide' by living on the run; again, this represents a mixture of the two modes, as an assumed gentile identity was supplemented by periods spent hidden away from view.

In this chapter, I will consider two novels – Louis Begley's *Wartime Lies* and Henryk Grynberg's *Child of the Shadows*[5] – in which the Jewish child protagonist lives openly as gentile; in both cases the cost of living in hiding returns in the form of particular textual effects.

Louis Begley, *Wartime Lies*

The 'lies' in the title of Begley's book refer simultaneously to its subject – Maciek passes for gentile; and to its genre – although its autobiographical origins have been eagerly sought by critics and reviewers,[6] it is a novel and it is in that sense composed of 'lies'. Begley's denials of *Wartime Lies'* status as memoir have the paradoxical effect of backing up such an idea: he may have altered certain relationships (it was his mother, to whom the book is dedicated, rather than his aunt who saved him) and details (which he claims to recall differently from his mother), but the fact remains that Begley did survive the war in hiding in Poland, just as his character Maciek does. However, the question of autobiography simply distracts the reader's attention from the most striking feature of Begley's novel, which is the extension of the notion of hiddenness to its narration.

The narration of Begley's novel is not as straightforward as it appears. *Wartime Lies* is prefaced with a frame-narration in italics and in the third person about a *'bookish fellow'* (3) of about fifty, whose present-day habits – a 'voyeuristic' interest in evil alongside an avoidance of the topic of the Second World War, and a conviction of his own inner sickness – are apparently *'the price to be paid for his sort of survival'* (4). This is the adulthood of a hidden child, someone who *'believes he has been changed inside forever'*. The narrator ambiguously claims that, *'[The man with the sad eyes] thinks on the story of the child that became such a man. For the sake of an old song, he calls the child Maciek: polite little Maciek, dancing tirelessly while the music plays'* (5). Although this italicizing narrator, who is 'bookish' in his turn, appears on two other occasions, at this point such a voice seems merely prefatory.

This introduction to Maciek's story preserves perfectly the entwinement of fact and fiction which characterizes *Wartime Lies* as a text. Is 'the story of the child' about the man's own past; or simply an apocryphal tale he is about to 'think on'? Is it even the story we are about to read, or another one which we never learn? The namelessness of both the man and the child is crucial; no definitive link is ever established between them. The man 'calls the child Maciek' after a character in a Polish folk song,[7] a fictive choice which, we imagine, bears no relation to the boy's actual assumed name. Maciek 'dances tirelessly' because as a fictional character he is a puppet, but also because as a hidden child he has to be unquestioningly obedient and good. In other words, the more fictional the *énonciation*, the more factual the *énoncé* appears: as a tale of a fiction which became fact – the man has 'changed inside forever' as a result of his 'lies'– fiction therefore takes on the status of historical discourse.

Narrating hiddenness

'Hiddenness' in *Wartime Lies* refers not only to the status of its child protagonist, but also affects the presence of the child's voice (it is hidden in a novel narrated by an adult); its generic status (fact is hidden within fiction); and its attitude to its readers (information is hidden from them). The character Maciek has already vanished by the time we come to read his story. We are both told this – 'And where is Maciek now? He became an embarrassment and slowly died' (198) – and perceive it: the narrative voice is an adult one, even if the viewpoint is a child's. The absence in the novel of direct speech from any of the characters may appear to support the idea that *Wartime Lies* is not fiction or even faction but a genuine record drawn from memory, as dialogue has not been invented. Reconstructed dialogue is often seen as a signal of generic hybridity, or of fact which has been treated in a fictive way;[8] but this technique is eschewed by Begley. However, dialogue is replaced with the supremely novelistic technique of dialogism: that is, with the representation of opposing discourses within an apparently unified discourse.

The presence of such dialogism is clear even in what appears to be the boy's own voice, for instance when we read about the preparation for communion Maciek undertakes as part of living in hiding, but which he also comes to believe in:

> I also found, as I studied the book [of prayers] and listened to Father P., that my personal situation was desperate and despicable. There was no salvation except through grace, and grace could be acquired only through baptism ... I asked Father P. whether savages living in our time away from the church could be saved if they were good, and he was very clear about it: the ministry of Jesus was complete. Virtue without grace could not suffice. (115–16)

However, as the past tense shows, this is actually the adult narrator's voice, not the child's. The phrase 'desperate and despicable' in particular reveals this, with its arch alliteration and dark humour. Yet the adult voice is shot through with the accents of childhood, while the child utters adult phrases. Maciek is clearly repeating Father P.'s words when he says, 'There was no salvation except through grace', and 'virtue without grace could not suffice'. Some childlike vocabulary is used, such as the word 'savages', and the phrase 'if they were good'. But these words are not directly cited – there are no quotation marks either for Father P.'s or the child's discourse; rather, they are embedded within the narration. Thus what we read is a mingled utterance, consisting of a dialogic clash between the child's and the adult narrator's voice, with the added accents of Father P.

The autobiographical effect of *Wartime Lies* is partly the result of its title and framing conceit. It begins with a meditation on the difficulty of recall and the rupture between a pre- and post-war self. The story which follows seems to be a genetic history and an explanation of these gaps; yet the story's very existence is a paradox which begs the question it sets out to answer. Among the text's final lines is the observation, 'Maciek was a child, and our man has no childhood that he can bear to remember; he has had to invent one' (198). This is ambiguous: is the narrative we have just read the invented childhood or the 'real' one? If it is the invented childhood, then 'the story of the child that became such a man' is just that, a story, one explanation among many of why the man 'has been changed inside forever' (5).[9] If it is an account of the adult protagonist's real childhood, then the adult narrator can remember with extraordinary clarity what his wartime childhood consisted of, but chooses to cut it off from his present, nameless[10] self. In this second scenario, the reader gains access to facts which are withheld from listeners within the text, including Maciek's father on his return from Siberia (195), and the narrator's 'beautiful' dinner-table neighbours (4). This ambiguity is crucial to the novel's project, and marks a moment where the leeway of fiction fulfils its potential.[11]

This paradox, in which the narrator describes his inability to relate a story but then does so in great detail, complicates the otherwise not unconventional structure of *Wartime Lies*. As is the case in any retrospective first-person account, the division between the adult narrator and youthful focalizer may be hard to detect because of the apparently identical and continuous self-reference: both are called 'I'. In *Wartime Lies*, however, the disjunction between these two entities is highlighted. In fact, the child's story can only be told by a radically split adult subject, and in *Wartime Lies* we see the process of Maciek's splitting.

In both *Wartime Lies* and Fink's *The Journey*, not only is the adult narrator divided from his or her youthful self; there is also present a *third* voice, which attempts to oversee the process of narration. In the case of *Wartime Lies*, this third voice, which frames the story, sounds similar to that of the adult narrator but speaks of both him and Maciek in the third person and in an exclusively adult, consciously poetic manner. In fact it is this third voice whose relationship to Maciek is ambiguous; the narrator of most of the text acts in a more stable fashion as the adult version of Maciek. The italicized third voice introduces the narrative and psychological problems involved in constructing the text, and mentions this narrator's reliance on myth and literary paradigm in understanding the Holocaust. By contrast, the adult narrator – the second voice – limits itself almost entirely to Maciek's viewpoint and his contemporary knowledge, apart from one overt flashforward.[12]

The third narrative voice appears only infrequently: at the beginning of the text, as we have seen (3–5); it intrudes with a meditation on self-pity and guilt (73–5) as a prelude to the death of Reinhard, Tania's German boyfriend; later it wonders why pity can only be felt for the defiant (120–2). In the book's final post-war chapter it reappears free of italics, come to fruition as the only kind of narrative voice capable of describing the end of Maciek's travails: it is acerbic, ironic, and so double-voiced that its own intonation is impossible to pin down (192–8). In other words, this third voice is the effect of the story it has told, the only possible outcome of this tale of performance, masquerade and self-fictionalizing. It is hard to categorize such a narrator, who bears some but not complete resemblance to the kind of 'frame-narrator' in Joseph Conrad's *Heart of Darkness* or Henry James's *Turn of the Screw*. Such narrative difficulty seems appropriate where Holocaust writings are concerned, as a representation of the traumatic fragmentation of subjectivity.

Most of *Wartime Lies* consists of a narrative voice which is split internally between past and present, child and adult. It is precisely the effectiveness of this construction that has led readers to want to read the novel as autobiography. The narration of *Wartime Lies* is a hybrid one: the perceptions are those of a child, the tone and vocabulary an adult's. This combination is of course not uncommon; various commentators have compared Begley's work to that of Henry James, and James's *What Maisie Knew* consists of just this rendering of childish perception in an adult literary discourse. The effect in James's novel is similar to that in *Wartime Lies*, since such a disjunction generates its own pathos and method of defamiliarization. However, *Wartime Lies* is distinctive in combining this method of conveying a child's perceptions with first-person narration, giving an impression of internal damage rather than external concern.

In *What Maisie Knew*, the eponymous little girl repeats, apparently innocently, the unflattering words spoken by one of her estranged parents to the other:

> 'And did your beastly papa, my precious angel, send any message to your own loving mamma?' Then it was that [Maisie] found the words spoken by her beastly papa to be, after all, in her bewildered little ears, from which, at her mother's appeal, they passed, in her clear shrill voice, straight to her little innocent lips. 'He said I was to tell you, from him', she faithfully reported, 'that you're a nasty horrid pig!'[13]

A similar impression is given in *Wartime Lies* by the appearance of a person's characteristic phraseology within the narrator's discourse, as if particular tones or words had stuck in the young boy's mind, as they clearly have in Maisie's. Both free indirect and the less usual free direct discourse occur throughout Begley's text as substitutes for direct speech. For instance, before the war a colleague of Maciek's father, a Catholic surgeon, recommends that a Polish rather than a Jewish nurse should take care of the boy:

> What Maciek needs, he told my father, is to touch our holy Polish earth [...] Give him one of our own. Salt of the earth. He will drink strength from her. (13)

Free direct discourse appears here shorn at first only of inverted commas, then blends seamlessly with the narrator's voice so that mediating verbs are also abandoned. This gives simultaneously an impression of immediacy and of uncertainty. It emphasizes the priority of the narrator's possibly faulty memory while preserving the different accents of various characters. Interestingly it is Hertz, in the wartime part of the novel, whose discourse most closely resembles direct utterance. He appears at first to be a blackmailer pretending to ask for money for his sick wife, and uses the first person although his words are not conventionally quoted: 'Hertz [...] commended Tania for her prudence. But Panna must not worry that we will lose contact. I have noted where she and the precious boy reside' (72). The bald shock of what sounds like a threat is preserved by the penetration of Hertz's self-reference into the narrator's indirection.

Just a page later, recounting Tania's sudden guilt at automatically having assumed Hertz to be a criminal, the narrator reverts to indirect discourse: 'Then she told me that [...] it was she whom Hertz and every decent man should flee' (73). This reversion acts ambiguously. It is clear, if we bear in mind 'she told me', that Tania's words about herself are being reported in her own tones but in the third person. If we forget 'she told me', then it sounds as if the narrator is making a damning statement *about* Tania rather than repeating her words. However, in *Wartime Lies* direct comment on a character occurs only within the speech of others, or by Maciek on himself. This makes the novel almost a textbook example of Bakhtinian polyphony,[14] and it is interesting that polyphonic character construction is the direct result of the narration in *Wartime Lies* – an adult speaks *for* but not *about* a child – and of the subject of the novel. Because Tania and Maciek are on the run and hiding their true identities, firm judgements about others are both crucial yet provisional, and much effort is expended by the pair on preventing others reaching judgements about them. As Tania puts it of the dangers of dinnertime conversations, 'one had to be ready to talk about oneself. Which self?' (107). Tania's question here goes to the heart not only of one aspect of her uncertain life with Maciek, but of the reader's uncertainty about the autobiographical nature of *Wartime Lies* and the relation of its three narrative voices to each other.

Polyphony is thus the logical representational conclusion of damage-limitation in such circumstances. Method and matter come together in this respect when Maciek is challenged by one of Pani Dumont's lodgers, Pani Bronicka, for his 'habit of insinuating flattery':

> It will not do, she told me, always to be trying to make oneself liked and then to ask whether one has succeeded. (106)

As readers, we have little sense of Maciek acting like this until we see him as if from the outside in Pani Bronicka's words. This is due to the polyphonic construction even of the narrator's young self; and the particular form his 'bad character' takes is determined by his circumstances and the need to dissemble so that even the reader does not gain the whole story.

The effect of free direct discourse in *Wartime Lies* is especially striking when it seems that the adult narrator is preserving a particular word or turn of phrase which has remained in the child's memory, and this applies particularly in Maciek's case to expressions to do with sexuality. Even an obscene song recited by the boys in the Kramers' apartment building in T. is quoted in indirect discourse, which greatly increases the gap between the reporting voice and reported words: 'We talked about women; they *explained* how one could *shove it in* between a girl's legs' (41, my italics). The narrator repeats Tania's analysis of the attention paid to her in Lwów as the Polish lover of Reinhard, an ex-Wehrmacht officer: 'let them mutter about the German's tart and her bastard, it will keep their minds off the Jewish question' (67). Use of free direct discourse again emphasizes more than reported speech would do the startling eruption of Tania's informal vocabulary into the usually precise and mellifluous narration.[15] Historical and personal imperatives are placed at opposite ends of a spectrum here by Tania; yet it is the words relating to the personal that Maciek has remembered. (Of course, part of the point of their plight is that the personal has become inextricable from historical concerns.) Similarly, the grandfather's voice is preserved in his description of a landlady: she is 'a pleasant old cocotte, he liked her' (97).

Another reason for the persistence of sexualized vocabulary is the oedipal dimension of Maciek's story; if this were a regular *Bildungsroman* or *Künstlerroman*, both of which it resembles, Maciek's love for his 'beautiful and brave' aunt, jealousy of her admirers and fear of her caustic tongue would have constituted the main part of the narrative. As it is, this sexual narrative occupies the interstices of the overshadowing historical narrative, literally so in the case of Tania's admirers, who are cultivated solely in order to help save her remaining family ('she claimed she had always had a heart of stone except when it came to grandfather and me' (69)).

Belated memory

The opening chapter of *Wartime Lies* concerns Maciek's privileged early youth, spent in a large house in the Polish town of T. Maciek's early years bear more than a passing resemblance to those of Sergei Pankiev, better known as the Wolf Man, one of Freud's most celebrated patients.[16] Sergei was the son of a Russian landowner and lived on a country estate in pre-revolutionary Russia; despite the fact that the 'Russian nobleman [was] the very image of anxiety for Eastern European Jews',[17] Sergei's early circumstances resemble Maciek's in several ways. Like Maciek, Sergei had friendships with his father's servants and a charged relationship – as Maciek's is with his nurse Zosia – with his nurse and a young cleaning woman. Maciek is much more unambiguously loved and cared for than Sergei, however, and while Sergei's father inadvertently frightened his son by telling him the tale of the Seven Little

Goats, Maciek's father devotes himself to his child after his wife's death. Although Freud's analysis of the Wolf Man concentrates on personal psychopathology, the third narrator in *Wartime Lies* offers a more historicized verdict on the man he is describing: '*Is that the inevitable evolution of the child he once was, the price to be paid for his sort of survival?*' (5). The costs of living in hiding under the Nazi occupation of Poland, it is implied, have been internalized. These costs are partly the result of the deceptions involved, but also, the overseeing narrator suggests, because of survivor guilt: he comments that 'our man' feels 'shame at being alive, his skin intact and virgin of tattoo, when his kinsmen and almost all others, so many surely more deserving than he, perished in the conflagration' (3).[18]

Like Maciek, Sergei Pankiev witnessed cataclysmic historical events, including in the latter's case the First and Second World Wars and the Russian Revolution, and the loss of family fortune and stability; it is as if in *Wartime Lies* the third voice's consciousness of his story's belatedness is so strong that he cannot help but model the early parts of his narrative on the *locus classicus* of that concept, Freud's case history of the Wolf Man.

In the case history 'From the History of an Infantile Neurosis' Freud introduces the notion of belatedness ('*Nachträglichkeit*') to explain the way in which the Wolf Man's childhood memories emerge during analysis. (I have already mentioned this notion in Chapter 1.) Freud argues that the Wolf Man witnessed scenes of a sexual nature in his extreme youth but was only able to understand their true significance *retrospectively*, in the light of his later knowledge. For this reason it appeared that cause and effect were reversed since the later event gave meaning to the earlier one. Eventually Freud could not decide whether the original events had actually taken place, or if they were simply strategic constructions. Belatedness is useful as a way of exploring how personal or historical narratives in general are constructed, which is often exactly as it was in the Wolf Man's case: a later event casts a quite different light on an earlier one, and its apparent innocence may retrospectively change into something more significant. In the case of *Wartime Lies*, the third narrator is understandably unable to disentangle the effects of belatedness from other causal relations. In the first chapter, he specifically asks whether 'our man', with his particular habits of reading, avoidance of intimacy, and interest in prisoners of conscience and the mechanics of torture, is the direct product of his wartime experiences. The result, that is, inevitably casts light on the cause: spending the Holocaust years in hiding turns out to have been damaging in unexpected ways, not physically but psychically. Belatedness saturates *Wartime Lies*. Knowledge of genocide is so general by the time the narrator comes to tell Maciek's story – 'our man' is in his fifties – that the backdrop of mass murder implicitly infuses Maciek's experiences as we read. We do not need to be shown a moment of revelation when Tania comes to learn of the death camps and the nature of the threat hanging over her and her nephew; on the contrary, when she is told a train is bound for Auschwitz she already knows perfectly well what this means (148).

Once more, a child's memory itself symbolizes belated knowledge. The narrative structure of *Wartime Lies* itself could be described in this way, as Freud's comment on the Wolf Man's memories suggests: 'The patient [...] puts his present ego into the situation which is so long past.'[19] This description fits aptly the relationship between adult narrator and young protagonist in *Wartime Lies*. Freud's later remark about the truth-value of the Wolf Man's memories from earliest childhood, particularly that of the primal scene, also casts light on the structure of Begley's novel: 'these scenes from infancy are not reproduced during the treatment as recollections, they are the products of construction'. In *Wartime Lies*, the distinction between early 'scenes' and later 'construction' is drawn between Maciek's viewpoint and the narrator's rendition of it. It is not that we can use Freud's differentiation of 'recollection' and 'construction' to judge the truth-value of Begley's novel. Rather, *Wartime Lies* works as an *imitation* of a case history in this sense. Freud goes on to assure his reader that he is not suggesting the analysand wilfully invents childhood material:

> scenes, like this one in my present patient's case, which date from such an early period [...] have to be divined – constructed – gradually and laboriously from an aggregate of indications.[20]

Exactly this split appears in *Wartime Lies*. It is not just memory-work but historical research that takes the place of the 'aggregate of indications'. Begley's mother recalls questions her son put to her about Polish vocabulary and songs during the writing of his novel;[21] while Ida Fink returned to the scene of a near-disaster in order to complete *The Journey*. Begley supplements what Freud calls 'the first dark years of childhood'[22] with the leeway of fiction.

The hybrid rendering of Maciek's story takes opposite forms at various times. Sometimes the adult narrator makes efforts to preserve a child's perception. Actions are noted simply and without comment or analysis: of Tania's suitor in rural Poland the narrator notes, '[Nowak] was calling her now by her first name only; perhaps saying Pani was too much trouble' (185). It is unlikely, of course, that laziness was behind Nowak's familiarity, and the suggestion is born partly of a naïve child's view, partly of the adult narrator's irony; the two modes inhabit the same phrase. At other times Maciek's own voice is briefly heard within the adult narrator's. His internal dilemma when he starts training for Communion is presented entirely within the purview, although not in the vocabulary, of a child, consisting partly of the words of Father P. and partly of the narrator's version ('I was') of Maciek's own reasoning:

> It was evident that every Jew, even if he did not break the Commandments, was damned.
> If that was true, my case was worse than that of a savage. [...] Bearing false witness was forbidden; serious lying and hypocrisy were the same as bearing false witness; I was a liar and hypocrite every day; I was mired in mortal sin on that account alone, even if all the other evil in me was disregarded. (116)

The opposite of this partial preservation of Maciek's voice[23] is the total abandonment of the child's-eye view in a sophisticated descriptive method, which reaches its apotheosis in the final chapter. This method is used exclusively to represent the views of the gentile Poles among whom Maciek's family are hiding, and marks another site of polyphony: such characters betray their inclinations on their own account without the need for any narratorial commentary. This occurs at a fairly reduced level when the grandfather is due to go ahead of everyone else to live on Aryan papers in Warsaw.[24] Interestingly, the double-voiced discourse which follows is said to issue from 'common knowledge', the Jewish counterpart to the communal voice of gentile Poles, later described as that of 'our neighbours' (103):

> It was common knowledge that the greatest dangers for Jews living on Aryan papers were being unmasked by the Polish police or denounced to the Polish or German police – either by Polish neighbours, *indignant* at the *usurpation* by some Rosenduft or Rozensztajn of an *honorable* name or identity, or by *dissatisfied* extortionists. (53, my italics[25])

The communal voice represented here economically conveys a rather complex view of the dangers of passing as Aryan, particularly in those words I have italicized. Use of the word 'indignant' dignifies bigotry sarcastically into righteous anger; 'usurpation' ironically retains the Polish subjects' own sense of right while remaining at a disdainful distance from the kind of word they might have used; 'honorable' preserves the Polish view of inherent Jewish dishonour; while 'dissatisfied' affects to elide the real meaning of blackmailers' activities and motivations.

The second occasion for a double-voiced representation of a particular Polish viewpoint takes place during Maciek's and Tania's 1943 sojourn at Pani Z.'s boarding house in Warsaw, from which the occupants had a good view of the Ghetto during the uprising. The adult narrator calls watching the Ghetto burning 'a special sort of social occasion' which Maciek and Tania cannot miss out on since 'at the dinner table the lodgers and Pani Z. talked of little else'. The discourse of this 'talking' is preserved here without direct quotation:

> Jews had *actually* attacked Germans, *even* forcing the SS unit that was sent to *restore order* to retreat. Some said that many of the SS had been killed. But now the Germans were teaching the Jews a *final lesson* [...] [Pani Z.] claimed it was the first *real entertainment* the Germans had provided in all this *sad time*. (102–3, my italics)

Again I have italicized the particularly striking instances of double-voiced discourse, where the neighbours' voices sound out from within the narrator's. In the first sentence adverbs registering awe at the Jews' daring co-exist with irritation at their disrupting good 'order'. *Schadenfreude* felt at the Jews' inevitable vanquishing and punishment ('final lesson' in combination with 'real entertainment') culminates in an expression of the irreconcilability of Jewish and gentile Polish experiences. The 'sad time' to which Pani Z. refers has nothing to do with the Nazis' treatment of the Jews; she means the war and the occupation of Poland.

Hidden meanings

In the final chapter, the narrative trajectory of *Wartime Lies* is replaced by a circling display of double-voicedness. The configuration of the three voices we have noted throughout – the frame-narrator, the adult narrator and the character Maciek – alters here. I would argue that, while Maciek is clearly transformed into a character narrated in the third-person, what we witness at the novel's end is the merging of the two narrative voices into one. This merging suggests two things. First, the triply split subject which began the novel has not been healed so much as papered over its own cracks. The self-questioning of the first chapter has been replaced by a more assured representation of a persona at odds with its history and inner life. Paradoxically, this merging of the two narrators is enabled by the constitution of the united voice out of a panoply of others' voices. When the narrator says 'Believe me' (192), this use of the first person does not signify a newly found self able to own its experiences, but a speaking position which is more settled than either that of Maciek, learning to lie, or the third voice's description of the evasions of 'our man' at the novel's beginning. It is simply a turn of phrase used with assurance.

In the final chapter a disavowal takes place, albeit one which demands to be decoded by the reader. Eric Santner calls such disavowals, which avoid the subject at issue by concentrating on red herrings, 'fetishistic narratives',[26] and this is how the narrator presents Maciek's post-war story. He tells of the 1946 pogrom in Kielce, 'the first in liberated Poland' (193):

> The behavior of our police was first-class: absolutely neutral, hands-off, yet how their fingers must have itched on the truncheon handles! (193)

The narrator signals here Maciek's outward identification with gentile Poland by describing 'our' police; yet this is not Maciek's voice – especially since Maciek is no longer a character described in the first person – but a confected, insinuating voice. It draws on the neighbours' talk at Pani Z.'s: a page later Jews in hiding are again described as 'usurping good Polish names', while others are said to have gone back to being called 'Rosenduft and Rozensztajn and think no one cares' (194).

In the quotation above about the Kielce pogrom the narrative voice acts out a fetishistic stance in its description of the police manfully restraining themselves from using their truncheons: it must have been the Jews their fingers itched to beat, not the perpetrators. This implication lies near the surface of the utterance, asking to be recognized, but another telling detail is more successfully buried. Maciek's father gives him an Alsatian dog:

> Maciek names him Bari, for one of the stations their new radio is supposed to catch but cannot, because Italy is too far away. (197)

Maciek successfully hides his real fear of this dog from everyone but a schoolfriend, and pretends to be heartbroken when the dog is run over; but the real fetishistic evasion here is Maciek's choice of name for his pet. 'Bari' is indeed the name of an Italian radio station; it is also the name of the dog owned by Kurt Franz, deputy commandant of the death camp Treblinka. This dog's savagery against prisoners and Franz's devotion to him are well documented in testimonies and histories of Treblinka.[27] Helen Darville fictionalizes this dog in her novel *The Hand that Signed the Paper*:

> Franz has a pet Saint Bernard, Barri, which [. . .] kills people at Franz's command, by tearing out their throats. But there is also a human dog in the camp, Ivan the Terrible [. . .].[28]

Darville makes implicit reference above to Franz's horrible inversion, described in Jean-François Steiner's factional text *Treblinka* (which she also appears to have read):

> As soon as [Kurt Franz] saw [a worker] who seemed to lack ardour, he would set Barry on him with the command, 'Look, man, that dog isn't working!'[29]

Maciek's act of fetishistic substitution – Italy for Treblinka – simply brings his true traumatic past out into the open. Unconsciously choosing to call the dog after Franz's emphasizes both Maciek's conviction that he has evaded the camps in a cowardly manner; and his desire to control his fate by allying himself with the winning side (see the bedbug-killing incident, 93, and his games with toy soldiers, 66). In contrast to the frame-narrator who began *Wartime Lies* and was willing to explore notions of survivor guilt, we end the novel with a more integrated but fetishistic narrator who can only unconsciously raise such issues.

Henryk Grynberg, *Child of the Shadows*

Grynberg's novel[30] is also about a young Polish boy living in hiding: at first literally, then by masquerading as gentile. In both texts a young Jewish boy lives as a gentile on the Aryan side in Warsaw, and finally in the Polish countryside tending cows; the resourcefulness of a female relative with long red hair (she is the child's mother, rather than his aunt, in *Child of the Shadows*) appears almost superhuman through the eyes of a child as she deals with blackmailers, confronts Nazis and is strategically flirtatious in order to protect her son/nephew; the child assimilates the illogical precepts he has to live with to the point where he can no longer distinguish truth from fiction; he gives his own version of biblical stories related by a priest,[31] and argues about Catholic doctrine with his mother/aunt, who tries to reassure him that he is not at fault;

and the narrator renders the clash of identities and allegiances undergone by such a child through a particular use of free indirect discourse. Indeed, in *Wartime Lies* Maciek actually meets a little boy named Henryk living undercover with his mother (109–11).

It is Grynberg's language and tone that show the greatest affinity with *Wartime Lies*. There is more direct discourse in *Child of the Shadows* than in Begley's novel – for instance, the malign intentions of a Polish forester are polyphonically revealed through his conversation with the child's parents (30–3). However, the child's own utterance and thought are conveyed either as free indirect – ('[Father] might not come back at all. It depended on so many things. If he should be caught, if he should meet someone he ought not to meet...' (34)) – or direct discourse without quotation marks ('All right, I said, I want to sleep, and I let go of father's hand and slipped into the snow' (41)). The absence of direct, reconstructed reportage conveys, in the first case, the child's adoption of his father's words and implicitly of his viewpoint – the phrases 'It depended on so many things' and 'someone he ought not to meet' are an instance of free indirect discourse in which the narrator is imitating a little boy's repetition of his father's phrases. The absence of quotation marks in the second case shows the provisionality of a memory about childhood: it is not clear whether these words were uttered or thought, let alone if they are accurately recalled.

Some of the most striking effects of Begley's novel, particularly its dialogic representation of non-Jewish voices, exist in Grynberg's in a less developed form. For instance, the narrator of *Child of the Shadows*, the older Henryk, reconstructs the thoughts of Podorewski, a wealthy and educated Polish landowner, as he prepares to betray two Jewish men, Abel and Manes:

> The peasants were ignorant and superstitious. A sin, they thought, not to help. But Podorewski had studied philosophy. Was it possible, he thought, to help at all? Perhaps only by shortening the pain of living... He did not care about the money, which would be his in the final event. He had enough of his own. But rather than that the money should fall into German hands, he thought, or be completely wasted... Podorewski had studied philosophy. (49)

Podorewski's reasoning is presented using a mixture of direct narratorial comment ('He did not care about the money') with heavily ironized free indirect discourse ('Perhaps only by shortening the pain of living'), and remarks which share both positions – 'But Podorewski had studied philosophy' is equally ironic if it is his own or the narrator's utterance. However, the narrator is still clearly present here, reporting the land-owner's thoughts ('Was it possible, he thought...'), while in *Wartime Lies*, all such narratorial moorings have been cut loose; in *Child of the Shadows* Podorewski's words are the product of pure speculation, while those in *Wartime Lies* are the public accents of received opinion.

For instance, the narrator of *Wartime Lies* reports, '[Blackmail] was open to all Polish connoisseurs of ineffably Jewish elements in physi-ognomy; perhaps ears were a trifle too large or too well articulated, or eyelids were heavier than was becoming to a purebred Slav' (54). Here, there is no pretence at reconstruction and the narrator gives no comment, but simply presents an ironized version of gentile opinion. The narrator chooses lofty terminology for base sentiments as a means of distancing and mocking ('connoisseur', 'ineffably', 'becoming').

Yet even in its rather rudimentary form the ironized double-voicedness in *Child of the Shadows* is the strategy of an adult narrator, not focalized through the eyes or voice of a child; in this sense, *Child of the Shadows* uses a blend of different narratorial voices – although their differences are more muted than those in *Wartime Lies*. Throughout, the narrator of *Child of the Shadows* (quotations in roman below) uses just the same blank, unadorned child's-eye view of threatening or horrifying events as the narrator of *Wartime Lies* (quotations in italics). The examples below are also coincidentally similar in content, but it is the narrative style that is most significant:

I knew that crying was forbidden, because I was circumcised. (80)
That I wouldn't go to school was understood between Tania and me; one couldn't take my penis where it might be seen, for instance to urinate in the common toilet. (92)

After some time Aaron came again with a lady, who addressed him as Janek. (60)
In the new papers, my name was no longer Maciek, and Tania was no longer Tania; I was to be called Janek. (85)

In this way, all the men and all the girls were shot. (64)
Instead, Dr and Mrs Kipper were shot by the Germans a few days later, together with some other Jews. (31)

Mama was walking next to me and even smiling. But her smile was of the kind I could still remember from the days when we went visiting. Therefore, we must be visiting, I thought. (70)

Tania laughed the long laugh she used when she teased people who weren't her friends. (87)

One had to talk a lot, too, for people don't like those who are silent and always suspect them of something or other. So one was forced not to shun people, not to avoid them, not to remain alone for a moment, to be on one's guard the whole time so as not to forget anything, not to commit a *faux pas*; and apart from all this, to be natural and at ease...And to play a part which one did not have time to learn. To play it day after day, at any given time, without any interval in which to collect one's thoughts, to breathe freely, or even to look at one's own face... (99)

One had to talk, one could not always talk about books, one had to be ready to talk about oneself. Which self? The issue was the limit of one's inventiveness and memory, because the lies had to be consistent – more consistent, according to Tania, than the truth. (105)

Most Begleyish of all, the narrator of *Child of the Shadows* reports on his wartime self that, 'I did not have to learn a part. I had been primed so well that in the end I could not distinguish between invention and truth' (99); the narrator of *Wartime Lies* says of his young self, 'I was chained to the habit of lying' (171). The invention of a Christian persona paradoxically creates real subjective problems for the masquerading children:

I was to take Communion although I was burdened with a sin. I had not been baptised. (114)

I was going to commit blasphemy, the gravest sin of all, when I took Communion without baptism and after a false confession. (117)

In all these cases, narrative voice is used to convey the viewpoint of a child without actually reproducing it. The techniques of reduced narratorial comment, added to free indirect and free direct discourse, *stand in for* rather than represent the lost child's voice. For instance, the reader is shown but not told about the young Henryk's unnatural understanding of causality (he must not cry *because* he is circumcised); about Henryk's and Maciek's knowledge of brutal facts, like the murder of innocent people and the need for false names; and both boys' sensitivity to unusual circumstances while only being able to comprehend them in terms of the social nuance of a vanished world.

5
Convent Children

This chapter is divided into two parts. In the first part, I will discuss the broad range of issues implicated in the subject of Jewish children living in hiding during the Holocaust years and how their conception of religious identity was affected by their experiences. To do this, I will refer to a number of fictional and testimonial accounts, as well as theoretical material on children and religion. In the second part, I will discuss novels by several of the 'thousands' of Jewish children who were placed by their parents in convents, monasteries, boarding schools, orphanages, or Catholic homes[1] during the war. My discussion will centre on two novels in particular, Frida Scheps Weinstein's *A Hidden Childhood*, Renée Roth-Hano's *Touch Wood*, and comparison with Elisabeth Gille's novel *Shadows of a Childhood*.[2]

The subject of Jewish children hidden in Christian institutions presents a challenge in narrative terms, as it demands the depiction of young children whose 'self-representation and identity formation'[3] were suddenly and radically altered. Unlike Ida Fink's novel *The Journey* about an external masquerade by late-teenage girls, these testimonies show children's *internal* worlds becoming coloured by the new rules and behaviour they must adopt in extreme circumstances. The novels are fictionalized testimony; despite the fact that Weinstein's and Roth-Hano's are cited in child psychology articles,[4] they are literary texts – indeed, fiction is the most effective way of presenting the high subjective cost and gains of Jewish children living as Catholics. The gradual encroachment and adoption of Catholic practice by these children living in extreme circumstances throws into relief the ordinary and everyday, including the psychological construction of Jewish identity, particularly in assimilationist or adverse conditions. In conclusion, I will argue that although Weinstein's and Roth-Hano's novels are about children living in hiding

in Catholic institutions, the most crucial hidden presence in both is that
of the adult narrator.

Hidden children are usually divided by historians and psychologists
simply between those who hid in secret and those who lived openly.
However, the binary of these two categories is more easily applied to
Jewish adults living in hiding, as matters were not this simple for
children. In his study of Jews living on the Aryan side of occupied
Warsaw, Gunnar Paulsson points out that most hidden children, unless
they were with their parents, had to hide 'on the surface' because they
might be a liability for themselves and others hiding 'under the surface':
thus 'nearly all children in hiding were represented as Catholics', living
in convents, orphanages or with a family.[5] It seems that the child
protagonists of fictionalized and autobiographical testimony who lived
in Catholic communities are of at least three overlapping types. The
first category consists of children who lived openly pretending to be
Christian, along with at least part of their family (Maciek in Louis
Begley's novel *Wartime Lies*, Henryk in Henryk Grynberg's novel *Child
of the Shadows*); second, those who lived as part of a Catholic family
(Marysia in Miriam Winter's memoir *Trains*; Sarah, her mother and
sisters in Sarah Kofman's memoir *Rue Ordener, Rue Labat* lived with a
Catholic woman); and third, those who lived in a Catholic institution
(Paul in Saul Friedländer's memoir *When Memory Comes* was alone in
a seminary; Georges in Georges Perec's novel *W or the Memory of Childhood* lived in a Catholic children's home and was visited by relatives,
while Juri in Shlomo Breznitz's memoir *Memory Fields* lived in a convent
orphanage with his sister). In all three categories, whether they remained
with their parents or not, children during the Holocaust years who were
exposed to, or taught to enact, Catholic doctrine, tended to internalize
it. This internalization occurred for a range of reasons, including the
children's own pre-war experience of their own and other religions,
their age and other circumstances during the war, and the appeal of
specific features of Catholic doctrine to Jewish children during the
Holocaust years.

'I feel torn':[6] between Judaism and Catholicism

Although they treat of shifts in religious allegiance, *A Hidden Childhood*,
Touch Wood, and other accounts of hidden children's experiences, do
not describe conversion in the sense of an adult choice to embrace
a particular religion, either as a wartime necessity or 'pro-forma affair',
or as the conclusion of a 'spiritual journey'[7] based on full knowledge and

acceptance of the new religion's rituals and requirements.[8] At first glance, it may seem that the reasons why hidden children were drawn to Catholicism were distinctive only in terms of historical and developmental context. In apparent support of this view, several of the features which Stephen J. Dubner describes in an account of his parents' conversion from Judaism to Catholicism are the same as those which drew the hidden children in wartime Europe. The possibility of prayer to a personal God, and worship of the 'mother figure' of Mary, were significant for these post-war American adults as they were for wartime children.[9] Dubner's parents' memories of their Jewish past, like those of hidden children, took the form of remembering snatches of Yiddish, and characteristic food. What is different in the case of hidden children, however, is the overdetermined historical reason for their adopting, or allowing the encroachment of, Catholicism, ranging from the substitution for lost parents to escaping negative constructions of Jewishness. The role of religion for children below the age of about thirteen is clearly also a distinctive feature of hidden children's experience; it partakes of uncompleted object relations and is experienced by the child in terms of his or her familial past and institutional, or adoptive, present, not as a religious experience *per se*. Added to this is the assumption, on the part of adults at least, that these children are incapable of making an informed decision about baptism or communion, let alone conversion. The adult narrators of texts about hidden children are divided about the matter of whether their younger selves were capable of independent religious belief. While the narrator of Janina David's memoir *A Square of Sky* is able to recall all kinds of external detail, her viewpoint seems entirely infused with retrospection and she claims that even before the war, the young Janie thought, 'Yes, as soon as I grew up I would become a Catholic.'[10] This is different from the blurred slide into Catholic practice recorded by the narrator of *A Hidden Childhood*, or Marysia in Miriam Winter's memoir *Trains*, who observes simply, 'My devotion grew along with my loneliness.'[11]

Hidden Jewish children's responses to what I have called encroaching Catholicism involved extremes of devotion, piety and pleasure (at his Communion, Henryk in Henryk Grynberg's novel *Child of the Shadows* reports, 'in spite of my heavy sin [in not having been baptised] I felt like an angel'[12]), as well as ambivalence, guilt and conflict, particularly in relation to losing their past and abandoning their parents. Henryk's experience of encroachment is different from that of, for instance, Paul in *When Memory Comes* because the former continued to live with his mother, whose Catholic persona was only external. Henryk's mother's responses to the child's newfound piety act as a bridge between the child's past and his present. In Grynberg's novel *A Child of the Shadows*, Henryk's mother tries for pragmatic reasons to reassure her son when he suffers from theological doubts:

> 'You must take Communion with the other children.'
> 'And carry a mortal sin?'
> 'If you don't do it, or if you say anything you shouldn't... you'll commit an even greater sin! Remember that!'[13]

The mother uses Henryk's Catholic vocabulary with a secular meaning when warning him of the possible 'sin' of exposing them both to danger. When Henryk's mother reassures him about the Jews crucifying Jesus her aim is to allay his worries for safety's sake, so that the very action of impersonation taken up by her and her son does not end up exposing them: ' "I think if he hadn't been born among Jews he would have been killed by non-Jews..." '.[14] In other words, what is a version of theological debate for the child is an external, pragmatic concern for the parent. Similarly, in *Wartime Lies* Maciek's aunt Tania tries to soothe the boy's encroaching Catholic guilt and thus preserve their gentile façade by encouraging him to take Communion, although he has not been baptised either: 'Her answer never varied: You have to do it, it's not your fault, if Jesus Christ allows these things to happen it is the fault of Jesus Christ, not your fault.'[15] In both these conversations, the adult has to persuade a child to act in a more consistently Catholic way than the Catholicism that is encroaching upon him would allow – by recourse to an *imitation* of the Catholic doctrine and vocabulary which the child has internalized. Perhaps the biggest discrepancy between vocabulary and reality occurs in *Child of the Shadows* when Henryk's mother takes him to see what she calls 'Jesus' grave' – this turns out to be the Warsaw Ghetto in flames, and she uses the sight as a warning to her son: ' "So remember once again, no one must know that you're a Jew! Ever!" '. Here, the phrase 'Jesus' grave' does have a meaning for the adult, however; Henryk's mother seems to be calling upon a notion of unjust death (' "behind this wall lived our uncles and aunts and your small cousins, the same age as you are" '),[16] and a sense of the death of Christian pretension to virtue.

It is this internalization that accounts for the moments in several novels about hidden children in which the child reproduces a version of Catholic doctrine in her or his own words. In *Wartime Lies* Maciek says, 'There was no salvation except through grace, and grace could be acquired only through baptism';[17] in Weinstein's novel *A Hidden Childhood* F. relates that, 'The Lord preached in Jerusalem. His mother was in Nazareth. She was sad because he'd left but he was the Son of God and had to obey' (27); Henryk observes, 'The most moving story was the one about Jesus who, although he was the son of the Lord God himself, had to escape with his distressed young mother from the soldiers of Herod, and had to hide all along the way for fear of being betrayed.'[18] This technique consists of a complex layering of different voices – the adult narrator's, the child's own repetition of a priest or religious teacher – which resembles direct utterance but has a forcefully dialogized meaning. Its effect is to reveal the logic of internalization: in each of these cases, the child is really speaking about his or her own concerns. Maciek fears being punished for his 'sinfulness' in lying about his background; and while F. is especially drawn by a story of Jesus being separated from his mother, Henryk is affected by one about Jesus living in hiding with her.

As Judith Kestenberg points out, Jewish children's perceptions of Christianity before the war were crucial in determining how their wartime experiences affected them. Such pre-war experiences did not involve the recognition of religious difference as such, but consisted rather of 'discrete, concrete events' viewed according to the 'egocentric mode of thinking' characteristic of children below the age of about ten.[19] Such events centred on children's awareness of the difference between familiar and strange behaviour, including distinctions between themselves and others in terms of language, dress and ritual.[20] These pre-war events included the celebration of Christian festivals by Jewish children (Anne Frank notes in her diary, 'Dearest Kitty, The closer it got to St Nicholas Day, the more we all thought back to last year's festively decorated basket'[21]) or not being allowed to do so (the child Gerhard in Gerhard Durlacher's memoir *Drowning* says, 'Though my mother sympathizes with my longing, Father gruffly brushes aside my wish for a fir tree; after all, we have Hanukkah'[22]); experiencing a loving relationship with a Christian maid (Maciek describes his in *Wartime Lies*: '[Zosia's] golden beauty filled me with wonder; I think that something literally moved in my heart'[23]); other children reacting abusively (André Stein reports such an incident in his memoir *Broken Silence*: 'my [Hungarian] classmates in Grade 2 called me dirty Jew, which made no sense at all since I was meticulously clean'[24]); and realizing that Catholic children did not share Jewish holidays. The psychologist Mortimer Ostow argues that after the age of five a child can distinguish between the Jewish and non-Jewish components of identity that she or he has incorporated, precisely through the kind of 'events' I have mentioned, and by associating with other children.[25]

Children's pre-war attitudes towards those outside or on the margins of the family combined with what happened within their own families to colour their wartime experience in Christian homes or institutions. For instance, Paul in *When Memory Comes* is grateful for the promise of love and protection from divine Christian figures in contrast to his distant Jewish father, while Sarah in *Rue Ordener, Rue Labat* detaches herself from her histrionic, emotive Jewish mother in favour of the more coolly supportive – and Catholic – Mémé.[26] Finally, the children's experience of Judaism itself affected their attitudes to their new homes. Kestenberg highlights the importance of a 'positive Jewish identity' in helping children to withstand both antisemitism and the threat to their own Jewishness.[27] Yet in *Rue Ordener, Rue Labat* the nine-year-old Sarah's 'detachment' from both her mother and Judaism takes place despite the fact that she is a rabbi's daughter who 'loved' Jewish festivals, that initially she sees 'the real danger' of the war as 'separation from my mother', and that her mother hid in the same place as her children;[28] in most other cases, attachment to another parental figure and/or to Christianity is the result of separation from the family. When Sarah does ambivalently return to her mother and to Judaism after the war, she describes this as a negative obligation: 'once again I obeyed all the religious *prohibitions* of my childhood' (my italics).[29]

Circumcision is of course noted as a liability by young hidden boys, even if they do not understand it as a sign of difference. Ostow argues that 'circumcision does not easily fall into the category of core Jewishness' as boys are not aware of it until they are eight or nine;[30] however, in the Holocaust world children did become aware of their circumcised state earlier than usual, even if they did not understand it. In Grynberg's novel, six-year-old Henryk thinks with childlike illogic when he got lost in Aryan Warsaw, 'I knew that crying was forbidden, because I had been circumcised.'[31] For the eight-year-old André Stein, in the absence of any religious observance at home, the external signs of circumcision and the taunts of others assured him that he was Jewish[32] – this is a reversal of an adult, peacetime view, which might rather see Jewishness as the reason for circumcision, and, instead of heeding the words of others, decide oneself whether or not to call oneself a Jew.

According to Ostow, a child 'becomes Jewish before [s/]he knows that Jewishness exists'.[33] Even very young children below the age of five have a 'core' Jewish identity established, for instance, by the child's 'use of sensitivity to language, names, dress and ritual as a means of establishing identification with family and community'.[34] Much of this identity may become and remain unconscious – although Ostow argues that, 'Being circumcised is never something relegated to the unconscious.'[35] This core identity is supplemented by the 'manifest identity', which 'may vary from time to time in response to external circumstances and the individual's current psychic state'.[36] The external circumstances during the Holocaust years of living in hiding, encroaching Catholicism, and antisemitism have such a marked effect that children's core identity itself is affected.

The components of the core that Ostow identifies are all to do with a positive establishment of heritage and community; during the Holocaust each of these aspects of Jewish identity turns bad, starting with what Ostow terms a 'principal component' of core Jewish identity, the name.[37] Just as it seemed that the attractions of Catholicism for wartime Jewish children were similar to those for adults living in peacetime, it may appear at first that during the Holocaust the role of 'the magical identifying device' of the name was simply a malign extension of its peacetime role. Ostow notes that even where Jews abandon their own languages, Jewish given and second names – 'signifying actual continuity with one's literal parents' – are less easily renounced. Ostow is describing here the (relatively) free choices of assimilation, particularly in the USA, but his words have a sinister and literal relevance for wartime Jewish children. In *Trains*, the narrator's given name represents the past she was for a while happy to forget: ' "How did your mother call you?" asked Romek. "Marysia", I lied. My name in hiding was Marysia Kowalska, but my real name was Miriam Winter [. . .] My mother called me Mirka. *They all* called me Mirka' (my italics).[38] Similarly, Ostow observes that in an assimilationist model, 'The first change to be made is to abandon clearly Jewish given names'; again, while Ostow envisages this occurring between the generations of a Jewish family, during the war these changes took place often several times within a few years in the lifetime of a single person. As Ostow points out, it is common Western practice for the initial letter of a person's 'English'[39] name to correspond to that of the 'Jewish' name of 'the ancestor who is being memorialized' and for whom the child has been named. During the Holocaust, however, it is the child's *own* name which is erased in this way, not that of a dead relation. Hidden children did often take up gentile names with the same initial as their own 'Jewish' name (Miriam becomes Marysia), although not consistently. As we saw in Chapter 1, there are different connections between the child's pre-war, wartime and post-war names for Pavel/Paul/Saul in *When Memory Comes*. Clearly, both the danger and the 'magic' of Jewish names during the war were increased by a potentially fatal highlighting of an unusually firm link between signifier and signified.

The significance of name-changes for hidden children during the Holocaust is represented in their texts by the act of narration itself. The reader never learns the real, 'Jewish' name of Maciek in Begley's *Wartime Lies*, nor of the sisters in Ida Fink's novel *The Journey*, as if these names can no longer be uttered; similarly, in Weinstein's *A Hidden Childhood* the distance between the author and her fictional younger self is signalled by preventing the reader from easily identifying one with the other: only the former is Frida, while the child is an abbreviated 'F.'.

During the war while living in Christian homes or institutions the discrete, concrete events marking out the difference between Judaism and Christianity for Jewish children were replaced by a linked series of responses to a new environment. This process is reproduced for the reader of fictional and non-fictional testimonies. As the narrator of Saul Friedländer's *When Memory Comes* notes about his younger self, children, after the trauma of separation, attached themselves to divine figures as substitutes for absent parents – 'Kneeling before the plaster statue [of Mary] with the sweet face [. . .] I rediscovered something of the presence of a mother.'[40] In an essay on group membership in which he compares the army and the Catholic church, Freud notes that, 'It is not without deep reason that the similarity between the Christian community and family is invoked.' The 'equal love' bestowed on all the church members by its leader, 'a substitute father', creates libidinal ties to the leader and to other members of the group. Freud argues that this principle of equal love was 'expressly enunciated by Christ: "Inasmuch as ye have done it unto one of the least of these my brethren, ye have done it unto me" '.[41] Under the special conditions of living without parents in a Catholic insitution, this effect is redoubled for Jewish children during the Holocaust. As an instance of the fact that the young Paul 'had passed over to Catholicism, body and soul', a scene in *When Memory Comes* represents Holy Week, 1944: 'Which of us was not gripped with emotion on reciting the last words of Jesus to the Apostles, on the evening of the Last Supper?: "As the Father hath loved me, so have I loved you: continue ye in my love" '.[42] The Biblical quotations chosen by Freud and Friedländer are very similar – but while Freud's emphasizes the shared nature of any offence within Catholicism, Friedländer's seems split between identification with Jesus on the brink of betrayal, and envying the apostolic security of divine love given by a human figure. The young Paul goes a step further than Freud's analysis allows for, as he does not experience God's love as equal or equalizing – precisely because he is Jewish, he thinks, 'Had God not tested me because he loved me *more* than the others, thus pointing out to me the road to sanctity?'[43]

Children in Catholic institutions felt the Christian God to be omniscient and benevolent ('By saving us, this new God was protecting us from evil, and we equated this new God with goodness'[44]), and identified with Jesus who they saw as similarly suffering and abandoned by his father ('If Christ was his son, why had he let him die?'[45]). Jewish children in hiding adopted the Christian habit of personal prayer (Anita, living with a Catholic nanny, prays for the return of a jacket with jewels sewn into the seams: 'The jacket had been Niania's. The treasure in its seams was Jewish. That may have been why the Holy Mother had ignored our prayers'[46]). They also adopted the habit of confession, which allayed the children's guilt at abandoning and then forgetting their parents. However, the very success of the Catholic environment 'created more guilt and conflict' for hidden children,[47] especially where their parents were concerned: Paul in *When Memory Comes* and F. in *A Hidden Childhood* in particular undergo guilt at this abandonment of the past. In *Don't They Know the World Stopped Breathing?* Renée's address to the statue of the patron saint St Francis leads to a conflation of narration and confession: ' "I knew you would want to hear my story. I am so glad I can speak to you" '.[48] Renée's 'story' is partly her recent activities, and partly the story that we are now reading. Placing St Francis on a level with the reader conveys the importance of Catholicism for the adult narrator as well as for the child. Renée also conflates narration with prayer in an address to a dead nun about her family and her religion: 'Sister Marie-Valentine, can you help me? [. . .] Find my Papa and my Maman, please [. . .] I miss them so, and I miss being what I was before.'[49]

In Catholic institutions, or in church for Jewish children living in Catholic homes, Rustow argues that 'a pre-ambivalent atmosphere of total beauty prevailed'[50] ('I was intoxicated by the splendor of the chasubles and ciboria'[51]) which allowed children to suppress any notion of historical or developmental conflict, sometimes with regressive effect, as 'everything "bad" – sexual, ugly, or aggressive – was rejected as sinful and banned from the mind'.[52] Such regression took the form of returning to behaviour appropriate to younger children (both Friedländer and Weinstein recount the agony of wetting the bed), and of 'blocking emotions and constricting cognition'[53] ('As if my previous life did not exist, I lived from day to day, without looking back'[54]).

By contrast, Judaism even before the war and before the period of hiding was often recalled by hidden children as alien (in *No Pretty Pictures* Anita remembers how her father 'rocked and mumbled in the mornings' in prayer[55]), painful (of the compulsory yellow star in Budapest 1944 André Stein notes, 'Until then, I knew only that to be Jewish was dangerous. On 3 April I learned that it was also shameful'[56]), only for men ('How I hated being forced to sit with the children and the women – away from Papa and his friends!'[57]), and as having an angry God who could not help them. Persecution was understood as the result of a misdeed ('And everything that happened later to this people was no more than they deserved!'[58]); 'Jewish looks' were seen as ugly and undesirable (' "What a pretty girl [. . .] She doesn't look like a Jewess at all" '[59]).

Hidden children's attitudes to Judaism conflate its features and their negative image with their own age; in other words, Judaism represents a lost, infantile realm while Catholicism represents a striving for adulthood. This confusion of developmental with external forces can be seen in the way Jewishness is recalled: as the voice of a parent ('I wasn't allowed to remember my father or grandfather [. . .] or any word they had ever said to me'[60]), family names (Marysia in *Trains* knows that her father's name was Tobiasz because she would add it to a poem he used to read her),[61] a smell (F. calls the odour of herring and onions, suddenly encountered in a Christian setting, 'The aroma of my memories', literally redolent of her 'Jewish home' (127); in *Trains*, the narrator says that the smell of *'czulent* is the sum and substance of my lost childhood'[62]). Once more it looks as if the experience of hidden children is simply a more extreme version of a well-known phenomenon. In this instance, it seems that these children are enacting the notion that the Old Testament will be superseded by the New, Judaism by Christianity. Indeed, several hidden children follow the trajectory outlined by Julia Kristeva in the sections of her *Powers of Horror* that concern Christianity's development out of Judaism. She argues that the Levitical laws of the Jewish Bible are material, organic and external, concerned with regulating the consumption of food, contact with the diseased and the role of women. By contrast, Christianity places emphasis on internal defilement, what Kristeva calls the 'interiorization of impurity', and the possibility of its remittance.[63] Within Christianity, guilt and sin can be absolved by the utterance of confession: 'Meant for remission, sin is what is absorbed – in and through speech.'[64] Kristeva contrasts the discursive confession with Jewish practices of 'bewailing, prayer or atonement'; 'acts of atonement, of contrition, of paying one's debt to a pitiless, judging God, are eclipsed by the sole act of speech. One slides over from the judicial to the verbal.'[65] Kristeva's terms could have been borrowed from one of the psychologist Flora Hogman's subjects, whose fear of the ritual of atonement seems rooted in her perception of it as non-verbal.

In the texts about hidden children discussed here, we can see the enactment of this shift from external prohibitions to internal. As part of her adoption of Christianity, F. in *A Hidden Childhood* eagerly transgresses kosher food laws – 'we feast there on the most delicious dish: pork' (82) – and notes the importance placed upon the inner life as well as the outer – showers on Saturdays 'cleanse our souls and our bodies' before High Mass on Sunday (40). Yet the narrator of *A Hidden Childhood* reveals that F.'s aspirations to Catholic spirituality are often subverted by the very 'material' world she has tried to renounce. Just after eating pork on Christmas Eve, F. is so nauseated by the milk she is made to drink – 'I don't like milk with cream in it, it's sticky [...] my head is spinning' (82–3) – that she cannot keep down her Christmas dinner.

But, fascinatingly, although she has transgressed one of the 'Levitical laws' forbidding the consumption of pork, this undrinkable glass of milk is the very thing that shows F. is not able to accede to Catholicism. It is similar to the milk that Kristeva describes at the beginning of *Powers of Horror* as an archetypal instance of abjection:

> When the eyes see or the lips touch that skin on the surface of milk [...] I experience a gagging sensation and, still farther down, spasms in the stomach [...] Along with sight-clouding dizziness, *nausea* makes me balk at that milk cream.[66]

By 'abjection', Kristeva means a sickening reminder of the human subject's bodily, rather than transcendent or spiritual, origins, often provoked by food. In F.'s case, the abjection-inclined, Levitical subject is still present, as her nausea and dizziness at the milk show, in constrast to the reaction of other – non-Jewish – girls at the convent school ('Everyone here likes it'):

> In the morning, when Sister Marie leaves, they fight beside the empty milk jug over who's going to scrape the hardened cream hanging over the edge like yellow strips of cloth. (82)

Clearly this does not mean that F. herself is the more primitive, Jewish 'being of abjection', whose transgressions of the Law are experienced bodily, and that she has failed to become the superior 'lapsing' Christian subject Kristeva describes, whose failings are those of rational choice – 'if Levitical taboo was what is excluded from a Law, sin, on the other hand, is a defect in judgment'.[67] Rather, both Jewishness and Christianity have a different meaning for a young child in these circumstances from the meaning they have for Kristeva. For F., Judaism represents the familial past, Christianity a new, safe, communal existence – but one which her mother cannot share. Kristeva argues that nausea at the skin on milk represents separation from 'the mother and father who proffer it' – it is 'that element, sign of their desire'.[68] For F., on the other hand, the milk acts as a cover for quite the opposite. It is the apparently neutral dairy product,[69] rather than the apparently 'delicious' pork, which makes F. experience the *'nausea'* of abjection. F.'s adoption of Christianity is necessarily at the expense of her parents, who she knows – as does Renée in *Touch Wood* – will be damned by the very religion that saves their daughter.

At mass after having to drink her milk, F. observes longingly the spiritualized interiority of the other girls, who are already baptised: 'The girls who are receiving communion take Jesus in their hearts. I envy them' (84). Kristeva claims that communion – 'to eat and drink the flesh and blood of Christ' – is also 'to transgress symbolically the Levitical prohibitions', this time against the ingestion of blood.[70] Indeed, hidden Jewish children's texts frequently do represent communion as if it were the transgression of a food prohibition. Renée in *Don't They Know the World Stopped Breathing?* reports that she and her sister were told of the wafer, ' "Careful not to bite it [. . .] or you will hurt Christ and blood will come into your mouth". '[71] By reporting the nun's words in this way, the adult narrator emphasizes the transgression involved in both eating a living creature, and consuming blood. F., who is not baptised during the course of her narrative, at first does not dare commit the 'sacrilege' of secretly tasting a wafer, because 'It will become the body of the Lord and His blood' (133). Only when she has partially returned to thoughts of her mother and the Jewish past does F. dare to taste one – the communion wafer itself represents Jewish ritual laws by reminding F. of matzah, 'unleavened bread' (147). That is, even the central Catholic rite of communion does not represent 'progress' but returns F. to the Jewish past – and to the Passover festival, a meal commemorating Jewish freedom from exile and slavery.

None of the various texts that I have mentioned is structured like adult accounts of living 'in hiding', in which a false identity is adopted and then shed at the war's end. Such a clear division between assumed and 'real' identity was not available to hidden children. Rather, these accounts represent a process of learning and internalizing certain habits and behaviours, whose religious, familial and even ethnic implications were not perceptible to the children themselves. Indeed, this confusion is increased by the nature of the external imposture and resulting internal encroachment: what seemed to be simply a new religious allegiance was meant to erase a prior overdetermined identity consisting of religious, national and racial aspects. Thus these tales of Jewish children living 'in hiding' in Catholic contexts are best – or can only be – told by an adult narrator, however hidden such an entity may also be, for an adult reader. I would argue that such a narrator has a religious orientation in its turn; in the case of Frida Weinstein's *A Hidden Childhood* the narrator is a principle of Jewish conscience and observance – both in a religious and in a watchful sense; while in Renée Roth-Hano's *Touch Wood*, the narrator is ambivalent and, like the child herself, 'torn' between two allegiances.

Elisabeth Gille, *Shadows of a Childhood*

These narratorial stances are quite different from that in Elisabeth Gille's novel *Shadows of a Childhood*,[72] which is told in a far more conventional manner. As the subject of *Shadows* is not hidden childhood itself but the effects of such an experience – which make Léa an emotionally inscrutable existential heroine – the novel does not match its narration to its content. Like *A Hidden Childhood* and *Touch Wood*, Gille's novel is fictionalized autobiography.[73] The novel recounts the youth of Léa Lévy, the daughter of recently converted Russian Jews living in France who placed her in a convent in Bordeaux when she was five, in 1942. Léa is befriended by a non-Jewish girl, Benedicte Gaillac, whose parents are in the Resistance; the Gaillacs adopt Léa after the war. When Léa learns that her parents are almost certainly dead, she becomes obsessed with the trials of Nazi perpetrators and collaborators in Bordeaux; just as she seems to be developing a way of considering her parents' and her own fate, Benedicte is killed in a car accident, leaving Léa bereaved again. The action is narrated in the past, rather than in the present tense. The third-person narrator in Gille's novel does not adopt varying degrees of distance from the protagonist, as do the narrators of Weinstein's and Roth-Hano's novels; rather, the narrator always views Léa from the viewpoint of an adult:

> Léa stood *revealed*. Her curly hair looked like a mat of brown wool. Her dark cheeks were flushed with exertion and her *small* face contorted with rage. (my italics)[74]

Thus the reader does not gain any internal view of what Christianity meant to Léa, as she/he does in *A Hidden Childhood* (F. gives her own idiosyncratic paraphrases of Catholic doctrine) or *Touch Wood* (Renée explains her attraction to Catholicism and the competing, residual pull of Judaism). Léa is never viewed ironically, although often tragically.

It is not so much that the child has been entirely subsumed by the adult narrator of *Shadows of a Childhood*; it is rather that the child and the narrator are indistinguishable. Their knowledge is identical; the child is already an adult, as shown by the way in which the narrator describes what Léa sees on newsreels about the liberation of Bergen-Belsen: 'The wasted bodies tumbled slowly over one another in postures like grotesque couplings.'[75] The same indistinguishability is notable when Léa is fascinated first by an ecclesiastical procession in 1944 celebrating the feast of Joan of Arc, and also by SS officers in the street; the narrator simply notes on the nuns' behalf, 'It was decided to interpret her fascination as religious fervor and to opt for Communion.'[76] Although it is clear that the narrator knows that the nuns are wrong – 'It was decided' – the significance of this occasion is not revealed for over fifty pages, when Léa tells Benedicte she has memorized the faces of priests and Nazis alike in order to give evidence against them.[77] Again, there is no difference here between the adult narrator's and the child's knowledge.

'Between two religions'[78]

Frida Scheps Weinstein's novel *A Hidden Childhood: A Jewish Girl's Sanctuary in a French Convent, 1942–1945*, is about a French child aged eight in 1942 who was sent by her Polish-born mother to a convent school at the Château de Beaujeu; her father had earlier escaped to Palestine. The novel alternates the present-time events at the convent school with F.'s memories, which are about her childhood in the area where refugees lived in Paris, the rue des Jardins Saint-Paul.[79] *A Hidden Childhood* is remarkable for its revelation of the way in which a young child swiftly learns and internalizes Christian ritual,[80] yet never entirely shakes off her Jewish past. This movement into and then away from Catholicism is described in a particular narrative technique: present-time, first-person narration, which is double-voiced but does not use free indirect discourse.

Like Renée Fersen-Osten's *Don't They Know the World Stopped Breathing?*, *A Hidden Childhood* is written in the present tense in an effort to recreate the subjectivity of the child, whom the narrator calls 'F.'. In this way, the older F. is present only as a narrative construct – the implied entity who has chosen and written down the events we read – and the little girl reveals her experience and preoccupations without the commentary of an adult. Seen from the viewpoint of a child psychologist, this structure represents an unhealthy allegiance to the past. According to Yolanda Gampel, the act of describing a past as if it is present, in 'a manner unsuited to [the survivor's] present chronological age and reality', and visualizing and describing scenes as they were 'experienced in the past, not as [they are] interpreted today',[81] are signs of pathology. However, in a literary text these methods are obviously very *well* suited to representing a lost historical and developmental past; this is shown in *A Hidden Childhood* by the novelistic exaggeration of the past's present-ness, as if the reader were an interlocutor the child must fear: 'We are Jews, too. Didn't want to say it before – got to be careful, you never know' (7).

Such moments represent an apparent supersession of adult interpretation by childhood experience, to use Gampel's distinction, but from a *novelistic* viewpoint the two voices and times are always present throughout *A Hidden Childhood*. Strictly speaking, there are two entities – adult narrator and child character – in Weinstein's apparently univocal novel just as there are in the more obviously split *Wartime Lies* and *W or the Memory of Childhood*. We may see events through the eyes of the young F., and in a version of her voice, but we know that this is a retrospective narrative constructed by an adult. At times the adult narrator's input is implicit; at other times, it is clearly present and creates a stark gap between the child's viewpoint and its meaning. Mikhail Bakhtin notes that novelistic first-person narration is characterized by 'an intention on the part of the [narrator] to make use of someone else's discourse in the direction of its own particular aspirations'. In the case of *A Hidden Childhood*, the 'tones and intonations truly characteristic'[82] of a child's-eye view conceal within them the 'aspirations' and ideas of the narrator. In *A Hidden Childhood*, the effect is largely ironic, although at the expense, rather than in support, of the child. The silent adult narrator also alerts the reader to subtexts, particularly about F.'s buried Jewish past, of which the child herself is unaware. Bakhtin says of Dostoevsky's *Notes from Underground* that it is a 'confession', as it is a first-person self-revelation, but 'not in the personal sense': 'this is not a personal document but a work of art'.[83] The same could be said of Weinstein's novel; it is a 'testimony' but not in the 'personal sense' as it is a work of art: like Elie Wiesel's *Night*, it is a highly structured text, offering a stylized, fictional child's voice in its effort to represent the past.

At certain moments in *A Hidden Childhood* the co-presence of adult and child is highlighted, for instance in the bathetic clash – set up by the invisible narrator – of childlike and Christian discourse in F.'s utterances:

Alice says they ate a lot of sugar-coated almonds at her [baptismal] ceremony. They all have a baptismal certificate. I myself have nothing but a paper from the dispensary saying I have a spot on my lungs. I also have spotty freckles, but it's the spot on one's soul that counts. (31)

Indeed, the reader might question whether this is really a clash of discourses or the reduction of Catholic sentiment to the level of freckles and spots – in other words, the subliminal discrediting of the very creed that F. is striving to live by. The same debasing and funny slide from religious to bodily discourse occurs when F. mentions one of the nuns: 'We are sure that of all the saints in the château Sister Marie will have the best place in heaven. What's more, she has tuberculosis' (110); and when F. wishes not to wet her bed at night: 'I hope the Last Judgement will come soon. So long as there are no more mornings!' (125). These instances may seem typical of a child's confusion of levels of discourse; however, they are not artless at all, but further evidence of the adult narrator's hidden presence. In the case of F.'s idolizing thoughts about Henriette, another hidden child, the subtext that the corporeal language represents becomes clearer:

We're both descended from the Ancient People. Oh, Henriette, I'll feel proud with you! I'll knock on doors; we'll spread the good word and people will know us. Oh, God! I feel feverish, my hands are clammy, my mind's wandering. I don't want to be sick for Christmas. (81)

The unsettling consciousness of F.'s Jewish ancestry disrupts her efforts to become a real 'French' girl (67): the contradiction between the image of Henriette as a missionary and as another hidden child causes F. to feel feverish. This ironic and 'sickening' juxtaposition comes from the adult narrator, suggesting that it is this narrator who is really the text's 'hidden', Jewish presence, and who orchestrates without comment such ironic self-revelation on the child's part. Just before the extract quoted, F.'s vision of her future with Henriette seems to be transposed to a Middle Eastern setting, paradoxically both the birthplace of Christ and refuge of her father David:[84]

The two of us walk lightly along in the sun, singing my favorite hymn: 'Flowers of Israel...look from heaven and hear our prayer...'. When we get to the desert, I kneel down and wash her tired feet with warm sand. (81)

Throughout *A Hidden Childhood,* F.'s Jewish ancestry exerts a residual and disruptive pressure on the child and her language. Indeed, as we have seen in the case of F.'s favourite hymn and feelings about her father, the two religions are not separated but awkwardly superimposed in F.'s mind. In each instance, the disruptive recalled Jewish detail is also a sign of the adult narrator's fictive choices: these two meanings inhabit a single signifier. In one episode, F. is upset by denied memories of her mother and gets into a fight with another girl over – significantly – a nativity scene; she takes out her anger on an ant hill,[85] both seeing the ants as Jews (they are at her mercy, and act like refugees in carrying 'bundles') and denying this equivalence (they are not usurers):

> I squash [an ant]. 'There, that'll teach you!' I say out loud as I wipe the blood off my knee. Another one, a big one, moves ahead with a white bundle on its back; I know it's been preparing all summer. I flick it off my finger – it's so small – and say, 'The ant is not a lender!' as Yvonne, the little girl from Marseilles does. (78)

Finally, it is revealing that the 'direct, unmediated discourse' of Hogman's psychological account of 'Frida' is quite different from the fictive representation of F. in Weinstein's novel.[86] Most strikingly, although Hogman concludes her discussion by stating that Frida's mother died in Auschwitz,[87] this fact is never revealed in *A Hidden Childhood.* In Weinstein's novel, F.'s feelings towards her mother at first move negatively from relief at separation ('I felt rid of her', 11), to associating her mother with Jews while asserting her own Christian identity ('My mother's not a French mamma', 77, 'I don't belong to that people anymore, not since I left my mother', 98), to attempting to substitute the church for her mother ('But she is no longer my mother: I want to be a daughter of the Church', 50, 'on letter-writing day I don't write [to my mother] anymore, I study the life of St Teresa', 85).

However, as with her Jewish identity generally, F.'s efforts at denying her mother often serve in fact to highlight her allegiance. Throughout the novel, the memories which alternate with the present-time account of life in the convent school are always of the child's mother, and are often triggered by the kind of repudiating sentiments quoted above. This pattern of over-emphatic denial followed by guilty restitution in memory is halted by a moment, like the one following the fantasy of acting as Henriette's disciple, of confronting the brutal possibility of deportation: 'I have a dreadful feeling my mother's not in Paris anymore' (103). From this moment on, the past in Paris and rue des Jardins Saint-Paul is not separated from – either structurally or psychologically – but incorporated into the present:

> Why don't I remember Yiddish anymore? I can hear again in my memory the voices of my mother and aunt, some sounds and bits of phrases, but I don't understand what they mean. (119)

In remembering the voices of her mother and aunt speaking the Jewish language which she can no longer recall, F. acknowledges what she has lost. In tandem with this imperfect maternal retrieval is one of retrieving Jewishness. F. recalls a comment once made by a teacher as she says the Hail Mary – ' "you can't convert *those* people!" ' (146) – but unlike the moment when she heard this remark (138), the comment now sounds not like a reproach but like a promise, and subverts F.'s prayer. At the same communion F. notes that the host tastes like unleavened 'Jewish bread' (147).

The mother's death is not narrated in *A Hidden Childhood*, in order to preserve the consistency of the child's-eye, present-time view, but the novel's ending points towards two unresolved events: reunion with the mother ('I don't know what has become of my mother. I don't dare ask. Deep down inside me I'm afraid; I don't want to know' (151, the book's last lines)); and F.'s attitude towards her newly acquired Catholicism ('The multiplication table is in my pocket, next to the rosary, Sister Marie's gift of fidelity and farewell', 151). *A Hidden Childhood* appears to be an elegy for F.'s mother; it is harder to tell whether it is also an elegy for F.'s Jewish or her Catholic identity.

'Identity confusion':[88] Renée Roth-Hano, *Touch Wood*

Renée Roth-Hano's novel *Touch Wood: A Girlhood in Occupied France*[89] concerns the fate of three young girls whose Hungarian-born parents moved from the Alsace to occupied Paris during the war. In 1941 the children are sent to hide in a Catholic women's residence, La Chaumière in Normandy, where, like F. in Weinstein's novel, Renée is drawn to Catholic doctrine and practice. *Touch Wood* is narrated with more clarity than *A Hidden Childhood*, partly because of its protagonist's age (Renée Roth was born in 1931, F. in 1934, and, as Wreschner Rustow argues, 'the older [children] were better able to conceptualize their identity struggle than the younger ones'[90]) but also because Roth-Hano is clearly indebted to Weinstein's novel. Many features of *A Hidden Childhood* appear here in starker form.[91] The present-time narration of the latter has become a fully fledged fictional diary in *Touch Wood* ('I chose the diary format as the best way to portray the climate of the times...I tried to keep the entry dates as close as I could to the events as they occurred', v). The fact that the diary is a narrative conceit is not concealed, and there are several impossible entries: '*Tuesday, June 6 [1944]*. I think I'm waking up from a nightmare' (238), reports Renée of the Allied bombing of Normandy at a moment when writing a diary entry would have been unlikely. In contrast to the internalized viewpoint of *A Hidden Childhood*, where the whole narrative takes place after F. has been separated from her mother, *Touch Wood* is full of dialogue, most of it clearly reconstructed, interaction with other people, including Renée's family and schoolmates, and greater self-awareness.

Similarly, the signifiers of Jewishness which kept troubling the eight-year-old F. are also present in the ten-year-old Renée's story, but in such a self-conscious manner that it is hard not to detect Weinstein's influence – and also that of the child psychologist Flora Hogman, herself a former hidden child, who Roth-Hano thanks alongside Weinstein in her acknowledgements as 'faithful members of my writing-group' (ii). The apparently strict boundaries between child psychology, autobiography, testimony and fiction in the work of Weinstein, Roth-Hano, Hogman and Wrescher Rustow threaten to disappear, in the face of the kind of generic collapse signalled by an error of Hogman's: she refers to *A Hidden Childhood* and *Touch Wood* as 'autobiographies' (531).

In *A Hidden Childhood*, F. bemoans her 'very curly' hair as the only feature that stops her appearing 'French': 'All Jews have curly hair, that's how I recognize them' (8). At the Catholic school, F. repudiates another hidden child in order to claim a distinction between them: '[Rachel] has very black, tangled, curly hair and her skin is sallow, not white like *ours*' (39, my italics); when another child admires F.'s hair, F. tries to rid herself of the sign of difference: 'I grab a lock, pull it out by the roots, and look at it in my outstretched hand' but adds, 'I feel funny' when she sees her own hair, in an image of dispersal and death, blowing away (59–60). After the partial reclamation of her mother and her past, F. is proud of her difference: 'I'd still like to be the only one with curly hair', she observes of another girl whose grandmother is black (89). In each of these instances, however, the child's voice is stylized and invites a response: F.'s rejection of Rachel is clearly as partial as her claim that curly hair is the way one recognizes Jews.

In *Touch Wood*, however, these tropes are self-conscious and the reader is encouraged to identify with Renée's self-doubt. The controlling hand of the adult narrator, with her extra psychological and retrospective knowledge, is nearly always perceptible in the plethora of hair-related instances, which seem overtly to benefit from Hogman's observation that '[the children] wanted to look like Christians, not like Jews' (523). Renée is dissatisfied with her appearance when looking into the mirror on two occasions: she notes at the outset of the novel that 'my hair [is] too curly' (15); and that when she has to wear a yellow star 'the whole world will know that I am a Jew' not just for that reason but because of the 'dark curly hair I've tugged so many times to try to get it straighter' (97).[92] Renée envies both the rest of her family for their less 'dark and curly' hair (98) and another Jewish girl with straight hair (50), and is asked to take the role of Judas in a play at La Chaumière 'because of my black curly hair' (195). She describes the French police (227), and German (261) and British soldiers (280) as 'blond' to signify their various kinds of difference from herself, and wishes to have been born into a 'blond and blue-eyed family' (115, also 146, 201). Eventually Renée too wishes to save her 'fashionable curls', as her 'only asset' (200). In *A Hidden Childhood*, these details of Jewish identity have a more internal, implicit resonance than they do in *Touch Wood*, where symbolism is spelled out.

While the story of F. in Weinstein's novel did not conform in all details to Hogman's account of 'Frida's' experience, Renée's in Roth-Hano's novel does conform more closely to Hogman's account of 'Renée': it is as if in *Touch Wood* we are given fictional versions of details in the psychological account, which was published in the same year. Hogman notes that her interviewee 'Renée' did not see Jewish women as role models, and was delighted to find in Catholicism a religion that valued a woman (512). In *Touch Wood*, Renée says:

> Jewish women can never become saints. They aren't even sup-posed to touch the Torah or to pronounce the name of God, and they don't count at all when it comes to a minyan, the quorum of Jews required in order to worship. It's Maman who told me this!
>
> At least here [at La Chaumière] God is nicer to women. He made Mary the mother of Jesus and little Thérèse de Lisieux a saint!
>
> I look at the statue of Mary – her face soft and smiling, her hands stretched out and welcoming. I feel torn. I don't know which way to go. (161).

At first this passage is related from the child's viewpoint in her own words – 'Jewish women can never become saints' – although interference from the adult narrator, this time in didactic mode, breaks through – 'the quorum of Jews'. In her article 'The Experience of Catholicism for

Jewish Children During World War II', Hogman's commentary concludes with an almost direct quotation – 'Renée was torn between the Jewish and Christian faiths' (513) – of Roth-Hano's novel, where the fictional Renée notes, in the extract above, 'I feel torn.' Hogman describes 'Renée's' wish for an 'elegant' mother 'like the French ladies' (512); again, this is an almost direct quotation of Renée's thoughts about her mother in *Touch Wood*, who is 'plump, with fat legs and fat knees', in contrast to her non-Jewish friend Pepée's mother, who is 'always so elegant' (77).[93]

Unlike *A Hidden Childhood*, the narrator of *Touch Wood* is not a hidden Jew but a more ambivalent presence, prompting Renée – if in a self-conscious manner in contrast to *A Hidden Childhood* – to reveal the contradictions and conflicts of her situation. These revelations are mostly ones of which Renée too is aware, apart from one instance. It is the title of Roth-Hano's novel which most resembles the narrative stance of *A Hidden Childhood*, where F. frequently gives herself away without realizing it. 'Touch wood' is the catch-phrase of Renée's mother, and she is quoted using it in the hope that Jews will be better treated in Paris than in the east (17); that Renée's father will not be betrayed by his boss at a new job (127); and that Renée's grandmother will be safe from the Gestapo in an old people's home (218). It appears that both Renée and her mother are ignorant of the thoroughly Christian origins of this phrase – that it is good luck to touch the wood from Christ's cross. However, it seems that the adult narrator does know this, and shares the irony with the reader over Renée's head on her first night at La Chaumière:

> My eyes fall on the cross hanging over my bed. Maybe – just maybe – Jesus on his cross could help me long enough to face Mother Superior.
> But I decide that's not a good idea. Instead, I reach out to the armoire with my fingers, touching wood for good luck. (137)

This moment apparently tends away from Christianity, as Renée touches the 'armoire' and not the crucifix, but it is part of a process that turns out to have permanent effects ('something is shattered for ever and we will never again be the same', Renée says after the sisters' baptism, 231). It is as if the occasions on which Renée's mother wished for luck, each of which concerned avoiding the Nazis' racist activities, turned out well – the girls and their parents survive the war – thanks to the Christian rather than the Jewish God; Renée compares the two Gods, to the latter's disadvantage (170).[94]

6
Masquerading as Gentile

In this chapter I will discuss two texts about living 'openly' in hiding during the Holocaust years, in which the central characters masquerade as gentile. In both Ida Fink's novel *The Journey* and Solomon Perel's memoir *Europa, Europa*[1] the protagonist is a teenager, and for this reason their experience contrasts with that of young children hiding in Christian institutions, or young children hiding openly with family members. Rather than simply living 'on the surface', in Gunnar Paulsson's phrase,[2] both teenagers enact multiple and sometimes conflicting performances on the basis of racial, national, class and gender stereotypes.

Because they are adolescents, the protagonists of Fink's novel and Perel's memoir have to harness to their masquerades such age-specific issues as developing independence from the family, concerns with personal appearance, gender role and sexuality, identity formation, becoming part of a group, and not appearing different from that group's members. Each of these developmental categories is taken to its extreme; it provides the backdrop and even impetus for the protagonists' masquerade. Independence is thrust upon these adolescents whose parents are absent or dead; concerns over personal appearance and self-esteem are interwoven with the denigration of Jewishness; blending into a peer group is a matter of life and death when the others in the group are gentile. In this sense, the circumstances and responses of Fink's and Perel's protagonists are akin to those of the thirteen-year-old diarist Eva Gold, of whom the child psychologist Theresa Cahn says, 'Eva does not stop her adolescence to cope with the Holocaust. Rather she experiences the Holocaust through the lens of the developmental issues that impinge on her.'[3] For Fink's nameless female protagonist and Perel's young Solomon, age-specific issues are inextricable from the detail of their masquerade, just as for both gender-specific signifiers become inextricable from those of 'race'.

'Womanliness as a masquerade':[4] Ida Fink, *The Journey*

Much has been written in recent years about the interrelation of Jewish identity and constructions of gender;[5] but there has been little attempt to explore the pressure on these categories in the Holocaust years. In this section I will consider the notion of passing for gentile during the Holocaust, and the attendant danger of being unmasked as Jewish, in relation to Ida Fink's novel *The Journey*. The central characters in Fink's novel are women and so do not risk 'the simple, logical invitation' frequently directed to men: 'If Pan is not a kike, a *zydlak*, would he please let down his trousers?'[6] – a scene which occurs, with variations, in many texts about men passing for gentile. Instead, *The Journey* shows the specifically feminine constructions of both Aryanness and Jewishness which took hold in exaggerated form during the Holocaust years.

Ida Fink is one of a number of eye-witnesses who have chosen the freedom of fiction over the strictures of memoir when writing about the Holocaust.[7] Her work is published as fiction, although in interviews she has mentioned what many readers must have suspected: that it has factual and autobiographical origins.[8] The leeway fiction offers is clear in Fink's texts. The short stories in her collections *A Scrap of Time and Other Stories* and *Traces: Stories*[9] rely on hearsay, rumour and other insubstantial sources, and they are told from a range of different viewpoints, Jewish and non-Jewish, male and female, survivors and the dead. Fink's novel *The Journey* reads as if it is autobiographical, although it does not entirely tally with the biography given in her books: Fink, born in Poland in 1921, 'lived in a ghetto throughout 1942 and then went into hiding until the end of the war' (i). It is left characteristically unclear here whether 'into hiding' refers to entering a hiding-place, or starting to live openly but as a gentile.[10] Choosing to classify her work as fiction allows Fink to retain ambiguity about the relation between her writing and her life; and it foregrounds the writing itself, making, for instance, imperfect recall in *The Journey* a narrative puzzle rather than an authenticating device.

The Journey relates the story of two young Jewish girls, whose real names and ages we never learn, masquerading as gentiles in occupied Poland. They work as forced labourers within a Nazi scheme which recruited 'volunteers' from occupied countries for labour in Germany,[11] and have to flee each place when their true identity is uncovered. The story is told (mostly) in the first person by an adult narrator about her younger self. The protagonist and her sister leave their Polish home-town for Germany in 1942, with false documents naming them Katarzyna Majewska and Elzbieta Stefanska. At first they work in a munitions factory in the Ruhr valley; then they flee to Iserlohn with another young woman, Marysia, after their co-workers make clear they suspect them of being Jewish. Katarzyna, the protagonist, turns herself into Joanna Pilecka, Elzbieta becomes Jadwiga Kotula, while Marysia is Anna Kloc. After handing themselves in at a local *Arbeitsamt* (work office), the three young women are sent to different farms. The danger of betrayal arises again, and the sisters flee once more – as Maria Walkowska and Barbara Falenska – to Karlsruhe. They are separated from Anna and never see her again. In Karlsruhe the sisters give themselves up to the police and are nearly handed over to the Gestapo before being sent to different farms, where they work until the liberation in April 1945.

The subjective splittings and masquerades that I discuss below are female adolescent reactions to hiding in Nazi-occupied Europe: not hiding away out of sight, but hiding something of one's self. The 'internal fortification'[12] possessed by the protagonist in *The Journey*[13] makes the shifts in identity undergone by the two sisters external ones; when alien selves threaten to become internalized, the protagonist is on guard against this. The clear return of the girls' own selves at the war's end is signalled by the astonishment of Hermina, the farmer's wife, that 'Maria' wants to leave: 'She had thought I would wait at least till the harvest' (239). Hermina's belief in Maria's masquerade is so strong that she cannot see the 'real' person underneath it. Nonetheless, the assumption of different personae, or fragments of personae, does have an internally splitting effect on the protagonists of *The Journey*. Because of their gender and particular circumstances – they are Polish city Jews masquerading as gentiles, alternately Polish or German country girls – the precise detail of the sisters' appearance is often as important as their accents, false papers and invented biographies. Whereas attention is ultimately focused on the bodily mark of circumcision in order to determine the 'true' identity of a man, such attention may take in any part of a female body.[14] In *Wartime Lies*, for instance, Maciek's grandfather speculates that a co-lodger may also be Jewish, based on the evidence that, 'probably she bleached her hair to make it less red, and there was something too tender about her eyes'.[15]

This means that in *The Journey* the young, unattached[16] sisters have a range of identifications to call upon, even if the suspicious gaze of informers and bystanders singles out Elzbieta's dark hair, a faulty accent (the protagonist mispronounces 'Karlsruhe') and particular surnames as weak spots in the façade. The protagonist uses the word 'recognize' (77, 82) in a particular way to signal her perception that other women are Jewish, whether they are pretending to be something else or not. She uses the term to mean the opposite of the psychoanalytic 'misrecognize'; in *The Journey*, the protagonist must know who she and others are – there is no option for the 'misrecognition [...] of Jewish self-alienation'.[17] Jacques Lacan emphasizes the close relation between recognition and misrecognition:

> Misrecognition is not ignorance. Misrecognition represents a certain organization of affirmations and negations, to which the subject is attached. Hence it cannot be conceived without correlate knowledge.[18]

This explains the various scenarios of suspicion, unmasking, informing and betrayal which take place in Fink's novel. Although the seven Jewish girls in the munitions factory are officially Aryan, everyone else knows or learns who they 'really' are. As Lacan argues, knowing is inseparable from not knowing, especially in these circumstances where the difference between knowledge and the lack of it is also the difference between life and death. In other words, the strict separation of Aryans and non-Aryans paradoxically does not guard against but guarantees the recognizable presence of Jews. In *The Journey* the protagonist's knowledge simply precedes that of everyone else. The following snippets of dialogue from the sisters' time in the factory all concern this kind of suspicion and knowledge: ' "Ladies, may I have a talk with the two of you?" ' (54); 'If she came from our town, she'd know who we were' (72); ' "They say that you... and the other one... and one more... the tall one with dark hair... and – " '(86); ' "He *knows*" ' (90); ' "Let them sing by themselves. Let's see how much they really know" ' (102). These phrases represent an overdetermination of seeing, knowing, telling, guessing and (mis)recognition of the truth. As Lacan puts it, 'There must be, behind misrecognition, a knowledge of what there is to misrecognize',[19] and these instances in *The Journey* represent moments when recognition emerges inevitably out of misrecognition.

To follow Joan Riviere's argument in her essay 'Womanliness as a Masquerade', the people best at seeing through the masquerade of others are those who have put on a similar front. In Riviere's examples, it is women who recognize each other's masquerade,[20] while in *The Journey* a disguised Jewish woman recognizes others in the same state. However, in their first placement at the munitions factory, everyone eventually sees through the girls' masquerade; and the narrator notes that the other Jewish women in the factory camp are not all masquerading at the same level. Stefa, for instance, is 'still herself' (74) and recognizable simply for looking out of place. Marysia does not bother to cover up either, while out on a walk with the protagonist and the camp director: 'One real, the other pretending, and all for nothing' (88). There are, however, two central differences between Riviere's template and that in *The Journey*. First, in 'Womanliness as a Masquerade' moments of unmasking – in which a woman may forget to 'put on' a guise – alternate easily with moments of successful masquerade. In Fink's novel, letting the mask slip could result in deathly recognition and the end of the whole process. Second, the front put on in *The Journey* is a consciously assumed one, in contrast to the involuntary, unconscious assumption described by Riviere.[21]

The split subject

The protagonist of *The Journey* has her pre-war identity sundered on several occasions, precisely at those moments when, concerned to present a seamless false self, she *hopes* for misrecognition from herself and others. In a reverse of the mirror stage pattern described by Jacques Lacan, in which the 'jubilant assumption' of the 'specular image' compensates the child for 'his motor incapacity and nursling dependence',[22] in *The Journey* the empowered self in the mirror has been purposely crafted that way, for instance when the protagonist adjusts the Polish peasant's floral headscarf she will wear on the first stage of her journey:

> With each of these tiny changes, the face in the mirror changed completely. I studied it carefully. It belonged to a girl I didn't know, and as I looked at her, smiling, colourfully dressed, I wondered: Which looks better: bangs down, or pulled back? Which looks more Aryan? (19)

Here, it is not simply an illusory specular effect which makes the protagonist fail to recognize her own reflection ('a girl I didn't know'), but a carefully constructed façade aimed to provoke misrecognition in the viewer as well. This act of masquerade appears similar to the ones described by Joan Riviere: a front of femininity is constructed by women who feel they have appropriated masculine power, in order to soothe their own 'anxiety' and avert male – or, in this case, Aryan – 'retribution'.[23] Looking 'better' here does not mean more seemly, or more attractive, but, as the protagonist herself acknowledges, 'more Aryan'. However, although the subject's anxiety and fear of retribution are certainly present in *The Journey*, the masquerade does not conceal the 'nothing' of femininity that Riviere describes,[24] but the 'something' of Jewish identity. Later in her journey, it is the Germanic effect of the protagonist's dress which must be verified in a mirror:

> Brown suited me; the bunches of flowers pinned to the rim of my hat were fresh and cheerful. "*Zweimal bitte, dritte klasse,*" I said and smiled at the mirror. (217)

Just as in the originary mirror stage, in this moment seeing the self as a – feminine, Aryan – whole enables the subject to speak: in German. The self's 'foreignness' is again used strategically; a new, albeit temporary, subjectivity is constructed by repeating the mirror stage of infancy. In this instance the protagonist is pleased with the 'citation'[25] of a German look and can almost view herself as a primarily gendered, rather than racially defined, being. The feminine glance in the mirror reveals, as with the Aryan bangs, something other than simply gender reassurance: 'Brown suited me...'. In this context, what 'suits' people is no longer primarily subjective or sexualized, but racialized. On the other hand, the very possibility of this masquerade as a gentile Aryan by a Jewish woman manages to undermine the ideal towards which she must aspire: Aryanness is no more real than Jewishness, and can be imitated or 'put on' in the form of a hat and gloves. It can also be removed; when the protagonist wishes to abandon her middle-class German masquerade and appear as a simple Polish country girl, she hides her hat under her coat (226). The insubstantiality of racial identity is made most apparent during a time of essentializing frenzy.

In these circumstances the wrong kind of masquerade can reveal rather than conceal, as Michasia, a Jewish peasant, discovers when she borrows a dress to wear instead of her usual plaid shawl:

> It was no longer Michasia! [...]
> 'When you put on something new, you look like a completely different person', she said, suddenly serious.
> Someone burst out laughing. 'Different? Like Jews are different!' (105)

This is a version of an ur-scene of revelation – changing or undressing to intensify the feminine masquerade[26] – which reveals a different truth in Michasia's case. While the codes stay within the realm of gender in Riviere's analysis, here they shift alarmingly from sexual to racial identity.

Jewishness as gender

Such a confusion of sexual and ethnic identity also threatens when the protagonist and her sister illicitly travel by train in Germany. In this case getting the detail of feminine dress right may not betray but substitute for a real, outlawed identity: 'I'm convinced that it was because of the hat and the gloves that the ticket clerk did not ask for identification' (193).[27] On the train and taken for 'a German girl – *ein deutsches Mädchen*' (220), the protagonist suddenly fears that the woman sitting opposite will see what is hidden under her gloves. Just as in the gender-masquerade the feminine body 'takes on the attributes of masculine desire',[28] here the protagonist takes on the attributes of what Aryan eyes want to see. The gloves suggest the innocent masquerade of Germanic femininity, covering nothing. But in the protagonist's case the gloves cover hands blackened and cut by potato-peeling, the task of 'savage foreigners from the East' (221). Once more the masquerade of femininity *itself* constitutes the disguise for a 'racial' secret, although both are simply performative.

The masquerade of femininity, however, must always include a racial dimension, and this is revealed here. Dressing, posing and performing interweave codes to do not only with gender, but also with class, age and ethnicity. Riviere prioritizes gender, and notoriously does not integrate into her account the racial dimensions of a dream that one of her analysands reports about a black man in the American South.[29] However, *The Journey* is set in a world where racial difference has been maximized alongside gender difference.[30] Freud's remark, 'When you meet a human being, the first distinction you make is "male or female?" and you are accustomed to make the distinction with unhesitating certainty',[31] was, according to Sander Gilman, based on a rather different question, which Gilman quotes from a 1927 guidebook to Vienna: ' "Is he [sic] a Jew?" '[32] It is not so much that the world of *The Journey* marks a return to a world divided along racial rather than gendered lines, but that the two systems fatally interconnect. The ideal to which the protagonist and her sister aspire registers such an intersection: it is an ideal of Christian, Aryan femininity, which, as the encounter with the German 'hag' on the train shows, is patriotic and devout, with 'Nordic looks'. Desirable racial and gender features share the same adjectives: 'ash-blond [...] Tall, fair-skinned and slender [...] slender and Nordic' (220).

It is harder to identify the features of Jewishness in the case of women, especially as the *racial* identity of the male body is conveyed by *gendered* traits. Michael Rothberg puts forward as definitive features of the Jewess the shaved head of the orthodox woman or 'the ubiquitous Jewish mother's body',[33] but of course the former is only a temporary feature, the latter rather unspecific. In Andrzej Szczypiorski's novel *The Beautiful Mrs Seidenman* the eponymous heroine notes that during her interrogation an SS officer examined her ears, but only as if impelled to invent a bodily equivalent for the covenantal sign of circumcision:

> They had men unzip their trousers. With women, they looked for something on their earlobes. They themselves didn't know what it was they were looking for.[34]

Critics describing nineteenth- and early twentieth-century representations of the *belle juive* all cite the same stereotypical details as definitive: Oriental, sensual, exotic looks, particularly dark, tender or otherwise alluring eyes.[35] These epithets are notable for their imprecision; although eyes might seem to be promising as the definitive feature of a Jewish woman, they are not sufficiently gender-specific.[36] For instance, Gilman cites Freud on the (male) Jewish 'vivacity of the eye',[37] and Nechama Tec, in an article on passing as Aryan during the Holocaust years, observes that, 'Jews [male and female] were known for the sadness of their eyes. Some were even recognized by their sad eyes and perished.'[38] The main difference between male and female Jewish eyes is subjective (and seen from a masculine viewpoint): men's eyes are sinisterly defining, to the point of association with the evil eye,[39] while women's are alluringly so. But the desire expressed for the Jewish woman and her eyes is just the lining of the fear and revulsion expressed at the Jewish man's eyes;[40] as Sara Horowitz points out, Nazi antisemitic propaganda drew out this lining to emphasize how 'the Jewish woman's physical beauty veils her racial repulsiveness'.[41]

One could draw a distinction between the definitive weight placed on circumcision for Jewish men, and alluring eyes for Jewish women: while the former is a 'cultural operation', the latter is a 'natural embodiment' of Jewishness.[42] However, this distinction tends to collapse when we note both that circumcision has often been taken as a congenital feature of Jewish men, and that circumcision itself need not be present to be seen.[43] This act of racializing a culturally acquired trait lays bare the even greater impossibility of racializing an organ, like the eye (or nose, ear, mouth, and so on). Gunnar Paulsson argues that in occupied Warsaw women were exempt from the bodily scrutiny undergone by men, and instead, 'The standard method was to quiz the suspect on aspects of the Catholic religion.'[44]

Indeed, in *The Journey* the moment when the German widow on the train tries to unwrap the protagonist's finger acts as a feminized version of the threat of unveiling circumcision. The 'German mother' tries to undo the gauze around the protagonist's finger, but she resists: ' "It hurts, it hurts, please don't untie it all the way" '. The protagonist fears that what will be revealed is the wound of difference. Rather than having injured her finger 'bravely' working in a munitions plant as a German woman, as she tells the widow, she has a 'blackened finger, cut by the paring knife' from working on a farm as 'a savage foreigner' (221). The irreducibility of Jewishness in the eyes of this German woman, and by extension the whole of Nazi-dominated society, is symbolized by the phantasy that Fink's protagonist picks up: an uncovering will reveal circumcision, the marker of male Jewishness, even on a female body. Interestingly, the German woman's own fingers are subject to the protagonist's scrutiny – what they might metonymically reveal, however, is neither the mark of a forbidden wound, nor the sexual sign of marriage, but that of legalized robbery and murder:

She had white hair, and wore a velvet ribbon round her neck, and a ring on her finger. Was it an old family ring, or a gift from her son on the Eastern Front? [...] Perhaps it was her son who pulled the ring off the finger of my dying mother? (219–20)

Conclusion

The masquerade and staged misrecognition of the mirror scenes in *The Journey* have a narrative counterpart. This is hinted at in the way that the narrator throughout meticulously uses the character's false names and not their real ones. Indeed, as in Begley's *Wartime Lies*, we never learn either the protagonist's or narrator's real names. This narrative habit shows partly that the need for consistency in assumed identities was so great that it only makes sense to share renaming with the reader, but withholding the Jewish name. The fact that the protagonist exists only as a first-person utterance emphasizes this: a Jewish woman referred to by her own name is an impossibility within this text. This is shown graphically twice, first when the protagonist dreams that her boyfriend Marian 'was calling my name', a gesture which is not a romantic but a racially dangerous act she must repudiate: ' "That's not my name", I said, and woke up. My heart was pounding' (127). On the second occasion, the narrator describes the moment the girls are reunited with their father also in terms of being reunited with their own identities – 'Running, he called their names' (243) – but these real names are not heard within the text.

The textual splitting of the subject in *The Journey* occurs most clearly when the first-person narrator refers to the protagonist, her former self, in the third person. There are two protracted instances: the novel begins in this way, and there is an interlude (154–61) when the narrator gathers together her memories and in doing so transforms herself into another person ('She observed, imitated, hid, protected herself with laughter and jokes' (155)). Third person narration is made to do extra work in this first-person novel: to convey alienation and division, but also a crucial critical gaze at the self.

As we have seen, the logic of passing for gentile during the Holocaust years follows the logic of (un)veiling: either a lack or an unwelcome presence is concealed and therefore runs the risk of being uncovered. This pattern is the reverse of the orthodox Freudian model of gender difference: here it is the Jewish man who is shown to be lacking when he is unveiled, whereas in uncovering a woman's hidden Jewishness a presence is revealed.

Circumcision is mistaken in the symbolic order for a mark of *racial* difference. This is especially so in the world of *The Journey*, where signs of gender difference have been racialized; the excessive emphasis placed upon the trope of circumcision – which we have seen played out on a woman's hair, fingers, voice, and whole body – is the *reductio* of this process. Indeed, the ability of gentiles to 'smell out'[45] both male and female Jews during the Holocaust years without recourse to any bodily inspection at all reveals that circumcision, as the ultimate mark of Jewish difference, was always an imposture: not that this notion would help anyone subject to its strictures. Ida Fink's *The Journey* – innocently but also aptly bearing the title of an ordinary *Bildungsroman* – enacts and exposes this imposture.

Masculine masquerade: Solomon Perel, *Europa, Europa*

Solomon Perel's *Europa, Europa* is an account of a teenage boy's adventures in occupied Europe. Perel is at pains to emphasize the factual nature of his account – 'My Holocaust experiences recorded here are true. These events actually happened to me' (ix) – not only because his story is so unusual but also, presumably, to reassure readers that his wartime behaviour was no worse than what he describes:

> Did I really have the right to compare myself with survivors of the Holocaust? [. . .] with their last ounce of strength they had succeeded

in retaining their Jewish identity, their humanity. I, on the other hand, had gone about among the Nazis at this same time, unmolested, had worn their uniform that included a swastika on my cap, and had yelled '*Heil Hitler!*' as though I really identified with their criminal ideology and their barbaric goals. (xi)

Not only did the Jewish Solomon pretend to be gentile, he also claimed to be a *Volksdeutscher* named Josef Perjell, nicknamed Jupp, and was accepted into a Hitler Youth school. There can be no doubt that Solomon's masquerade was just that: a superficial pretence adopted to save his life. However, the text skates over moments of particular contradiction between Jewish Solomon and Aryan Jupp and does not really represent the internal cost of this masquerade.

Perel's memoir is better approached as a 'comedy of horror', as he puts it (29), that is, a hybrid text, rather than as a straightforward memoir about ambivalent behaviour. If seen as a hybrid, *Europa, Europa* appears bold and experimental, rather than anomalous and uncomfortable to read.[46] Perel says that *Europa, Europa* is a European version of Elia Kazan's similarly *Candide*-inspired screenplay and film *America, America* (1963) and that Agnieska Holland, who directed the film *Europa, Europa* (1990) based on Perel's book, saw him as 'the Candide of the twentieth century' (xii). In other words, *Europa, Europa* is an example of what Mikhail Bakhtin calls an 'adventure novel of ordeal',[47] which concentrates on the external aspects of its characters and plot, stark contrasts and fantastic coincidences. However, *Europa, Europa* combines this form with saturation by historical and autobiographical specificity. It also combines temporal and spatial markers in equal measure, contrary to Bakhtin's insistence that literary chronotopes always subordinate space to time.[48] As the title of a memoir, *Europa, Europa* clearly links a time (*A Memoir of World War II*, as the subtitle has it) with a place (Europe) in a perfectly balanced chronotopic mix.

No subject, in fact, could be better suited to the violent contrasts of the adventure novel than a Jewish teenager joining a Hitler Youth school. The title of the German translation of *Europa, Europa* is *Ich war Hitlerjunge Salomon* [I was Hitler Youth Solomon]. It shows clearly the shock value and farcical humour of even placing the name 'Salomon' alongside 'Hitler Youth' in a single sentence (this is an irony only apparent in the German title, which also makes ironic reference to Karl Schenzinger's 1932 novel, *Der Hitlerjunge Quex*;[49] by contrast, the French original is also called *Europa, Europa*). The genre and subject of *Europa, Europa* make it hard to read it as any kind of comedy, as it is a memoir of the Holocaust years which recounts the death of Perel's parents and sister. Yet its breathtaking juxtapositions – the Jewish Solomon, in disguise, is called upon to rehearse the reasons for the Jews' extermination in class (180); a girlfriend's mother asks him, 'Why are you Germans so cruel to the Jews?' (51); the commanding officer in his Wehrmacht division arranges to adopt him after the war, and Solomon imagines becoming 'Josef von Münchow' (39); a classmate, inflamed by an antisemitic poster, exclaims to Solomon, ' "If only I had one of these Jews here right now...!" ' (133) – are so ludicrous they are almost funny. The two generic strands of Holocaust memoir and picaresque novel battle against each other throughout the text.

Solomon Perel, the protagonist of *Europa, Europa*, was born in 1925 in Peine, Germany, into a Jewish family who had left Poland only seven years earlier. The Perels fled back to Lódz, Poland, in 1936. When war broke out in 1939 Solomon's mother urged her two elder sons to leave for Russia, where Solomon lived in an orphanage in Grodno and joined Komsomol, the communist party youth movement. In 1941, when Germany invaded the Soviet Union, Solomon managed to pass himself off to a Wehrmacht officer as an ethnic German from Grodno, called Josef Perjell. Solomon was promptly nicknamed 'Jupp', and adopted as a mascot for the battalion of the 12th Panzer Division in Minsk. He was then sent back to the Reich to a Hitler Youth training school, where he remained until the war's end. In 1947 Solomon emigrated to Israel.

Many of the subjectively inflected concerns of Ida Fink's *The Journey* appear in *Europa, Europa*, but in externalized form. Like the protagonist of Fink's novel, Solomon undergoes moments of internal division when, as a Jewish subject, he sees his gentile reflection, for instance when he first wears a Wehrmacht uniform:

> Looking at myself in the rearview mirror of a parked vehicle was like getting a slap in the face. [...] On my chest I saw an insignia with the Prussian eagle holding a swastika in its predatory claws. They had given me a cap with a black-white-and-red band, and that sobered me totally. All around little Solomon – me – a bloodthirsty war was going on, and here I was in a Nazi uniform! (25–6)

Indeed, at times Solomon says that, due entirely to 'their uniforms and their insignias' (58), he ' "looked like a German" '(70). In other words, the political Nazi façades and signifiers offer a specifically *racial* protection, and can make even a Jewish boy like Solomon, whose appearance was characterized by non-Aryan details preventing his entry into the SS (63), appear like 'one of them' (58). In *Europa, Europa* this paradox – a boy of 5'2" with 'pitch-black hair' (96) is warmly accepted by the Nazi hierarchy – acts with the dark humour of extreme irony, rather than undermining the terms of such difference, as happens in *The Journey*.

Throughout *Europa, Europa*, Nazi uniforms and insignia are usually enough to outweigh Solomon's other features. During a lesson on the 'Characteristic and Distinguishing Features of Jews' at the Hitler Youth academy, at which 'industrious Jupp [...] copied everything down with a steady hand', Solomon notes, 'I resembled many of the prototypes they showed us, and I had many of the "distinguishing Jewish features" that were described to us' (94). The remarkable fact that Solomon's Jewishness has become in effect invisible is less important here, however, than that this invisibility offers another occasion for blackly comic irony. When it is Solomon's turn to have his racial characteristics discussed, he fears the worst, but gets miraculously out of the trap: 'The teacher said, "Class, take a look at Josef. He is a typical descendent of the Eastern Baltic race" ' (96).

It is naturally the removal of Jupp's protective uniform in the shower or toilet that threatens to turn him back into Solomon, who possesses a ' "dangerous body part" ' (74). As in *The Journey*, racial and sexual characteristics overlap, and one is often read as the other. In *Europa, Europa*, however, the 'danger' of Solomon's circumcised state being uncovered also becomes the opportunity for farcical and ironic juxta-positions (even more so in Agnieska Holland's film). When the medical officer Heinz Kelzenberg follows Jupp into the communal Wehrmacht bath and finds that he has actually approached Solomon, Solomon's rejection of Kelzenberg's sexual advances is indistinguishable from trying to evade the older man's racial scrutiny:

> I felt a naked body pressing against me. I froze. Thousands of alarm bells went off in my head. [...] I jumped as though a snake had bitten me. It would have been smarter just to stand there, with my back to him, but I had instinctively freed myself from his embrace. Jumping out of the tub, I turned around. (43)

Kelzenberg's unexpectedly generous reaction is ambiguous. It sounds as if he is promising sexual restraint and racial protection, but the two are blurred: ' "I won't hurt you, and I won't betray your secret" ' (44).[50]

Bakhtin describes several features of the 'adventure novel of ordeal' which perfectly fit *Europa, Europa*, even though it is non-fiction.[51] He emphasizes the fact that such texts combine both the '*random contingency*' of 'chance *simultaneity* [meetings] and *chance rupture* [nonmeetings]',[52] with an apparently paradoxical sense of predestiny. In *Europa, Europa*, the overwhelming effects of randomly contingent events make Solomon think he must have a predetermined fate. As Bakhtin puts it of the characters in Achilles Tatius' Greek romance *Leucippe and Clitophon*, 'The entire escape is built on a chain of random "suddenlys" and "just at that moments" that benefit the heroes.'[53] In accord with Bakhtin's observation that 'moments of adventuristic time [...] provide an opening for the intrusion of non-human forces',[54] Solomon imagines that, precisely because his luck is so contingent, there must be a plan behind it. The notion that 'an angel of liberation was watching over me' (20) first strikes Solomon when he is in a queue of refugees near Minsk after the Nazi invasion of the Soviet Union, and his situation seems at its most hopeless ('My life hung by a thread'). Not only is anyone circumcised or otherwise unsuitable shot in a nearby forest, but 'unexpectedly' a Polish man in the queue with Solomon points him out as a Jew to the German soldier in charge. The soldier's decision to believe Solomon and not the Pole is a contingent incident set in adventure-time. It is so charged with biographical and narrative significance that the soldier's faith in Solomon's story seems preordained: 'What was going in this [soldier's] heart at that decisive moment? Did some divine voice whisper to him, "This boy must live"?' (21). Later, when Solomon finds himself confessing his Jewishness to his girlfriend Leni's mother – although not to Leni herself – Solly[55] wonders at Solomon's sudden recklessness: 'Was it faith that my lucky star wouldn't desert me this time either?' (117).

As Bakhtin points out, many moments of happy chance may indeed point to an underlying plot: 'chance is but one form of the principle of necessity and as such has a place in any novel, as it has its place in life itself'.[56] Such an observation has especially stark implications for Holocaust literature, where retrospection transforms contingency into necessity and can make survival look like the result of virtue, or successful choices. While in an adventure novel of ordeal moments of 'meeting/parting (separation), loss/acquisition, search/discovery, recognition/nonrecognition and so forth' are simply formal 'motifs',[57] in a Holocaust memoir or novel they are crucial events signalling the difference between life and death, and the continuation or end of the narrative.

In Holocaust narratives, the effect of such 'chance simultaneity' is even greater. It guarantees a plot about escape and life; indeed, except for unusual cases such as Anne Frank's, we do not read about stories governed by malign simultaneity. Inevitable retrospectivity gives these moments of positive simultaneity their narrative significance, as the narrator of Fink's *The Journey* says of an accidental meeting at a crucial moment with a friend who owes her money:

> A miracle had occurred. If I had walked that way a few minutes earlier, or a few minutes later, if that insistent gaze hadn't driven me from the streetcar ... (45)

However, in *The Journey* such chance simultaneities do not have the breathtaking comedy of those in *Europa, Europa*, but rather emphasize how tragedy was only narrowly averted (in the quotation above, the ellipses take the place of imagining how things might have turned out). Near the end of Fink's novel, the narrator describes 'the place where everything nearly ended' (226), an instant in a police station where a policeman was prevented from calling the Gestapo by another fortuitous 'suddenly':

> He dialed the number, and at that very moment, the station commander opened the door. Sheer chance, the perfect concurrence of two events. The policeman put down the receiver. (224)

The precise relation between the masquerading gentile persona and the Jewish teenager underneath is left unclear in *Europa, Europa*. This is understandable, as we have already seen the possibility of encroachment inwards by external performance, both in relation to *The Journey* and to narratives about children hidden in Christian institutions (see Chapter 4). But the contradictions in Perel's memoir are not so easily explained. At times the narrator uses a temporal notion of internal division, as if 'Hitler Youth Jupp', free from worries by the time he joins the Hitler Youth school, had completely supplanted the younger 'Shloimele', the boy who wet his bed in the Grodno orphanage (88). At other times the narrator speaks as if Solomon has not been left behind, but coexists with Jupp in a single unit: 'Hitler Youth Jupp and Solomon the Jew got along like fire and water. Still they existed side by side in the same body, in the same mind' (77). The image of fire and water here is distracting, as it does not convey the 'coexistence' Solly mentions so much as supersession of one by the other – and it is not clear which.

On certain occasions Jupp does take over, for instance when Solomon is asked to present his documents on a train, and when Brunswick is bombed. Solomon meets a young woman on a visit to Lódz, but he calls her 'Jupp's girlfriend' (171), as the woman does not even know of Solomon's existence. Solly claims that the urge to hear from the soldiers of his battalion after he had left them shows that 'Solomon had turned into Josef the Hitler Youth' (85), and adds that 'I became convinced that a superior people had the right to rule [...] Day by day Jupp remembered Solomon less and less' (100). However, although Solly claims that Jupp had replaced Solomon at this time, third-person narration is always used for the Hitler Youth member, first person only for Solomon. This is because Jupp is a construct without an inner life. Solomon surfaces whenever the inner life of fear or loss is triggered on occasions when he thinks about the past and his family (90, 114–16, 129). On his trip to Lódz, when Solomon is near the surface, Solly describes the relation between Jewish inner self and Hitler Youth persona in terms of a hybrid, not the replacement of the former by the latter:

> At least half of me was beyond reproach; I was wearing a uniform, and I had genuine documents. But the other half might easily arouse suspicions through his highly unusual behaviour. (145)

Indeed, despite Solly's claims to the contrary, it seems that this is how Solomon and Jupp interact throughout *Europa, Europa*: as two halves of a hybrid. This echoes the text's mixed generic form, just as the novelistic narrative of *The Journey* mirrored its concern with masquerade and self-fictionalizing. Only Jupp – a fictive character – appears in the picaresque novel. Jupp is not Aryan; even as a fictional character his existence depends on a hidden Jewishness. Jupp's very name suggests this, with its echoes of '*Jude*' and 'Jew', as does his knowledge of Solomon's existence:

> Jupp would never forget his primary commandment – to protect Solomon. The spark of Solomon's Jewish origins would continue to glow, never to be extinguished. (112)

Only Solomon, however, as the narrator's younger, Jewish self ('I'm of pure Jewish blood, from head to toe!', as Solomon tells the Race Education teacher after the war (96)), features in the Holocaust memoir.

There are moments in *Europa, Europa* where this division of generic roles – fictional, picaresque Jupp versus autobiographical Solomon – is particularly clear. The students at the Hitler Youth school are told that Hitler sees them as future leaders of the Reich: 'And even Jupp mumbled to himself, "Did you hear that, Shloimele? Some day even you may become a little führer"' (112). Jupp's remark suggests that one day even Solomon might be part of an adventure novel, the only fitting location for a Jewish Führer.

The farcically incongruous situation and events in *Europa, Europa* depend on an unlikely fact. It turns out that Solomon's brazen masquerade – as a Jew in a Nazi uniform – was extremely successful, despite the great risks of hiding in 'the lion's den' (62), as Solomon describes the Hitler Youth school. Solly himself comments on an 'extra-ordinary paradox', when a guardian from the Hitler Youth school is appointed for Solomon: 'An SS-officer was – unknowingly, of course – taking a Jewish child under his wing, in effect legally becoming his father.' As a result, Solomon enjoys a moment of eugenic fantasy, as if he, and therefore hybridity, is in fact the future of the Aryan race: 'In their eagerness and goodwill, would they one day marry me off to a blue-eyed girl with blond braids?' (102).

Solomon in effect hides not only in the open, 'on the surface', but on display. This is rather like the case of the purloined letter in Edgar Allen Poe's short story of that name, which escaped detection because it was simply displayed in a letter-rack rather than ingeniously hidden from sight. Jacques Lacan explains the failure of the police investigation in Poe's story to find the letter in terms of 'a glance that sees nothing',[58] in the way that Solomon's Nazi colleagues see but fail to 'recognize' him.[59] As with Solomon's Jewishness in *Europa, Europa*, it is the fact that the letter is a signifier (that which produces certain effects) and not a signified (something which possesses intrinsic meaning) that causes it to be overlooked.[60] As we saw in *The Journey*, the fact that Jewishness is constructed out of a range of signifiers in unwitting substitution for the absence of a signified – an 'essential' Jewishness visible from the outside – is starkly revealed by the masquerades and performances of 'passing for gentile' as a teenager in the Holocaust era. However, in *Europa, Europa* this fact becomes the site of comedy, in constrast to *The Journey*'s revelation of a tragic irony.

7
Present-Time Narration: The Holocaust Diaries of Children and Teenagers

In this chapter, I will discuss diaries by children and young people – those Holocaust works which appear most fully to unite the time of events with the time of writing. The strong appeal of Holocaust diaries in general arises from the fact that here alone, of all the literary genres I have discussed, present-tense narration does not entail the temporal separation of character from narrator. Diaries written by children and teenagers during the Holocaust years are striking and unusual documents *and* texts. They offer the impression of a return to the moment of events unfolding. Yet the writers of the diaries I discuss here are conscious of the limitations as well as the possibilities of the diary form, and all take this form to its temporal and structural limits.

Introduction: documentary or testimony?

The diary as a genre has been little considered in literary-critical terms.[1] Even the fictional diary has not been widely analysed.[2] In general, the diary is viewed as an artless, amateur form which is neither literary nor historical. Most studies of autobiography tend not to mention the diary;[3] while autobiography and the diary are not synonymous, the '*journal intime*' in particular has a strong autobiographical strand in its focus on the writer's subjectivity. Alain Girard argues that the '*journal intime*' is characterized by an emphasis on the diarist's private rather than exterior life, on public events as they affect him or her, and that the diary's 'privacy' is guaranteed by a lack of intention to publish. The counterpart of the '*journal intime*' is the '*journal externe*' or chronicle of public and historical events without emphasis on the writer's life or subjectivity.[4] This absence of critical attention is surprising, since the diary has great narrative potential in its representation of time, voice and viewpoint.

Although the fictional diary has been criticized for avoiding 'the laborious tasks of narrative focalisation or temporal reconfigurations of plot',[5] both fiction and non-fiction diaries possess a distinctive narrative structure. While the memoir is characterized by retrospection, overview and integration, an awareness of historical irony, and the creation of suspense, the diary is characterized by a focus on temporal duration, accumulation and extent. Even at this level, however, the Holocaust diary does not follow the usual pattern; as Lawrence Langer points out, it is characterized by *dis*integration – of the familial, communal and even personal continuity usually presupposed by the *journal intime*[6] – and by narrative disintegration, as I shall argue.

Susan Rubin Suleiman argues that the non-fiction diary is also characterized by contingency and factuality: contingency in the sense that 'the day-to-day unfolding of the story [...] necessarily escapes the foreknowledge and control of the writer', factuality because the diary '*guarantees* that an event took place, on the date indicated [...] I who am writing now was there to *witness* it or hear about it or experience it'.[7] Suleiman's plea for contingency supports Michael André Bernstein's notion of the diary as the ultimate expression of sideshadowing,[8] in the sense that it must present a range of outcomes and cannot prioritize those that turned out to take precedence.[9] However, Suleiman's assertion of the diary's factuality is less compelling. The only event 'guaranteed' to have taken place by the diary is the act of recording itself, as all accounts of events must be *interpretations* due to the diary's part-subjective, part-historical nature, and to its writer's proximity to the events recorded. One of the diaries I discuss below, Ana Novac's record of Auschwitz and Plaszów,[10] shows this clearly, as the diarist is aware that the act of writing in the camps is itself worthy of note. Novac also puts into question the very notion of an 'event': most of the 'facts' of Novac's diary involve subjective accounts of other inmates and the camp personnel, details of food and clothing. Similarly, an anonymous diary written by a boy in the Lódz Ghetto[11] consists largely of commentary on the difficulty of keeping a diary, and meditations on the 'rumours' – as opposed to news or facts – that the ghetto inhabitants are subject to. Indeed, James Young argues that while Holocaust testimony, including the diary, endorses the authenticity of an account – in its eye-witness proximity to the events recorded – it does not necessarily endorse that account's *factuality*.[12]

Equally, there are few studies of Holocaust diaries[13] – of which children's and teenagers' are a subsection – although a relatively large number of such diaries exist, of which a substantial percentage has been published.[14]

This lack too is surprising, given that Anne Frank's *The Diary of a Young Girl* remains the best-known work of Holocaust literature in general;[15] and that the most detailed records of Jewish life during the Holocaust take the form of contemporary chronicles and archives from the ghettos of Warsaw, Lódz, Vilna and Kovno.[16]

The general critical neglect of the non-fiction diary is partly due to the fact that it is a mixed genre: it is seen as a historical document but also as a cultural narrative. Historical claims are made for Holocaust diaries, although these are often couched in terms which reveal the form's uneasy division between documentary and testimony:[17] Daniel Grinberg describes the 'exceptional value' of unpublished diaries held in Warsaw 'in view of the data they contain *or* the literary skill with which they were written' (my italics).[18] Some commentators make claims for the diary as a historical record: given the fallibility of memory which must affect retrospective accounts, 'we prefer diaries written during the war, when the events were actually taking place', as in this way details of 'chronology' and 'common events' are preserved.[19] Others recognize that diaries are not the first recourse for factual detail about the Holocaust, although they still claim that the 'private and intimate diary' is the privileged source for 'the individual experience, the individual fate, in brief, the individualization of the Holocaust'.[20]

Views of the Holocaust diary are thus divided between the notion that although the diarist does not suffer the 'lapses' of memory that a memoirist might, he or she is subject to 'limitations' of factual knowledge.[21] However, as I will argue, it is the diary's *form*, as much as these content-based issues, that is truly distinctive. As well as the two poles of historical and cultural value, some commentators see the preservation of diaries as a 'moral duty';[22] while others view the Holocaust diarist's impulse to write as covenantal, even if the content is not overtly religious.[23] I will argue in this chapter that it is precisely the formal and narrative features of the diary, in so far as these form a coherent list, that are taken to an extreme or defamiliarized when these appear in diaries by young people during the Holocaust years. In this chapter I discuss several non-fiction diaries and one fictional example, respectively by and about children and teenagers, in an attempt to explore the subversion of the diary's form by its content.

Hybrid diaries: Mary Berg, *Warsaw Ghetto: A Diary*

Mary Berg's diary is one of the first accounts by a witness of the Warsaw Ghetto to be published in English.[24] As Alexandra Zapruder points out,

Berg's diary is actually a hybrid of diary and memoir.[25] Berg rewrote the text from its original Polish note form[26] when she arrived in the USA in 1944; it was published as a Yiddish serial, then in English a year later. Whether or not Berg continued to write after her arrival in the US, it is only the part of her diary that takes place – or is set – in occupied Poland that is of interest to the reader.[27] This suggests that although her diary, like others I discuss here, possesses the features of the *'journal intime'*, it is readable only as a *'journal externe'*.

Berg was born in 1924, the daughter of an American mother and a Polish father, and began the diary on her fifteenth birthday, 10 October 1939. Her family lived in the Warsaw Ghetto until 1942, when they were sent to Pawiak prison to await exchange for German prisoners of war, on account of Berg's mother's American nationality. In 1943 the family was sent to a French internment camp at Vittel, and they left for the US in 1944. Berg began her rewriting immediately on arrival.

Although Berg began to edit her diary before the war ended, it shows clear signs of its hybrid nature through knowledge of how events will turn out. The last entry is for 5 March 1944, but this has an obviously retrospective viewpoint: Berg writes here that, 'On March 15 our ship approached New York'. It seems from the diary's last line that the writer knows the war will soon end: 'A little more patience, and all of us will win freedom!' (253). Equally, it is hard to know whether various of Berg's convictions – even in 1941 that the Allies will win the war (93); that 'something terrible' is 'in store' for her and will 'separate me from my friends' (126; in fact it is something terrible for them, not for her) – are evidence of foresight or of rewriting.

Even the layout of Berg's diary shows its combination of present-time diary with retrospective memoir. It is set out in the form of daily entries, but the entries themselves are grouped together into chapters whose very titles – 'Life Goes On', 'Another Year' – reveal a summarizing view. It is hard to credit some of the moments which emphasize the diary's presentness, particularly those which mention the moment of writing. On 26 June 1941, for instance, the entry begins, 'I am writing this in the bomb shelter of our house. I am on night duty, as a member of the home air defense' and ends, 'I think there is an alarm now; yes, a long blast of the siren. I must run to awaken the commandant' (75–7). Berg even picks up her pen on the train taking her family from Pawiak to the internment camp in France: 'A few minutes ago I woke from my sleep [...] Our train is moving in the direction of Poznan, not Oswiecim' (216); and again on leaving Vittel en route to the ship for America: 'We are in the train! We are going despite everything' (249). It is as if an impression of great contemporaneity – in which the moment of action and of writing are as close as possible – is used to displace the retrospection of rewriting.

'I'm alive! I'm writing...' (150): Ana Novac, *The Beautiful Days of My Youth*

While Berg's diary is a hybrid of journal and memoir, Ana Novac's remarkable diary, *The Beautiful Days of My Youth: My Six Months in Auschwitz and Plaszów*, reads as a hybrid of diary and fiction. Although it is a genuine diary, it uses novelistic techniques. The literary status of Novac's text is revealed by its ironic and clearly retrospective title,[28] a marked contrast to those of most of the other diaries discussed here. While *The Beautiful Days of My Youth* should suffer from the same effect as Berg's rewritten diary, in Novac's case the literariness is so self-conscious that it is as if the erasure of the 'trace' of contemporaneity is flaunted.

Novac was born in Transylvania in 1929 as Zimra Harsanyi, and deported to Auschwitz in 1944, then to Plaszów, then taken back again to Auschwitz. Her parents died of typhus after the liberation of the camps, and Novac (as I will refer to the retrospective editor of the diary) believes her younger brother was killed in the gas chambers (9). Zimra (the diary's protagonist and author) left Romania in 1963 to live in Paris. She wrote her camp diary with a pencil-stub found in the ground at Auschwitz, on scraps of paper – including posters declaiming 'WORK WILL MAKE YOU FREE' which she tore off the walls at Auschwitz (7), and a notebook she was given by a Lagerkapo at Plaszów (35). When her shoes became too full of the paper she hid in them, Zimra learned each 'chapter' of her diary by heart and reconstructed it in the next camp (7–8). In the introduction to the English edition, Novac describes how she reconstructed and 'awakened' her diary by translating it from the original Hungarian notes into French. Zimra recounts how her diary was smuggled out of Plaszów to the home of a former concierge for safekeeping (171–5).

But despite the unusual nature of *The Beautiful Days of My Youth*, as a diary written in a death-camp by a teenage girl, its ability to record often seems subordinated to concern with the very act of writing. This is partly due to the rarity of such an activity in the camp, and to the value Zimra placed on writing as a means of survival: 'there's only one matter that concerns me here: my notebook' (66). In the introduction, Novac describes her 'benign amnesia' about the journey to Auschwitz, and adds, 'My first memory is of a pencil stub I found in the sand', as if only the memory of a writing-instrument – the pencil stub – can prompt recall. Novac adds that she was already used to writing and 'living for that journal', so that from June to November 1944 'my story was the story of my journal' (7).

These formulations suggest the transcendence of the journal itself over what it recorded; the train journey to Auschwitz cannot be recalled because it was not written down, and Novac adds, 'Of the eight camps I passed through, I remember only the ones that appear in my journal, during the time when I still had the energy to write' (8). As Gérard Genette argues, 'The paratextual message of writers' journals . . . is less dedicated to setting forth the truth than to producing an effect on its author.'[29]

While Zimra speaks of her diary in a way that is familiar to readers of other Holocaust diaries – that she lives to write and record what is happening – the terms of this notion are reversed in *The Beautiful Days of My Youth*. She does not live to tell posterity in general about her experiences ('I dwell on myself, on details that concern only me', 69), but to assure *herself* of their reality, as Novac notes in the prefatory paragraph to the first diary-entry: '*It's a stranger [i.e. Novac] who deciphers these pages . . . I'm only recopying*' (15). This is not so different from Primo Levi's comment that, 'writing the book [*If This is a Man*] has worked for me as a sort of "prosthesis", an external memory set up like a barrier between my life today and my life then. Today I relive those events through what I have written.'[30] However, in the teenage Zimra's diary the gap between experience and its record, between present and retrospection, is very small. To reassure herself after a nightmare about losing her pencil-stub, Zimra notes, 'Now I'm writing. I'm writing that I'm writing' (20). At other times she writes *about*, and also *at*, the moment of hearing the summons for roll-call (32): story and plot are thus united, in a fashion closer than that Berg's diary strove for. Whereas the latter united the moment of writing with a particular historical event – such as travelling to Vittel – Zimra simply writes about the event of writing.

The tense Novac uses – taking advantage of the resources of the diary's French-language 'awakening' – is the narrative present for most events, even those, such as memories of her brother, from the pre-camp past (33). It is as if Zimra is both emphasizing the presentness of events, even when they are literally past (they may have happened earlier that day), and paradoxically making the diary seem more literary, as if she is using the 'classical narrative *figure*' of the 'narrative present, or historical present'.[31] At the same time, the reader knows that there are gradations of time within the apparent unity of the present tense. 'I don't have anything to write with' is clearly a past event, since the lack is recorded, as is, '[The Lagerkapo] rummages in his pockets and manages to extract a pencil' (37). But Zimra's statement, in a camp hospital, that 'I'm writing all this secretly, on toilet paper, which makes funny scribbles' (278), does take place in the present, that is, unites the moment of action and that of writing. Indeed, only the act of writing itself can be a fully present-time action; so the ultimate diary would be one that consisted simply of writing (about) writing. This is especially true, paradoxically, of diaries written in the Holocaust years, during which the act of writing itself is at once unusual and dangerous.

While the present tense combines these moments, the unfamiliarity and chaos of events pushes them apart, as if Zimra were a real-life Tristram Shandy: 'I have to hurry; new material is accumulating danger-ously, and I'm barely able to keep up with the daily events that besiege me' (46). It is clear that the horrifying nature of what Zimra witnesses is what drives her diary, as she notes of a brutal scene: 'I'm afraid [the details will] never stop rolling through my head, for as long as I have one' (184). However, other entries seem entirely metatextual – one written after Zimra's return to Auschwitz consists of twenty-four lines, mostly about the act of writing itself: 'I write little, and with difficulty' (191). Zimra calls her diary a 'testimony', and in a sense what it testifies to is the struggle to write in such circumstances.

Zimra's style – a matter of constant concern to her ('the style is careless, in places', she notes, due to 'lack of inspiration' and hunger (69)) – reads, like her self-consciousness, in a literary[32] way which is undercut by its subject. In a sardonic glance at an everyday adolescent diary, often interrupted by the demands of adults, Zimra writes, 'They're "calling". I'll continue after "lunch" . . . Oh, the "menus" at Auschwitz!' (61–2).[33] In another parody of more usual adolescent concerns, Zimra turns the demand of the Nazis at Plaszów to record new arrivals' profes-sions into a darkly humorous acknowledgement of the lack of such a future: 'we only have ten minutes to decide whether we want to be dressmakers, nurses, dancers, or typists' (82). This becomes carniva-lesque as the Kapo demands to know 'who it was that put down: Jüdin, Häftlinge, Hure, Hexe,[34] and Dolores del Rio' (83). The rhetorical effects in these examples – irony, parody, the 'impudence' of black humour – seem to be a way of controlling and distancing uncontrollable events. As we have seen in the chapter on split narrative, such 'constriction of affect', in Teresa Cahn's phrase,[35] often results from the distance of retro-spection; here, constriction is evident even at the moment of recording.

Zimra's diary is characterized by dissonant qualities. She cannot date her diary entries ('what day is this?', 102) nor verify duration, even after the war ('I'm unable to recall, for example, how long the woman doctor kept me in hospital', 294). However, the diary entries are her life ('Breathe for one more day, one more page!', 170), its paper a 'second skin' (25). The text is characterized by linguistic and stylistic knowledge and control despite its lack of chronological specificity. When Zimra meets another writer in a camp hospital, their rivalry is of such a farcical nature that it subverts any notion of literary mastery of the camps. Zimra is enraged by this balladeer's 'burlesque' pretensions to representing suffering and violence – using 'no end of vampires and other tortures' (285) – and records the following carnivalesque dialogue when challenged to name another composer of ballads:

'Well, a Frenchman, for instance. Villon.' [said Zimra]
'I know', said the author, 'he's from Camp B.... Was he a Jew?'
'A crook, a complete scoundrel.'
'Well! He wrote his poems between heists?' (286)[36]

While the camp balladeer was asking her a question about other balladeers in the camp, Zimra answered with reference to literary history and the fifteenth-century French poet François Villon. This clearly ironizes Zimra's own production. She is a writer herself, but even those who write camp ballads provoking 'cries and wails' (285) from their audience cannot recognize the name of a canonical French author; the camp has become the only reality; and, like the imaginary Häftling Villon, Zimra herself has been writing as if 'between heists'. The relation between camp writing and canonical literature is often debated in the former itself. As Jean Améry notes in his collection of essays *At the Mind's Limits*, 'No bridge led from death in Auschwitz to *Death in Venice*';[37] in *The Beautiful Days of My Youth* this debate has itself turned into 'burlesque'.

'It's bad enough for a girl of thirteen that her Papa and her bicycle have been taken away from her' (76): *The Diary of Éva Heyman: Child of the Holocaust*

Éva Heyman's diary is formally the antithesis of Zimra Harsanyi's, despite some coincidental similarities. Both were born in Nagyvárad, Zimra in 1929, Éva in 1931; both kept 'diary notes'[38] of their experiences after the Nazi invasion of Hungary, Zimra from June to November 1944, Éva from February to May 1944. Both were deported to Auschwitz; while

Zimra began to write her diary there and survived, Éva stopped before her deportation and died at Auschwitz in October 1944. The diaries of both exhibit such precocity for young women of, respectively, thirteen and fourteen, that rewriting by adults has been suspected. Novac notes in her introduction that in editing and translating her diary into French, 'I can say in all honesty that I did not "doctor" my account, or impose on it a false maturity' (13). The editor of Éva's diary, Judah Marton, includes a caveat in his introduction: 'it should be remembered that the diary was in the possession of the Zsolts [Éva's stepfather and mother] – Béla the writer, and Agi, an intellectual with a literary bent – for almost three years before it was first published (in Hungarian)', but adds that Jewish children in Europe at the time were very 'mature' (17). However, it is not the 'maturity' of Éva's diary which might raise questions about authenticity but its combination of this quality with its opposite, an apparent – and sometimes self-conscious – naiveté, as the quotation in the subheading to this section shows.[39]

In fact, it is precisely on the question of literary and rhetorical 'maturity' that the differences between Zimra's and Éva's diaries turn. It is often hard to detect a youthful element in Zimra's diary, apart from its 'impudent' tone; indeed, she repudiates the label 'child' or 'kid' when it is applied to her in the camp (263, 289). As we have seen, Zimra parodies elements of traditional adolescent diaries in a sideways glance at her own official age. In Éva's case, however, we witness clearly several of the effects that characterize children's Holocaust writing, for instance, what I have called 'ironic ignorance'. (The irony here is not strategic, unless Marton's suspicions of editorial intervention by Éva's parents are justified.) Éva's habit of repeating adults' words – in this case, her mother's – provides a perfect opportunity for ironic ignorance: 'they could still take us to Poland in a train just because we were Jews and because there was Fascism here. I don't know what Fascism is, but one of the things it probably means is deporting Jews to Poland' (33). Moments of childhood ignorance are represented but not glossed, nonetheless allowing the adult reader to supply the missing – nearly always malign – meaning.

Other features of Zimra's self-conscious and metatextual diary appear in apparently simpler form in Éva's. Zimra focused on the paradox of the diary existing in two time-frames – the moment of composition and the moment of action – particularly in the camp. While Éva also addresses her diary it is in a more usual way, her words given an uncanny quality by their setting: 'I will lock you so that no one will ever know my secrets' (28), she says of 'secrets' which are both those of adolescence (a crush on Pista Vadas, an older boy) and those of the Nazi occupation (her mother is a socialist). While Zimra described her diary in terms of her own body – its removal a 'wound' (171) – Éva personifies hers in a more recognizable way, as if it were a younger child: 'dear diary...I felt so sorry for you because I'm hardly writing anything in you that can give you some pleasure' (53). This difference in technique is partly due to the respective circumstances of the two girls: Éva lived at home with her family for most of the diary's duration, entering the ghetto on 5 May 1944, while all of Zimra's was written in death- and labour-camps when she was on her own. The same is true of Éva's view of historical events in terms only of her own present – 'I thought that the Unknown Soldier probably was some good friend of Agi's who was buried in Paris' (60) – a habit not repeated but exposed by Zimra in the Villon incident cited above.

The structural effects of Éva's child's-eye view of events include several that we have already seen in other kinds of text, as well as the irony of ignorance and pathos. For instance, once more sexual innocence acts as an analogy for political innocence, functioning in its way akin to pathetic irony – Éva is too young to understand adult sexuality, but not too young to die. Of a neighbour who offered to shelter Éva, the child observes, '[Mrs Jakobi] is a very good woman, and I don't even understand what Grandma meant when she did say that Mrs Jakobi would sell me to men. Nobody is buying Jewish girls nowadays' (80). Éva's view of Jewishness is constructed by the current propaganda and restrictions. She declares her intention to marry someone as un-Jewish as possible, 'an Aryan Englishman' (13, 63). She associates mourning with Judaism, as she notes of her nanny Juszti: 'Her eyes were as red from crying as though she were also Jewish' (65), and of the failure of a family friend to provide them with forged documents: 'Uncle Zoltán is sad, just as if he were Jewish, and he is a real Aryan!' (77). In all these cases, irony and pathos – and humour – arise from the clash of childhood and adolescent concerns with those of adulthood, within the diarist's voice itself and not just in the reader's response. Indeed, it often seems that Éva is drawing attention to this clash between her youthful frame of reference and her unprecedented circumstances as, for instance, when she describes life in the 'ghetto-camp':

> The most awful thing of all is that the punishment for everything is death. There is no difference between things; no standing in the corner, no spankings, no taking away food, no writing down the declension of irregular verbs one hundred times the way it used to be in school. Not at all: the lightest and heaviest punishment – death. (89)

Even within Éva's childlike voice some signs of Zimra's self-conscious and literary techniques are perceptible.

'The everyday life of tyranny':[40] Dawid Sierakowiak, *The Diary of Dawid Sierakowiak*

Dawid Sierakowiak began his diary in the Lódz Ghetto in June 1939, at the age of fourteen; the last entry is for April 1943, and he died of tuberculosis in August of that year, weakened by the starvation he records in his diary. In this case, the forward-looking, cumulative, progressive aspects of a diary are replaced by focus on individual days; the potentially lifelong diary form is balanced against not wanting to look ahead, and an increasing certainty of premature death, as Dawid puts it in the final paragraph: 'In politics there's absolutely nothing new. Again, out of impatience I feel myself beginning to fall into melancholy. There is really no way out of this for us' (263). Paradoxically, the diary form is used to convey the pointlessness of recording the days at all: 'Time is passing to no avail' (163). Dawid's tone is an analogous mixture of anger and the boredom of despair: during 1939 his remarks on nepotism in the ghetto ('This is the rotten, bourgeois-bureaucratic basis on which the ghetto exists, and on which it will perish', 79) alternate with impatience at enforced inaction ('I'm still bored at home', 72).

Especially at first, Dawid's political interests ('The most important things are schoolwork and Marxist theory', 93), and caustic commentary on ghetto and world affairs, stand out – of Roosevelt he says, 'Listening to this disgusting blabber drives you crazy' (96), and he calls the Eldest of the Jews in the ghetto 'The sadist-moron [Chaim] Rumkowski' (102). Dawid describes fury at the 'unmitigated egotism' (93) of his father, who seems keen that his wife be deported so that rations will go further, and steals sugar from visitors' bags. However, the distinctive timbre of Dawid's adolescent voice declines due to the degenerative effects of attrition by hunger and cold which only a diary can effectively convey: 'And so it goes, day by day, ration by ration, deportation by deportation, until the end of the war, or departure to Marysin, or perhaps until we go into exile' (171). Here, Dawid mimics the very form of a diary ('day by day') to show not hopes for what he might be or do,[41] but the staving-off of death; the diary, a form usually used to chart life, instead charts the gradual 'stifling' of life.[42] Dawid's habit of listing the necessarily limited concerns of the ghetto conveys both its deathly boredom, and during 1941 and 1942 provides a malign imitation of the metonymic form of the diary as a genre, which consists of strings of days: 'The only subjects now are food, work, workshops, rations and potatoes' (135); 'May there be no deportations, and may something substantial arrive to eat. Potatoes are the main thing. To eat, think, study, write, and work. Just to get to the end! . . .' (151). The 'end' here suggests at once the end of the war, of the current situation, and perhaps an end to the impulse to write a diary at all, which was born out of extreme conditions. Matters can only stagnate or get worse: 'There are no new food rations. Extermination is approaching' (259); 'The weather's most lovely, simply charming, but in politics there's nothing new' (263).[43]

Dawid records facts from the external world[44] as well as his own increasing 'melancholy', and although his diary reads as a chronicle of slow death, in which, as Lawrence Langer points out in his foreword, food is the only 'hero' (x), its very existence suggests rebellion against constraint. Just as Dawid reads to try and forget his physical circumstances – 'As usual in the times of hunger, I have to turn to forced, intensive reading to drive away the sense of deprivation with this "opiate" ' (244) – he also writes. Even the uncertain future, when it is invoked, is seen in terms of food (and perhaps revenge), as Dawid notes wryly of a visit to the dentist in June 1942: 'Should I, however, get out of here, I'll need to have my teeth in good shape to be able to bite without any problem, to bite all the way!' (189). Although Adelson observes that, 'Dawid seems to take it as his personal duty to record the process of his people's destruction' (12), the diary is both more and less than this. Partly due to his youth, Dawid focuses more than, for instance, Chaim Kaplan, on his own responses to domestic, ghetto and world events, which makes him an exemplar of 'his people's fate' just as he is a chronicler of it.

Yitskhok Rudashevski, *The Diary of the Vilna Ghetto*, June 1941–April 1943

Yitskhok Rudashevski's diary, like Dawid Sierakowiak's, conveys the inadequacy of the diary form by again being at least partly *about* that form.[45] Yitskhok was born in Vilna in 1927 and lived with his parents and grandmother until the establishment of the ghetto in September 1941. Yitskhok's diary consists of two parts: a retrospective summary of events following the Nazi invasion of the Soviet Union (June to December 1941), and a daily record from September 1942 to April 1943. It is clear that Yitskhok was impelled to start writing by the Nazi occupation, as he puts it: 'I consider that everything should be recorded and noted down, even the most gory, because everything will be taken into account' (84). The diary ends several months before Yitskhok's deportation to Ponar in September 1943, where he and his family were killed by shooting. This premature ending to the diary, as Tsvi Shner speculates in his introduction, could be due to missing material, or to the diarist's falling into 'a state of despair' (11) during the raids and mass shootings of the ghetto's last months: it is as if, like Éva Heyman and Anne Frank, he could no longer record a reality that had finally outstripped the diary form. As Victoria Stewart points out, this begs the question of what constitutes 'completion' or an ending in a diary, and in Holocaust diaries the most striking disjunction is between the diary's conclusion and the 'post-textual fate of its author'.[46]

Like Dawid, Yitskhok is a committed communist and sees events through this lens ('Never did life possess such joy and freedom from care as in the Soviet summer of 1941', 23); he also criticizes corruption within the ghetto ('in the ghetto the vitamin P, as it is called, is victorious; "pull" or "pleytses", in other words strong shoulders', 118). In more structural terms, however, Yitskhok uses the diary form to lament the passing of the time that he is also recording. This takes the form of boredom ('There is nothing to do', 'you waste days on nothing', Yitskhok notes on two consecutive days in 1941, 53); of wishing time would pass ('time does not stand still as long as I progress normally with [my studies]', 104) and fearing its passing ('I wish to shout to time to linger, not to run. I wish to recapture my past year and keep it for later, for the new life', 104). Yitskhok's ambivalence about time – the familiar past, threatening present, uncertain future – is also conveyed by the mixture of tenses he uses in the diary. Like Novac's diary, the English translation of Yitskhok's diary shows his use of the narrative present tense, even – or especially – in the first, retrospective half of the text, often shifting abruptly in its effort to convey both immediacy and more recent knowledge: 'I meet my friend Benyke Nayer...He too spent the night in a hide-out. It was the last time that I saw him' (38).[47]

Yitskhok records what Bakhtin would describe as a shift from one chronotope to another. In his essay 'Forms of Time and the Chronotope in the Novel', Bakhtin uses the term to refer to the combination of time and space markers in any text; his examples include the chronotope of the road, in the seventeenth-century novel, and that of interior spaces such as the salon and and drawing-room in the eighteenth-century novel. Yitzkhok's chronotopes are historical ones, and he records a shift from the chronotope of the past (the schoolroom) to that of the present (the ghetto): 'When I used to go to my lessons, I knew how to divide the days, and the days would fly, and now they drag by for me grayly and sadly' (56). As if in acknowledgement of Bakhtin's observation that in a text – here, a diary – 'spatial and temporal indicators are fused into one...concrete whole',[48] Yitskhok notes the spatial reason for the undifferentiated passage of time: he claims that the ghetto is, 'not a painful, squirming *moment* of a dream...but is a large *swamp* in which we lose our days and weeks' (104, my italics). It seems that here space represents the loss of ordinary time, possibly of life itself.

Clearly the diary in general, which records time in a spatial manner – as Zimra noted, a page is equivalent to a day – itself constitutes a chronotope, one that is disordered here under the pressure of what it represents. When school resumes in November 1941, Yitskhok writes, 'The days pass quickly' (72), as if time spent studying – and writing – cannot be 'boring' time. Underlying this awareness of time and its passage is uncertainty about the future and a fear of death, as Yitskhok records in September: 'It is dusk. "We have staved off another day", the women say to each other' (28). Indeed, Yitschok repudiates the present, which the reader might expect the diary to focus on (and it does so in terms of factual detail: memorials, club evenings, festivals and even plans for resistance[49] are as frequently noted as edicts and atrocities) in favour of the future, as if his diary were not just about but *facilitating* the passage of time itself:

> My determination to study has developed into something like defiance of the present which hates to study, loves to work, to drudge. No, I decided. I shall live with tomorrow, not with today. (120)

This commentary on diurnal composition suggests a new relation between the diarist and time. It is not just recorded, but – as if this were a new kind of relativity – the diarist implies that the act of daily recording itself may have an effect on the speed at which time passes. In this way, present time transcends space by becoming the future more speedily: 'Time runs by so quickly and there is so much work to be done, lectures, social gatherings. I often forget that I am in the ghetto' (135). Yitskhok acknowledges the new chronotope he is writing in by hoping that, 'Next year we shall eat Hitler-tashn' (137): he predicts an end to the current outrages by trying to place Hitler in the future-past of religious observance. Jews – and especially children – eat 'Haman-tashn' (that is, pastries shaped like 'Haman's ears') at the Purim festival to commemorate the defeat of the genocidal minister Haman in the court of the Persian King Ahasuerus. In Yitskhok's analogy Hitler too will be consigned to a liturgical past.[50] This future-perfect hope sits alongside the more fearful conditional future of the last line of Yitskhok's diary: 'We may be fated for the worst' (140).

'So write children, whose only school was Teutonic life' (11 July 1944): Anonymous, *'Les Vrais Riches'* Diary

This anonymous diary was composed in the Lódz Ghetto by a young man or boy, whose fate is unknown but who is assumed to have perished in the liquidation of the ghetto in late 1944. The diary is written in four languages, in a disordered fashion on the endpapers and around the text of François Coppée's 1892 novel *Les Vrais Riches*. The diarist's gender is apparent from a stray remark ('I [am] a man who am entrapped by the German snare', 15 May 1944).[51] The boy's age is unknown, although it is clear from the diary that he had a sister of twelve and that they had lived with their father until he died of starvation.

If the diary form constitutes a chronotope, in which the pages are space, the daily entries time, then *'Les Vrais Riches'* offers a new version of the 'diary chronotope' in its configurations of multiple and disordered levels of both time and space. The order in which the entries appear is dictated by the blank pages of Coppée's novel, rather than by the order of events and progression of time. The present-day reader of the *'Vrais Riches'* original can make sense, or keep track, of the diary's disorder by four different methods of noting time's relation to space: the dates of entries; the order of the pages of the diary itself;[52] the page numbers of Coppée's novel; and page numbers added to the manuscript in pencil by an editor to every recto and verso of Coppée's novel on which the diarist has written.[53] (Each of the three translated versions of parts of this diary puts the entries into chronological order; but this is not how they appear to a reader of the original or reproduced text.)[54] As is the case with most of the diaries I have discussed, the primary method of measuring time while reading the diary is of course the dating of entries, and even in the case of *'Les Vrais Riches'* this allows a chronology to be established; the anonymous boy wrote during the spring and summer of 1944, in Hebrew, Yiddish, Polish and English, sometimes composing entries in several languages on one day. However, the entry which appears on the first page of Coppée's novel is not the first one to be written. Zapruder notes that, 'the diary opens in May [1944]', but the book in which it is written does not 'open' here: the first entry that we read is from 17 July 1944. This has the disconcerting effect that the introductory entry appears three pages into Coppée's novel, two into the diary: 'I decided to write a diary, though it is a bit too late. To recapitulate past events is quite impossible so I begin with the present' (5 May 1944).

Yet this disorderly means of recording is clearly an appropriate one. The boy appears to have been prompted to write by his sense that it is 'too late', time is running out and many noteworthy events have already been lost (it is 'impossible' to 'recapitulate' them). The diarist's sense of time on a threshold is partly historical; while the Nazis' defeat seemed inevitable by mid-1944, the liberation of the Lódz Ghetto was not assured. (The boy's last entry in English ('I cannot write more') was made on 3 August 1944; although the Red Army reached the Vistula near Lódz on 1 August, they did not liberate the city until January 1945.) His diary is the means of recording – and even hastening – the passing of time, which, as he notes, in itself might save lives: 'When I write these lines, I don't know for sure if the outsettling [deportation] has been wholly stopped – or partly only, but it is after all good news, because *time plays a considerable part at present*' (undated English entry, after one in Hebrew for 15 July 1944, my italics). While specific events which took place after May 1944 are noted, the diary is not a linear account so much as a repetitive,[55] angry and bitterly irreverent[56] polemic on life in the ghetto, the attitude of the outside world and the Nazis' behaviour during their last months.

Even if, like Novac's undated diary, they do not consist of sequentially dated entries, diaries usually follow the linear structure of the pages on which they are written, whether this is in the form of a bound book or not. In the case of '*Les Vrais Riches*', this orderly arrangement too is absent. While the diarist's record is dictated by Coppée's novel in varying ways – he writes around and not over the novel's title on the title page (5 July 1944), and around text set in large print, but over smaller print which allows his writing to be read – he does not follow the pages of the book in order from left to right. In other words, the diarist does not follow the 'plot' of Coppée's novel, but imposes on it his own 'story': and this is to use these terms purely formally.

This formal disruptiveness matches the diarist's constant refrain that writing is nearly impossible, either because of his own mental and physical state (hunger, disheartening rumours and international news mean that, 'it is now impossible for me to write down a few decent lines because of the utter destruction of my nervous system', 9 July 1944), or because reality outstrips both precedent, language ('To say that it is unimaginable, undescribable, unspeakable, un...un...un...etc. and etc. is to have said nothing!', 12 July 1944), and his own ability to record ('I dream about telling to "humanity" but should I be able, should Shakespeare be able? and

what yet I who am only a little proud of understanding Shakespeare?!',
11 June 1944 – and, presumably, proud of having such a nuanced grasp
of Shakespeare's national language). Like Novac's ambivalent burlesque of
the notion of a ballad in the camps, the anonymous diarist's invocation
of Shakespeare in the ghetto both questions and continues the notion
of a literary representation of the Holocaust.

Langford and West describe the '*Vrais Riches*' diary as, 'a highly literary
meditation upon the relation of everyday writing to canonical texts
which appear to have proved inadequate in describing, let alone resisting,
the political perversions of civilised nations'.[57] It is true that the diary-
entries written or scrawled on the pages of Coppée's novel often produce
effects which are almost self-evidently ironic (and on which the diarist
himself never remarks): the world of the nineteenth-century French
romance seems grotesquely irrelevant to the boy's life in the ghetto. For
instance, the diarist writes carefully around an illustration which shows
a young man petitioning a mother for her daughter's hand in marriage,
captioned, 'Vous pouvez d'un mot me rendre le plus heureux des
hommes.'[58] The diarist is himself temporarily an 'homme heureux', in
incomparable manner, on hearing a rumour that deportations have
ceased: 'a few hours later this joy of mine was spoilt – by being told
tha[t] someone read a letter which was hidden in the waggon of the
outsettled – that they were travelling to Kolo; and this is a terrible name
for us, the name of this town because there was the abbattoir for the
Jews [i.e. Chelmno]' (15 July 1944). But it is as if the diarist's sentences
clash without interaction with Coppée's. The orderly chronotope of the
classical novel and its paratextual apparatus is at odds with the disordered
diary and the unpredictable reality it records. Perhaps most meaninglessly
ironic of all is the juxtaposition of a handwritten inscription on the
novel's flyleaf, reading, 'A ma chère soeur, pour le bon souvenir' (To my
dear sister, for good memories), dated 5 February 1918. Not only does
this appear above one of the boy's entries lamenting the murder of
'7000 of our co-sufferers' (17 July 1944), it also reminds the reader of the
boy's relationship with his own sister (the quotation in the subheading
to this section is by the diarist about her efforts at writing) and the very
bad time through which they are living, without really shedding any light
on either. The reader might, however, be reminded of the First World
War by the fact that the year of this inscription is 1918, and of the
Armistice of 11 November which is yet to come; this makes Coppée's
world seem suddenly less divorced from that of the diarist.

Furthermore, not only does the diarist himself wish for 'beautiful
things'[59] including books like Coppée's novel in the ghetto. He also

seems to be struggling with the relation between 'canonical texts' and 'political perversions' in a less conclusive way than Langford and West. To convey precisely the terrible brink between liberation and annihilation on which the ghetto stands, the anonymous diarist implicitly continues his question about Shakespeare's fitness to represent events by quoting from *Hamlet*:

> The only care is about our future; the nearest future; because every one i[s] convinced that the war is decidedly approaching its end; Fears are aroused by rumours according to which the G.[ermans] destroyed tens of thousands of Hungarian Jews. When should this question of 'to be or not to be' be taken off our shoulders? (19 July 1944)

The diarist quotes Hamlet's words – 'to be or not to be' – in awareness of their change in meaning, from a question about individual 'self-slaughter' to one simply about being slaughtered en masse. A few days later, after the attempt on Hitler's life on 20 July 1944, the diarist quotes from *Hamlet* again:

> It is 2 o'clock after midnight – I cannot lie in my Getto bed for it is full of merciless bugs with whom I have no means to fight – so I have time for sombre thinking – I think about the "[defeat of Hitler]"[60] which is going to take place in the nearest future – but if we shall be present . . . if we shall live? this is the rub, this is what makes us shudder all over . . . (23 July 1944).

Once more, the quotation is moved from its original context – where Hamlet is paralysed into inaction by uncertainty (the 'rub') over what happens to suicides in the afterlife – to the present context, where the diarist ponders the enforced passivity of ghetto inhabitants who cannot predict their *earthly* fate. I think this recontextualization itself registers the diarist's ambivalence about 'canonical literature'; while the context of Hamlet's original dilemma is not applicable to that of those the diarist calls 'Gettonians', his phrases are, as is the notion of suicide (which the diarist mentions as a possibility on 1 July 1944 in Polish[61]). When news of the fighting which preceded the Warsaw Uprising reaches Lódz in late July 1944 the diarist is impelled by sudden hope to repudiate the notion of poetry altogether, rejecting its tropes:

> Oh! If I should be a poet I should say – that my heart is like the stormy ocean, my brains a bursting volcano – my soul like . . . forgiveness. I am

no poet. And the greatest of poets is to[o] poor a fellow in word even to hint, only to allude at what we passed, and are presently passing by – Never has any human being been put into such a state of 'the profundis' as we have been. (29 July 1944)

Rather, the diarist claims that 'imagination' is reserved for those Jews who hear the 'few magic words' that fighting has broken out around Warsaw. At this moment, history supersedes poetry.

Conclusion

The most distinctive feature of these young people's diaries is their interweaving of personal and public concerns, often in favour of the former. While the adult Chaim Kaplan, in his Warsaw Ghetto diary, declares his intention to write impersonally – with 'objectivity', as Abraham Katsch puts it[62] – and rarely touches on personal details, for instance, his diabetes, the 'uncanny' quality of teenage diaries arises precisely from their combination of domestic, subjective or developmental issues with unprecedented public events. Anne Frank's diary often reveals an intersection between adolescent concerns and those about living in hiding. Her frequent wish for adulthood and self-determination is barely distinguishable in these examples from fears about the war and hopes for its end:

Now I think either about unhappy things or about myself. (73)

I'm longing – really longing – for everything: conversation, freedom, friends, being alone. (182)

In other words, reversing the pattern we have seen, Frank's is an archetypal adolescent diary *because of* the extremity of its historical setting.

Philippe Lejeune notes that, 'the private diary is a *practice*. The text itself is a mere by-product, a residue'.[63] It is perhaps this notion of a 'residue', or 'trace of the past',[64] that exerts the strongest appeal of the Holocaust diary to its reader. Reading such a contemporary account can appear either to restore the loss it records ('but for [the diary] Dawid Rubinowicz would have perished without trace'[65]), or to figure that loss (as Hanno Loewy argues, Otto Frank's reading of his daughter's diary after the war 'must have been unspeakably excruciating', as a reminder of his losses[66]). A striking instance of such a 'trace' is perceptible in the very handwriting of an entry by Anne Frank, which begins, 'My hand's still shaking' (56). Frank's fear at hearing someone knocking on the attic door continues to affect not just the moment, but the mark, of writing itself, two hours later.

James Young has argued that the content and tone of children's and teenagers' Holocaust diaries vary according not only to the circumstances of historical reality, but to their own preconceptions and background. He uses a comparison of Anne Frank's and Moshe Flinker's diaries to support this; the secular Frank sees room for hope where the orthodox Flinker sees religious apocalypse.[67] I would argue that there is a dialogic relation between the writer's inner and outer worlds which is reflected in the particular formal details of each diary. For instance, Novac's literary aspirations (borne out in her post-war life, as she is a playwright and novelist) partly determine the impressionistic way in which she describes her six months in Auschwitz; while Sierakowiak's daily entries are fitting as a way of recording the piecemeal wearing down of the ghetto inhabitants. Yet of course the circumstances also shape the diaries' form. As I have noted, Novac is unable to supply dates for her entries, increasing the episodic and literary appearance of her diary; while Sierakowiak's gradual debilitation – his frostbite (247), scabies (250), inability to walk due to hunger (263) – makes short regular efforts at writing more possible than a sustained or retrospective account.

The diaries I have discussed here clearly exhibit great variety, in terms, first, of language: Rubinowicz writes in Polish, Moshe Flinker chose Hebrew over Flemish, Anne Frank chose Dutch over German, Ana Novac translated her diary from the Hungarian of her youth into the French of her post-war life, while the '*Vrais Riches*' diarist wrote in Yiddish to express his 'true inner self' (371),[68] English to prevent his sister reading those entries, Polish and Hebrew 'because [it] is the language of the future'.[69] The diarists' circumstances were determined partly by their nationality or where they lived. On the other hand, the diaries of children and teenagers do have traits in common. While Sierakowiak and Rudashevski explicitly state their disdain for religion, all the diarists address and question God in some manner. The diarists also share features appropriate to their ages and circumstances, such as love for inspirational teachers, stultification and boredom without school, quarrels with parents and siblings, and recording in great detail the amount and cost of whatever food was available.

The readership of these Holocaust diaries is even more unspecific,[70] or radically uncertain, than is usual in the diary. Anne Frank moves between doubting that anyone 'will ever be interested in this drivel' (259) and believing in the value of her writing for future readers: 'ten years after the war people would find it very amusing to read how we lived, what we ate and what we talked about as Jews in hiding' (240). These comments show a clash between Frank's view of the quality of her writing, and her view of its historical significance. The diarists wonder whether they, let alone posterity, will ever read what they have written, due to life-threatening events that take place between entries, as the '*Vrais Riches*' diarist notes of a forced labour edict: 'I write and I don't know if tomorrow I shall be able to read it' (18 August 1944). As well as invoking and doubting canonical literature from the Bible to Dante, Shakespeare to Villon, most of the diarists here exhibit their own literary inclinations, as Marie Syrkin puts it of Moshe Flinker: he was 'obviously an *Ilui* (prodigy)'.[71] In fact, the diary can only record the experiences of children and teenagers during the Holocaust years through being taken to an extreme – an extreme which, rather than distinguishing the Holocaust diary from all others,[72] lays bare the formal construction of all diaries.

Appendix: the page order of *'Les Vrais Riches'*

In the following columns of page numbers and dates I have used as a 'base' order the editorial page-numbers pencilled onto each folio of Coppée's novel on which the diarist wrote. I have chosen to present the columns in this way because such an order differs from the published translations (as I have noted, these are chronological). The columns show clearly the relation between the structure of the book, the language of an entry and the date of composition, and the order of the pages of the boy's diary. As I have said, the *'Vrais Riches'* diary is a virtual construct and exists as a separate text (with its own pagination and sequence) only as a projection of these other elements.

This diary could be described as a chronotope, constituted from the space of another text's pages and the time of dated diary entries. The relation between these space and time markers varies according to other spatial and historical factors, such as which language the boy uses (as can be seen, the entries for the last week of July are written from the end of the book inwards, as the Hebrew the boy uses runs from right to left), and where the blank pages fall in *Les Vrais Riches* (these are at the beginning and end of the book). Yet even these unusual and distinctive features mean that the *'Vrais Riches'* diary emphasizes what is typical of the diary in general: chronology and sequence are present through their very disorder.

Diary[73]	Editorial[74]	Date[75]	Novel	Languages[76]
xxx	1	17.7	dedication	H, E, P[77]
xxii	2	10.7	blank page	P, Y
i, ii	3	5.5, 15.5	blank page	E
v	4	31.5	blank page	E
vi	5	1–11.6	blank page	E
xi	6	25.6	blank page	E
xii	7	26, 27.6	[ibis engraving]	P
xiii, xix	8/9	1.7, 5.7	title page	P, E, H
xx	10	6.7, 8.7	[engraving]	H, P
xxi, xxii	11	9–11.7	blank page	H, E, Y
xxiii	12	11.7	[note on paper]	E, H, E
xxiv	13	11.7, 12.7	blank page	E, P, H
xxv	14	12.7	blank page	H, Y
xxvi	15	12.7, 15.7	blank page	E, P
xxix, xxxi	16	16.7, 18.7	[ch. title]	P, H, E, P
xxxii	17	18–20.7	blank page	E, P, E, Y, H
xxxiii	18	21.7	1	H, P
xxxvi	19	21.7	2	P
xxxvii	20	21.7	3	P
xxxviii	21	22.7	4	P
xxxix	22	23.7	5 [engraving]	P, E
xlv	23	26.7	6	P
xliii	24	26.7	7	P

Appendix   (Continued)

Diary[73]	Editorial[74]	Date[75]	Novel	Languages[76]
xlvii	25	27.7	8	P
xlviii	26	27.7	9	E
xlix	27	28.7	10	P
li	28	29.7	11	P
liv	29	29.7	12	E
lv	30	29.7	13 [engraving]	E, P
lvii	31	3.8	14	E
lviii	32	3.8	15	E
lix	33	3.8	16	E
lx	34	3.8	17	E
lxi	35	3.8	18	E
lvi	37	31.7	253	H
liii	38	29.7	254	H
lii	39	29.7	255	H
l	40	28.5[78]	256	H
xliv	41	26.7	257	H
xliii	42	25.7	258	H
xlii	43	24.7	259	H
xxxviii	44	23.7	260	H, Y
xxvii	45	15.7	261 [engraving]	E
xviii, xl	46	4.7, 15.7	262	H, E, H, E, Y
xvii	47	3.7, 4.7	263	P, E, H
xvi	48	3.7	264	P
xv	49	2.7, 3.7	table	H, H, E, P
xiii	50	26.6, 30.6	date	H, E
x	51	22.6	catalogue	H
ix	52	19.6, 20.6	catalogue	E, Y, H
viii	53	16.6, 18.6	catalogue	E
vii	54	16.6, 17.6	catalogue	H
v	55	9.6, 12.6	blank page	H, Y
iii	56	24.5, 31.5	blank page	Y, H
xxvii	57	20.7[79]	blank page	Y
xxviii	58	20.7	blank page	Y

8
Fragmentary Narration

Introduction: fragments or episodes?

The psychoanalyst Dori Laub says the following of Holocaust testimony: 'personal historical testimony emerges as a composite, a mosaic of... existential, detailed and profound knowledge, side by side with vast voids, absences and ignorances'.[1] Although Laub is discussing oral testimony, the features he mentions are also, more specifically, characteristic of fragmentary Holocaust narratives by or about children and young people. In the latter, profound knowledge of detail can only exist alongside 'voids, absences and ignorances', because the effects of trauma are compounded by the necessary incomprehension of youth. It could be argued that fragmentary form and the notion of lost plenitude characterize all representations of childhood memory; these features appear, for instance, in the opening of James Joyce's *Portrait of the Artist as a Young Man*. However, the loss and brokenness in the texts I am discussing depend precisely on the overlap of developmental with historical trauma and amnesia.

In many Holocaust accounts personal disruption is not matched by a fragmentary form, despite the titles of such memoirs as Hedi Fried's *Fragments of a Life*. Hana Greenfield's similarly titled *Fragments of Memory* is related in an episodic but not fragmentary way: according to the blurb, it is a 'collection of articles' rather than a single, fragmented work.[2] I would distinguish episodic from fragmentary narration on the grounds that the latter consists of instances broken up by gaps of lost or repressed memory which are as significant as what is present. Episodic narration, on the other hand, consists of self-contained, teleological stories. The gaps occur within and not between episodes, and may constitute deliberate rather than unwitting omission. Marga

Minco's novel *Bitter Herbs* is an instance of episodic narration, although it might at first appear to be fragmentary. It does represent the viewpoint of a child, but not in the radically discontinuous manner of fragmentation.

Marga Minco was born in Breda in the Netherlands in 1920; she, alone of her family, survived the war by living in hiding in rural locations. As I noted in the introduction, although the novel follows the details of the author's life, the unnamed first-person narrator is clearly several years younger than Minco, increasing the effect of an innocence which implicates others. Throughout *Bitter Herbs*,[3] the episodes conclude with a moment of irony in which teenage character and adult narrator are closely united. In other words, the irony is not at the expense of the child, as it is in Jona Oberski's *A Childhood* (a text which *Bitter Herbs* otherwise resembles). For instance, in the episode 'In Safe Keeping', the irony of the title is carried over into the story itself and shared by the child. In the story, a neighbour visits the house where the child and her brother are hiding and takes away a bagful of their possessions on the pretext of looking after them until the war's end. The child reacts ambivalently to this: she appears naively to encourage the neighbour when the latter laughingly says she should have brought a sack: ' "But, of course, you didn't know you'd have so much to carry. After all, you only came for the [tennis] racket, didn't you?" ' (46). This remark is ambivalently presented. It represents at once the child's innocence and her irony. Indeed, it is the neighbour's dishonesty, rather than the child's misunderstanding, which has been revealed, and this notion of the incomprehension of neighbours, or even rescuers – which is both a theme and a device – appears in several stories (see 'Someone Else', 107, and 'Epilogue: The Tram Stop', 114).

The correction of misunderstanding is not presented as a developmental theme in *Bitter Herbs*, as it is in Oberski's *A Childhood*. Indeed, it is sometimes hard to tell in Minco's stories whether it is the child or adult narrator who explains facts to the reader. For example, after the arrest of her parents, we read, 'I thought of the Hollandsche Schouwberg, the former Jewish theatre to which all our people were taken to begin with' (78). Technically, this is the adult narrator's utterance, but using the child's discourse – 'to begin with' is characteristic of her unwillingness (rather than inability) to describe the Jews' fate. As we will see below, it is precisely the identity of the Schouwberg that the nameless protagonist of *A Childhood* cannot supply. That ignorance in itself creates fragmentation, as the boundaries of factual knowledge are missing and can only be supplied by the reader.

Fragmentary narration: 'Bits and pieces of a memory'[4]

In this chapter I discuss four texts which use a fragmentary method of narration: two memoirs (Francine Christophe's *From a World Apart* and Isabella Leitner's *Isabella*), and two works of fiction (Jona Oberski's autobiographical novel *A Childhood*, and Binjamin Wilkomirki's *Fragments*).[5] By 'fragmentary narration' I mean a narrative that is continuous, although not necessarily chronological, and which consists of the 'mosaic' tiles, in Laub's phrase, of incidents and images without the framework of explicit analysis or context. Fragmentary narration offers the potential for representing disrupted temporality and viewpoint in a way that is perfectly suited to children's-eye views. In each of the four texts we see the same pattern. The child's viewpoint is represented by first-person narration usually in the present tense, through isolated episodes or impressions. These fragments replicate *both* the child's-eye view and the narrator's memory of it. Where the child is very young, as is the case in the fictional texts by Oberski and Wilkomirski,[6] the narrative mode stands for the child's-eye view itself, while the fragmentary form constitutes a means of memory, and is thus from the adult's viewpoint.[7] Clearly, both first-person narrative through a child focalizer and fragmented narrative form are the result of the adult narrator's choices. But it seems equally clear that while the former shows what remains of the past (represented by incidents which are misunderstood or unexplained), the latter reveals what has been lost in the recall (represented by the gaps between episodes).

The fragments in all four texts stand for all that remains of the past, although this limited knowledge is in practice supplemented in varying ways. In *From A World Apart*, Francine's knowledge is filled out by endnotes, and although the gaps between the fragments of the memoir convey her incomplete understanding as a child, details such as quoted speech, dates, locations and other facts are supplied by the adult narrator (for instance, it is the latter who notes, albeit in the present tense, 'After 11 November 1942, the invaded Unoccupied Zone surrenders its cargo of refugees', 60). In *A Childhood*, the onus is more fully on the reader to supply contextual information which the unnamed boy cannot, in ways ranging from working out the rules of the camp world, to decoding unnamed historical locations. The implied reader of *Fragments* is similarly made to take on a burden of interpretation, partly to emphasize the child's innocence and inability to understand the meaning of his early experiences. However, the child's view is inconsistently rendered. Sometimes the impression of immediacy is preserved by showing the child's ignorance – he refers to the 'wooden boards' (141) used for skiing, and the occupying forces' vehicle, a 'gray black monster with a round lid that was standing open' (33) – but elsewhere the knowledge of the adult narrator reminds us that this viewpoint is retrospective, for instance, 'I left the *inner fence perimeter* along with a women's *work detail*' (40, my italics). In *Isabella*, the eponymous narrator's memories are those of a young woman, so are more complete than those of the three children; she also relies on the anachronous[8] narration of flashforward and flashback to order her fragments, which means information is often supplied in the plot of her memory before we reach it in the chronological story.

Although there is by definition in these retrospective texts a split time-scale – at least between the time of the events and the time of writing – this is not the division focused on in these texts. Fragmented works foreground gaps and divisions in perceiving the events themselves. They do this instead of focusing on the distance between adult and child, which is both taken for granted and denied. It is as if both the narrative mode and the 'fragments' themselves are constitutive of a child's voice, whereas they are in fact both signs of a later organization. The failure to see such aesthetic organization is typified by the blurb for the British Picador edition of Binjamin Wilkomirski's fictional *Fragments*, which describes the text as 'unselfconscious'; and Jonathan Kozol, reviewing *Fragments* in 1996, claimed it to be 'free from literary artifice of any kind'.[9] Even before it became clear that *Fragments* was fictive and not testimonial, its nature as a highly patterned and structured text served simply to give the *impression* of unselfconscious lack of artifice; and this construction holds good for all the texts I discuss here.

The radical distinction between character and narrator that we saw in Chapter 1 in the split-time narratives, often symbolized by their different first names, is much more muted in the fragmented texts. Indeed, occasionally the narrator tries to suggest that the distinction between times has vanished both by using the present tense and through a direct address to someone in the past, as in Christophe's *From A World Apart*: 'I'm hungry, Mother, I'm hungry. Yes, you can look at me oddly, I blame you, I blame you for my hunger' (106). Yet despite these differences – both the past and the present time of writing appear in split narratives, usually the past alone in fragmentary ones – both kinds of text register temporally the deformation of traumatic memory. In fragmentary texts, past and present are actually also both represented, as we are always aware of the adult narrator responsible for the story, however unobtrusive s/he may be. Here, the present-time writing adult is relegated either to the 'paratexts', in Gérard Genette's term for a text's 'accompanying productions',[10] such as its title, afterword, or endnotes (in the case of Christophe's *From a World Apart*); or to an apparently recuperative present which may or may not appear in the text (respectively, Isabella Leitner's *Isabella* and Jona Oberski's *A Childhood*).

'Fragmentation' as a concept appears both in psychological analyses of Holocaust survivors and their testimonies,[11] and in cultural and literary theory. In terms of the former, Laub argues that the 'extensive fragmentation' undergone by survivors can be partially repaired only through a 'testimonial process' that 'allows for the re-externalization or historicization of the event'.[12] In all four of the texts I discuss here, efforts are made in this way to construct 'an Other, a hearer who listens to the account of trauma': within the text, such an 'Other' is usually the child's own parent, but as she or he is already dead at the time of writing, or even at the time of the events that are narrated, such a hearer has to be replaced by the reader of the testimony or fiction. It is as if fragmentation itself provokes the address to an absent Other, one who might recreate the text into a coherent narrative whole.

In literary-theoretical terms, fragmentation is a term often used in relation to postmodernism.[13] Postmodernism is clearly not a unified body of thought, but the views of postmodern thinkers are divided between lamenting the loss of surety and stability conveyed by fragmentation, and welcoming the opportunity it offers to represent minority interests outside a hierarchical 'master narrative'. The latter approach is apparently at the opposite extreme to that I have just discussed, in which fragmentation is the result of trauma and constitutes an implicit appeal for a lost wholeness. However, rather than being simply a destruction of epistemology, fragmentation itself in these Holocaust texts could be described as a system of knowledge, as Dori Laub and Nancy Auerhahn put it: 'we believe that survivors know mostly through retention of fragments of unintegrated memories'.[14] The child focalizer seems an apt symbol for the overlap between the fragmentary Holocaust text and postmodern notions of fragmentation, as a being for whom 'the grand narrative' did not 'lose' its credibility: the child was simply unable to perceive an overview of its experience, whether offered by 'a speculative narrative or a narrative of emancipation'.[15] For the child in fragmented works about the Holocaust, such 'incredulity towards master-narratives'[16] takes the form of a failure to understand them; but the child can nonetheless represent the constituent parts of such a narrative. In fact, despite its apparently postmodern credentials, the fragmented Holocaust testimony or novel conforms rather to Lyotard's definition of modernism, which 'allows the unpresentable to be put forward only as the missing contents' while 'the form, because of its recognizable consistency, continues to offer to the reader...matter for solace and pleasure'.[17] In the texts discussed here, the 'unpresentable' – that is, full adult knowledge of atrocity – is literally missing, between the gaps and after the text's end; yet the text is 'consistent' as a form 'shot through with holes'.[18]

'Not a full account, but a series of snapshots' (1): Francine Christophe, *From a World Apart*

Francine Christophe's *From a World Apart*[19] is a memoir describing the arrest of nine-year-old Francine and her mother in the south of France in 1942, their journey through six French deportation camps and finally to Bergen-Belsen. In his introduction, Nathan Bracher mentions Christophe's term, ' "photos" ', for the fragments she presents: the text consists of 'snapshots of ordinary people' rather than a 'sweeping narrative' of the Holocaust (ix), assembled into the 'photo album' of the text. In a brief preface, the older Francine describes the process of assemblage: from the age of twelve (from her liberation in 1945 onwards) she 'noted down' her memories, that is, committed them to memory as images: 'This little book was therefore inside my head.' The written version of the photograph album is a chronological reconstruction: 'It only took me a few weeks to compose [this book] in 1967, bringing together my ideas and notes' (1).

The photograph analogy captures the striking neutrality of the narrator's tone throughout *From a World Apart* (the older Francine terms it 'totally without literary pretension' (1), although it is at least the result of textual decisions and structurings). Both of these techniques aim to replicate the view of a child, whose focus is on local detail rather than a wider picture; for instance Francine is shocked at a man who cries in the same way she does (92). This childlike focus blends with the camp habit Francine develops of living 'for the present moment, thinking less and less. I wait for my soup, I wait for bedtime' (60). The use of the present tense here is overdetermined; the child has chosen it as a means of protection, while the adult narrator also uses it, to represent both the child's world ('I wait') and the moment of writing: 'I have forgotten what everyday life was like in this camp', the older Francine says of Pithiviers (33).

The 'snapshots' of *From A World Apart* are arranged in short bursts of a sentence or two – which may themselves be verb-free fragments – with gaps between them representing the knowledge and context which the child did not have, as well as 'yellowed' memories discarded by the older

Francine. The outbreak of war is represented in such a fragmentary way, intruding on a holiday in Deauville, August 1939:

> And one day, when we come home, the radio is blaring in the house. Father and Mother go up to their room, very pale: Father comes back down wearing a suit and tie.
>
> Kisses, smothering kisses, arms wrapped tightly, hearts bursting. The station, the train. And the radio that blares on about pink and blue forms.
>
> I am six years old. (3, layout as in the original)

These fragments constitute an attempt at the replication of a child's view of historical events: images and sensory perceptions take the place of factual, ordered knowledge, and the spaces between the sentences stand for the literal absence of knowledge. Yet, as the present tense shows, this is a stylization of a child's viewpoint. The reader knows that it is in fact retrospective, a narrative of memory rather than the captured childhood present of a photograph; and the statement of fact here – 'I am six years old' – is clearly information given by the adult narrator but using the child's voice.

From a World Apart is arranged in unnumbered chapters with captions, ironically – particularly those in bold – imitating the layout of a photograph album: '18 August 1940. I am seven' (8); **'Drancy, August 1942'** (29). The gaps between the snapshots are, as one might expect, often as significant as the images provided. The effect of *From a World Apart* is not to confound and 'abandon'[20] the reader, as do the gaps between the memory and fantasy narratives in Perec's *W or the Memory of Childhood*. Rather than the reader becoming orphaned by the lack of a parental, omniscient narrator as in *W*, in Christophe's text the reader is transformed into a surrogate parent who can decipher the missing text and recognize the pathos of the child's situation – a technique shared with subtlety by *A Childhood*, more insistently by *Fragments*. While the notes to Perec's memories served to unsettle the notion of clear or accurate recall, the notes and chronology in *From a World Apart* attempt to buttress with fact what the child Francine remembers. They supplement the details that the older narrator has omitted apparently to preserve the consistency of the child's 'snapshot' views. Yet the notes to *From a World Apart* are in their way as inconsistent and destabilizing as those to *W*, if less self-consciously so. As well as explaining that, for instance, Léon Blum was an ex-Prime Minister of France, the notes (177–9) let us know that Francine's mother was a barracks head at the transit camp Beaune-la-Rolande and that the gift the inmates gave her was a flowering plant. This strange combination of different levels of information emphasizes the arbitrary line drawn between what would be natural for the young Francine to include in her 'snapshots' and what is contextualizing material, sometimes known only after the war.

The knowing, adult reader implied by *From a World Apart* is made clear, for example, when Francine and her mother visit her father, a prisoner of war, with a birthday cake for the child:

> At the entrance, the sentry on duty goes through all the parcels and shakes the cake box violently.
>
> 'The imbecile!' cries Mother. Then she blanches and adds, 'No, no, he can't have understood!' Neither did I. (8)

Here, the fragments that remain in the memory are shown not to be arbitrary but based on the child's knowledge that she has missed the meaning of a significant incident; the tense of, 'Neither *did* I' implies that now the adult narrator, like the adult reader, *does* understand. Misunderstanding is both an alibi for a brutal adult, and a reality for the child; later in her journey through the camps, Francine's viewpoint grows closer to that of the adults who surround her.

Indeed, the most striking aspect of *From a World Apart* is the overlap it presents between an uncomprehending child's viewpoint and the knowing amorality of a camp inmate's view. The lack of commentary by the narrator throughout the text economically signals both the decontextualization of a child's view ('in brief, Beaune-la-Rolande was good times' (40), Francine observes of one internment, preserving the child's voice in the phrase 'good times'), and that of a camp inmate ('Dead bodies pass by everyday on the central roadway [at Belsen]. It's their Champs Elysées' (86)). In both cases the 'abnormal' (40) has become the norm, and the two viewpoints – of child and of inmate – ironize each other.

In most instances the child's voice is uppermost, for example as Francine is surprised to discover that her mother feels as she does – 'So she's unhappy too, just like me?' (88) – and in her constant complaint: 'Mother, I'm hungry. I tell her every day, to make sure she knows' (90). We see a mixture of childlike and adult views in Francine's description as the 'privileged' inmates of Belsen are transported out of the camp by the SS and Francine views this in childhood terms – 'I think of

Tom Thumb, who left a trail of stones; we leave a trail of bodies' (121). Yet unlike the psychological imperative to 'experience traumatic events from their viewpoint as children' mentioned by Paul Valent in his discussion of child survivors,[21] the child's reference in *From a World Apart* is made with the ironic knowledge that it is bathetic. However, occasionally the questions of the child are exactly the same as those of adults; in Beaune, Francine's first-person plural signals the disappearance of a boundary between child and adult knowledge: 'What is deportation? We devise theories' (51). This overlap between child and adult is replicated in the fragmentary narration of *From A World Apart*: the viewpoint is a child's, the organization an adult's.

'Faded shreds of paper' (16): Isabella Leitner, *Isabella*

Isabella Leitner's *Isabella: From Auschwitz to Freedom* (1994) was originally published in two separate volumes, *Fragments of Isabella* (1978) and *Saving the Fragments*.[22] The earlier titles refer explicitly to the texts' composition: Isabella 'began to "speak" on little scraps of paper in my native tongue, Hungarian, using a pencil [...] I would write wherever I happened to be' (14). When she decided to write the first volume of her memoir, Isabella was 'afraid to rely on my memory only' and therefore 'reached for my box of faded scraps of paper, and began to translate them [into English]. Nearly all the words found their way into the manuscript' (16). *Isabella* is the product of reworking and its change of title is telling: rather than emphasizing a disjointed account of a fragmented subjectivity as in the earlier version, in which, as Laub puts it, 'the core [was] missing',[23] the emphasis in *Isabella* is on memorialization and attempted restitution in the USA (while imprisonment in Auschwitz merits 70 pages, America also gets its own chapter of 40 pages).

Isabella recounts the experiences of the teenage Isabella, who was born in 1924. She was deported from Kisvárda, a small Hungarian town, and arrived in Auschwitz three days before her twentieth birthday. Isabella's mother and youngest sister were killed soon after arrival in Auschwitz; another sister died in Bergen-Belsen after the camp's liberation. Isabella and her two other sisters and brother were eventually reunited with their father, who had been in the US for the duration of the war. Howard Fast's Afterword repeats the point that the narrator of a fragmentary text like *Isabella* cannot 'analyze', 'explain' or 'create historical patterns' as the action is seen through the eyes of a young girl (225); this emphasizes the double duty of fragmentary form in representing simultaneously retrospective adult memory and a child's-eye view of events. Although Isabella has just left her teens, she views herself as much younger than this; she describes herself and her siblings as 'children' on their arrival in Auschwitz (24), and herself as 'just a child' (65). This is partly because Isabella's primary identification in Auschwitz is that of a bereaved daughter; her determination to record the camp experience, and the fragmentary nature of her memoir, is the result of her mother's death.

Despite their shared fragmentary form, Isabella's account of writing *Isabella* is significantly different from Francine Christophe's of the genesis of *From a World Apart*. The older Isabella seems to have composed her 'scraps' as a way of speaking to herself about what had happened to her; in the absence of an interlocutor (her sisters knew too much, other people too little) she constructed one. Isabella's mode of representation is the rhetorical question, which at times attaches itself to a specific addressee. Throughout *Isabella* she appeals to the vanished, absent or unnamed: 'Have mercy' (65); 'Somebody, please help us!' (75); 'Cipi, how could you not have followed?' (79). Isabella also appeals to the reader, 'Have you seen a *Muselmann*?' (49) and even, after the war, to the infamous SS doctor Josef Mengele to witness the sisters' freedom (149).

By contrast Francine, who was younger than Isabella, survived the war in the company of her mother and returned afterwards to live in France; the frequent address throughout *From a World Apart* – 'Mother, I'm hungry' (90) – is to a mother who is alive (in memory), rather than to one who is already dead, as it is in Isabella's metaphorical address – 'my eyes are still burning, Mother' (11). Isabella's situation resembles more what Laub asserts is typical of the Holocaust world: the impossibility of witness in a situation where 'the very possibility of address, the very possibility of appealing, or of turning to, another' was extinguished.[24] Laub describes a child in wartime Kraków who was separated from his parents and used a photograph of his mother in just this way, by addressing it and thus 'creating his first witness'.[25] In Christophe's text such appeals appear to be directly quoted: 'every day I repeat, "Why, mother, why; tell me, Mother, explain"' (32); 'Mother, protect me; Mother, I'm hot; Mother, I'm cold; Mother, is it true that I'm a dirty Jewish swine?' (34). However, what these instances record is not Francine's utterances – she does not say whether she 'repeated' them aloud or to herself – but her urge to address someone, even if her mother cannot effectively respond (no replies are recorded). Indeed, the rhetorical questions become a refrain, usually without inverted commas, showing that Francine's appeal is much broader than that of a child to its parent.

Isabella's 'fragments' are not the neutral snapshots of Francine Christophe's text. They are as self-consciously characterized by narratorial rhetoric as Francine's were self-avowedly non-literary. In this way they also differ from the unevaluative fragments of *A Childhood*, in which childlike incomprehension is figured by lack of analytic or affective description. In *Isabella*, in the fragment entitled 'The Baby', for example, the older Isabella addresses a dead child in a highly stylized manner: 'And so, dear baby, you are on your way to heaven to meet a recent arrival who is blowing a loving kiss to you through the smoke, a dear friend, your maker – your father' (44). In this apostrophe, the narrator tries to lay to rest painful memories by veiling horrifying camp realities with poetic and religious abstraction. This mental habit, of dissolving atrocity in extended musing, apostrophe or rhetorical questions, itself gives rise to fragmentary narration, as individual memories are put to rest through distancing and defensive description. In 'Irma Grese and Chicha', the infamous SS officer is not addressed directly, as the baby was; instead, the reader is asked to witness, rather than answer, unanswerable questions: 'Is the face a mirror? Is that mirror capable of recording so much cruelty that it makes a complete turnabout and records beauty instead? How else could Irma Grese have been so completely beautiful? . . . Who made this beautiful beast? Who was responsible for this mockery?' (52). Once more, God is obliquely invoked *in absentia*, and stylized discourse is set alongside harsh camp reality. The abstract questions are a prelude to the description of an incident involving Isabella's sister Chicha in this fragment, which is notable for its reliance on the contrastingly ugly, functional language of the '*Lager* lexicon': '*Funferreihe* (rows of five prisoners)', '*Zahlappell*' (roll call), 'the *Kremchy* (the crematorium)' (53).

The excess of poetic language which constitutes Isabella's fragments acts as a defence[26] against nihilism, and abstract literary discourse often coexists with the direct description of atrocity, as if one balances the other: 'A silent prayer is etched into our footsteps as we heartlessly step over a decomposing arm, a hip, or a head' (98). This psychological and literary technique is the opposite of the one we have seen in many instances, of affect omitted or denied. At times poetic excess has the effect of blotting out the signified; for example, Isabella describes the objections her father raised to her sister Chicha's marriage to a non-observant sailor she met on the ship to America: 'May you live in peace forever, Romeo of the seas, Juliet of Auschwitz' (192).[27] This kind of discourse – at once inflated and bathetic – is perhaps the teenage equivalent of the child's plain language in *A Childhood*, showing once more the division in fragmentary narratives between focalizer and narrator.

Isabella's 'scraps' appear in an order which combines chronological progression with both flashforwards and flashbacks. There is a chronological thread running throughout the text – shown by the titles to such episodes as, 'May 28 1944 – Morning', 'May 28 – Afternoon' (the day of deportation), 'The Arrival' (at Auschwitz). However, there is no linking narrative thread between these chronological episodes, which are constantly interrupted by other, less orderly, fragments of memory, or meditations. One of the latter concerns Isabella's youngest sister ('My Potyo, My Sister', 36), another her mother ('Grave' 38), both of whom were gassed on arrival at the camp; these are laments which stand in for historical narrative. The effect of these fragments is to disrupt chronology and to remind the reader that the logic of memory as much as historical narrative lies behind Isabella's text. Rather than concealing information until it was learned,[28] Isabella narrates it immediately in recognition of its priority. The text's two threads – of chronology and of memory – are sometimes at odds with each other.[29] For instance, in the memory narrative Isabella describes the circumstances of her sister Cipi's death in Belsen and her sister's last words which Isabella learnt after the war (79), but in the chronological narrative the young Isabella is still waiting for news of Cipi several pages later ('Where is Cipi?', 93). Even after the war's end has been reached there are fragments which appear out of order, as if they were flashbacks: 'Manyi', about another prisoner who helped the sisters (126–8), and 'May', about the irony of being deported in the spring (194–5). Unlike the split-narrative texts, *Isabella* represents time itself in a fragmentary way. Whereas Friedländer and Breznitz distinguished past from present both narratively and typographically, here they are jumbled together. The only thread in *Isabella* linking the episodes from chronology with those of memory is association. The uncontextualized address to a baby who was born and died in Auschwitz ('The Baby', 44) appears immediately after 'Philip', as if linked to the latter episode by a suppressed notion of failure to save the baby's life, in contrast to the brother's success in helping his sisters survive. The fragment which explains and dates the baby's fate to November 1944 appears 14 pages and six months later (58–9).

'Disjointed memories that made no sense':[30]
Jona Oberski, *A Childhood*

Jona Oberski was born in the Netherlands in 1938, the only child of German-Jewish immigrants. The family was deported to Bergen-Belsen in 1943, and Oberski's parents did not survive the war; he was liberated from Bergen-Belsen in 1945 and was brought up by foster-parents. Oberski's novel *A Childhood* is not only characterized by the paradox I have mentioned – that the apparently authenticating fragmentary nature of a child's Holocaust text actually signals its aestheticization – but makes this paradox a part of its meaning. The novel exhibits features which could only originate in the organizing efforts of an adult narrator, such as 'chapter' headings for each fragmentary episode, and long sections of quoted speech. Indeed, in a reverse of the child's unanswered address in *From A World Apart* and *Isabella*, the frequent address of the mother to her son in *A Childhood* constitutes a way of conveying partial information to the reader as much as to the child, making our limited understanding match that of the small boy. In the opening episode, 'Mistake', mother and child are clearly in a barracks – 'The walls were wood. There was a funny smell', as the nameless child puts it – and the mother explains, calling upon the child's social knowledge in a new context: ' "They've made a mistake, so we'll have to stay here for a few days, visiting the way we visited with Trude a while ago. Remember?" (7). The mother reminds the child they reached the barracks on a train, and uses the word 'camp'; but even her explanation does not identify the situation for the adult reader. (It only becomes clear that in 'Mistake' the mother and boy had been in the transit camp Westerbork when the child and both his parents make the journey there for a second time, 31.)

The technique in each fragment of *A Childhood* is the same – an adult narrator describes the young boy's impressions, which depend on local detail without any framing or historical knowledge. The narrator uses a stylized children's discourse: sentences are short; factual and descriptive observations substitute for explanation; everything is reported as if on the same level. The 'chapter' headings themselves reveal this. Although their very presence emphasizes the existence of an adult narrator, they are couched in the language of a child, or a children's book ('Mistake', 'Mr Paul', 'White Dunes') even when the setting is a camp ('Soup', 'Soldiers', 'Nose Thumbing'). The child's viewpoint does not distinguish personal from historical events; this lack of distinction makes the reader suspect malevolence even when it is absent. For instance, 'Jumping Jack' opens with the child's mother saying to him, ' "You're good at keeping your eyes shut ... I'm going to carry you inside, and you can open them when I tell you. All right?" ' (10). Despite the reader's anxious expectation, this turns out *not* to be an example of calling upon the child's resources to explain enormity to him, as in the case of 'visiting' the camp or 'taking a trip' (27, 28) to Westerbork, but simply a birthday surprise. The reader is wrong-footed in just the way the child himself is, only in reverse: what the child does not usually recognize are ominous events, and he sees most things as part of a benign continuum ('I thought the [yellow] star was pretty', 24).

At other times, however, this radical defamiliarization is abandoned and a more usual developmental irony appears in instances where the reader can readily identify what the child cannot. In the fragment 'Muiderpoort', the boy's family is taken to 'a building'. The boy's father explains that the building 'was the theatre ... A place where they used to put on plays and people could go and see them': the boy is only interested in 'the stage and the curtain' (30), but the implied reader is invited to decode the building's historical identity. The Nazis used the Hollandsche Schouwburg (Dutch Theatre) as a gathering place for Jews prior to deportation to the transit camp at Westerbork.[31] The sinister bathos of the Nazis' actions – such as using the cycling track Vélodrome d'Hiver in Paris as an assembly point – is a frequent feature in defamil-iarized children's representations of the Holocaust, as we saw in the inspiration for Perec's sports fantasy in *W or the Memory of Childhood*, and in Clara Asscher-Pinkhof's allegory about the Schouwburg in *Star Children*. In *A Childhood*, citing the Schouwburg in this covert way subverts the text's dual strategy, of directing irony at the reader or at the child alternately. It may seem at first that the father calls the building a theatre to comfort the child, or that the child has misunderstood, since its present function is obvious ('At every table they marked our papers with rubber stamps', 30). The reader can decipher this fragment only through adult historical knowledge. In fact, what is expected of the reader changes from fragment to fragment in *A Childhood*; s/he is required to interpret ironic innocence, lack of historical context, material that has simply a domestic meaning and incidents that are genuinely incompre-hensible until made clear – by the child himself.

Although the reader's historical knowledge is relied upon in 'Muider-poort', such superiority of understanding is ironized in the fragment 'Kitchen'. It is clear that the boy and his parents are now in Bergen-Belsen,[32] in the 'Star Camp' for potential exchange prisoners (most of whom died before the war's end). The boy's mother insists that he help carry the empty cooking-pots back to the kitchen to prevent 'them' being angry with her, even though he is too small to reach the pot's handle (45–6). In the kitchen,

All the children bent over the edges of the pots. Some couldn't keep their feet on the ground. All I could see were their backs and legs.

Their heads and arms were gone. I would have liked to help with the cleaning, but I didn't know how. (46)

When the children are asked if they enjoyed the food, the boy notes of his investigation, 'I'd had my head in the pot so long that I hadn't noticed anything good being handed out' (47). At this point it becomes clear to the adult reader that the boy was sent to 'help' in the kitchen in order to lick out the cooking-pots, and, predictably, the boy's mother is angry with him for not eating the extra food.

A number of literary strategies help perform the cognitive trick in 'Kitchen' on the reader, in particular, the episode's strictly chronological narration – there are no flashforwards to represent a greater understanding, as there might be in a conventional memoir, and the incident is related as if unfolding as we read. Indeed, the very meaning of the fragment is that of misunderstanding – not only in the form of the boy's concluding epiphany, which reveals his former ignorance ('I'd never known what it was', 48), but also in the form of its narration where it affects the reader too. The act of misunderstanding is extended through the use of a child's viewpoint and language, as can be seen in the extract above describing – but not labelling – the children licking out the cooking pot. The effect of this misunderstanding, and placing such emphasis on a particular kind of literary technique, is similar but not identical to that described by Viktor Shklovsky in his discussion of Laurence Sterne's novel *Tristram Shandy*, in which 'awareness of the form through its violation constitutes the content of the novel'.[33] In other fragments, incomprehension and misunderstanding are shown simultaneously from two viewpoints, a child's and the adult reader's. For instance, the boy visits his sick father in the camp infirmary and is told, ' "He won't be here long, tell your mother to come quick" ... they put his shoes into my hand and sent me away' (65). What seems to be neutral or even positive information to the boy – the father will not be long in the infirmary – is for the reader clearly a prediction of the father's death. However, in 'Kitchen' there is a temporal gap before adult comprehension can take hold, which it does only half-way through the episode. The dual perspective here is out of kilter, not simultaneous.

'Broken images with no order to them' (90): Binjamin Wilkomirski, *Fragments*

Binjamin Wilkomirski's *Fragments* is notorious for its abrupt and shocking change of generic identity. Although it was published, originally in

German in 1995, to great acclaim as the memoir of a child survivor, and in English the following year, it became clear by 1998 that the text was fictional and that its author was Bruno Doessekker, a Swiss musician who was not a Holocaust survivor, nor Jewish.[34] Doessekker was born Bruno Grosjean in 1941, and adopted by the Doessekker family in 1946. Although literary commentary has formed a part of psychoanalytic and historical discussions of the text,[35] the representation of a child's-eye view – which contributed to the book's success – has not been fully explored. In this section, I will discuss the construction and effect of the text's fragmentary viewpoint.

In *Fragments* the opening discussion of memory and the past is mingled with *describing* that past, as the following sentence shows: 'If I'm going to write about [my earliest memories], I have to give up on the ordering logic of grown-ups' (4).[36] Here, the narrator writes simultaneously from the vantage-point of an adult, and in the language of a child speaking about those adults ('grown-ups'), in the fragmentary manner with which we are familiar. The first 'chapter' – each one is composed of several fragments, from varying periods in Binjamin's life – ends with what is apparently a reference to a therapist or counsellor, as if present-time adulthood can only be told in the same way as the childhood past, without giving identifying dates or names: 'this was the beginning of years that I only slowly came to understand, when *someone* tried to talk hope into me again, and took me on *another long journey*' (10, my italics). In other words, Holocaust memory here consists of broken pieces of mingled time-periods: its is both spatially and temporally fragmented.

As with the other texts I have discussed in this chapter, fragmentariness in Wilkomirski's text is associated with a set of interrelated narratorial techniques. It is a way of presenting a child character in – a stylized version of – his own terms, by using a reduced adult narrator; and a way of disrupting linear chronology. The adult narrator of *Fragments* draws attention to the lack of 'chronological fit' in his memories (4), to explain the textual patterning which follows. Unlike the metaphorical conceit of a photograph album in Christophe's *From A World Apart*, in *Fragments* the narrator's mention of 'isolated images' refers to a literal model of memory: 'My early childhood memories are planted, first and foremost in exact snapshots of my photographic memory' (4); 'The first pictures surface, one by one' (5); 'I can still see [the scene] exactly' (19). The images of a recurrent nightmare seem to the narrator to emerge from 'an unstoppable copying machine' (38).[37] Language itself is described in visual terms: 'I can only try to use words to *draw* as exactly as possible what happened, what I *saw*' (4, my italics).

The link between the text's reliance on a discourse of sight and the mechanical reproduction of images, and its narrative stance, is clearest when the child Binjamin notes, 'I'm just an eye, taking in what it sees, giving nothing back' (87): the absorption of light[38] is not accompanied by the reflection of interpretation and analysis. Indeed, on one occasion the child's memory is not even an image, simply 'a brief flash of light' (99). Like other instances of present-tense usage in *Fragments*, the remark about the absorption of events is ambiguous: is it the adult narrator or child character who sees himself as 'just an eye'? Similarly, in the orphanage Binjamin thinks, 'I had brothers too once, I did – I remember now' (116). This is a present-tense utterance which seems to emanate from the past but also refers to the moment of writing: 'now'. In fact, these instances indicate not just ambiguity but the merging of past and present that characterizes *Fragments* as a whole. It is the text's constitutive 'fragments' which allow for this merging. As we have seen, the fragments of narrative constitute the spatial equivalent of temporal disruption. For instance, Chapter 2 (11–25) opens with the mysterious Frau Grosz taking Binjamin to Switzerland. During the journey the boy thinks back to her coming upon him in the Kraków orphanage, is reminded of an incident from the camps when 'the big gray man' threw him against a wall, arrives in Switzerland without Frau Grosz which makes him cry, is reminded of 'the last time I'd really cried' when in hiding with his brothers, is taken by another woman to the orphanage, where he eats cheese rinds discarded by the other children and is ridiculed for doing so.

The contextless nature of these events, the way they are narrated and focalized through the child's eyes, increases their fragmentariness. But there are in fact associative links between each temporal and memorial shift – the time-scales in this chapter range from the early days of the Nazi occupation of Latvia, internment in the death-camp Majdanek, to the immediate post-war world – which appear even more clearly than those in *Isabella*. (*From A World Apart, A Childhood* and *Bitter Herbs* are each more continuously chronological than Leitner's or Wilkomirski's texts.) These associative links emphasize, surprisingly, the similarity of past and present, not their difference. The pathos of the scene in the orphanage, in which the boy eats cheese-rinds and then goes to sleep under a bed, arises from our knowledge that the boy imagines he is still in a camp where food is scarce and only the 'privileged' sleep in beds. This scene dramatizes what has earlier been made explicit: the present is the same – and as bad – as the past. The post-war train journey to Switzerland segues into a memory of the 'big gray man's' betrayal through

the boy's remark, 'That was the way it had been before, too' (15). Elsewhere, the boy states a positive preference for his 'images' of the camp
world: 'Yes, they were almost as unbearable [as this strange present], but
they were familiar, at least I understood their rules' (68). Indeed, the
text's structure as a whole emphasizes its lack of teleology. Through a
mixture of progression and regression – in Chapter 3 onwards, we read
more about the boy's post-war life in Polish and Swiss orphanages, but
also more about the past of the camps – the reader returns to the same
words uttered by Frau Grosz over one hundred pages earlier: ' "Switzerland
is a beautiful country" ' (12, 118). During our reading, time has in effect
stood still. This is not just the stasis of traumatized memory, but of literal
imprisonment in the past; as the boy thinks to himself in his foster-
parents' home, 'The camp's still there' (125), and that there was 'No
joyous liberation' (148). We might thus be tempted to liken *Fragments*
not to the broken patterns of a postmodern text, but to the disordered
plots and associative internal monologues of a modernist work. Binjamin's
nightmarish vision of the 'unstoppable copying machine' implies regret
for precisely the auratic, individual image of modernism.[39] But this regret
rests on a paradox, as we now know that 'copying',[40] and constructed
rather than authentic experience, were paradigmatic of the text's construction. Indeed, *Fragments* may actually be a ' "fragmentary collage" '[41]
in terms of its production, but aspires to be the healing process of
a modernist subject who can own and recognize all of his experience.[42]
The postmodern text's 'collapse of time horizons and preoccupation
with instantaneity'[43] appears in *Fragments* as a sign of historical and
psychic disturbance, not as a liberatory force.

The mingling of past and present in *Fragments* has two different
effects. It does represent effectively and accurately the psychological
state of many child survivors of the Holocaust. In *From A World Apart*,
for instance, Francine describes the reaction of a child after the liberation
of Belsen who is unable to adjust to the post-camp world: 'Little Michel,
on entering the hotel, overcome with panic, shouted, "My barrack-hut,
my barrack-hut, I want my barrack-hut!" ' (152); in the Kraków orphanage
after the war, Binjamin, also in a panic, demands, 'Where's my barracks?'
(115). On the other hand, particularly now that the reader knows of
Fragments' fictional status, the confusion of past and present means,
paradoxically, that the focus of the text is not on the Holocaust itself
but on an individual – and idiosyncratic – psyche. As Daniel Ganzfried
argues, 'This book had one notion: that a victim of the Holocaust is
forever a victim. It is forever a child, it is forever sick, not only in its
body but in its mind.'[44] However, reading *Fragments* as fiction might

lead us simply to value this literary construction of a child's-eye view, which consists of layered and complex narrative fragments. Although the tendency in *Fragments* is to encourage a blurring between narrator and author – as in a true memoir – it seems that it is only the former who says, 'I'm not a poet or a writer' (4).

Conclusion

Despite seeming an ideal way in which to present children's-eye views of the past, fragmentariness is not a common narrative mode. For instance, Ida Fink's collections of short stories are self-consciously composed of small segments of a bigger history, as their titles show – *A Scrap of Time*, and *Traces*[45]– and many of them have child narrators or protagonists. They also share some features with the works I have mentioned. Contextualization is absent, historical facts and details are sparse, several stories concern the logic of memory and of misunderstanding. However, many of these features arise because of the short story genre, of which we would not expect a connecting overview or consistent viewpoint. Although the same themes characterize many of Fink's stories – including betrayal, the relation of domesticity to death, seeing atrocity obliquely or from a vantage-point in hiding – they do not constitute continuous fragmentary narratives, but collections of self-contained episodes.

Fragmentary narration is uncommon partly because of its paradoxical nature: its obvious artifice undoes, or ironizes, any attempt to represent the immediacy of events and childhood incomprehension of them. At the same time, however, fragmentary narration does effectively convey children's views of the Holocaust. Its concealed temporal division, between wartime moments of incomprehension and their artful representation, accords with Cathy Caruth's temporal definition of trauma:

> For history to be a history of trauma means that it is referential precisely to the extent that it is not fully perceived as it occurs; or to put it somewhat differently, that a history can be grasped only in the very inaccessibility of its occurrence.[46]

In the texts I have discussed, moments of 'not fully perceiving' are represented through the eyes of a child or young person, while the adult narrator in each case – most explicitly in *Isabella's* – 'grasps' what happened only much later. Such adult understanding is signalled overtly only in the case of *Isabella*; in the other texts, its 'inaccessibility' is shown by a lack of commentary and a reliance instead on the reader to fill in the gaps. These gaps take the form of various kinds of developmental irony: irony's usual gap between ostensible meaning and actual sense takes on a specific slant, that of a child's viewpoint set against adult understanding. It may take the form of an 'irony of ignorance', in which the adult reader is called upon to decode events, as in the case of *A Childhood*; or 'pathetic irony', in which the child's misunderstanding is a site of pathos when viewed by the reader who understands not only the meaning of events, but their true impact on the child, as occurs throughout *Fragments*. The superimposition of time-scales in fragmentary texts mimics the form of a trauma, a perpetual present which is 'always there'.[47] Fragmentary narrative is as much a matter of temporality as of structure or form.

Conclusion

In the introduction to this book, I asked whether Binjamin Wilkomirski's fictional *Fragments* was as singular as it seemed on its publication in 1995, as the testimonial – but also literary – account of a child's perspective on the Holocaust. It is clear that Wilkomirski's text was not as unusual as it appeared. Even the anachrony of its form, in which three historical periods are narrated out of order, is simply an extreme version of the disordered memorial chronology to be found in many of the fictional and non-fiction texts I have mentioned throughout this study.

In concluding here, I will briefly discuss another work of fiction about children in the Holocaust, W.G. Sebald's *Austerlitz*.[1] I am ending with this work because it marks a new stage in the history of children's-eye views of the Holocaust, as a move towards fiction based not on the author's experience but on material from other texts. The protagonist of *Austerlitz* says that he has read Holocaust works such as Jean Améry's *At the Mind's Limits* and Dan Jacobson's *Heshel's Kingdom*;[2] its author has read many of the children's-eye-view texts I have discussed in this study, but alters their focus from the difficulty to the possibility of memory.

Apart from Wilkomirski, Sebald is the only writer I mention in the present work who has no personal *victim's* connection with the events of the Holocaust (he was born into a Catholic German family in 1944). *Austerlitz* is about the recovery of a former Kindertransport child's lost past. At the age of fifteen, the central character discovers that Emyr and Gwendolyn Elias, the Welsh clergyman and his wife who fostered him, have concealed his past from him: he was placed on a Kindertransport train by his parents in Prague in 1939 at the age of four, and his parents died during the war. His real name is not 'Dafydd Elias', but 'Jacques Austerlitz'. Austerlitz's discoveries are related to the reader by a nameless narrator, his friend.

It might seem odd to place *Fragments* alongside *Austerlitz*. The former is a generic oddity written by someone suffering from 'Holocaust envy',[3] ordered in the 'fragments' of childhood memory. As a fictional testimony, the text encourages the reader to identify the narrator with the implied author. *Austerlitz*, in contrast, is by a well-known novelist whose earlier work *The Emigrants*[4] won several literary prizes. Despite some reviewers' claims that the narrator who passes on Austerlitz's story is an unnecessary presence,[5] this German, non-Jewish figure is in fact a crucial mediating device, providing precisely the distance between character and implied author denied in *Fragments*. While *Fragments* represents the Holocaust in terms of its atrocious detail, *Austerlitz* represents it, in Sebald's phrase, 'from an angle'[6] and obliquely.

It is the particular use of intertextuality in *Austerlitz* that is its most striking feature. Such a method points towards a possible future for the representation of children during the Holocaust years when this can no longer be accomplished, either testimonially or fictively, by survivors themselves. Sebald claimed in interviews to have based the details of Austerlitz's life on the stories of 'two or three...real persons. One is a colleague of mine', and another was Susi Bechhofer, whose story was recounted in a television documentary and in Jeremy Joseph's book *Rosa's Child*.[7] Many details of Susi Bechhofer's story appear in transmuted form in *Austerlitz*. Like Austerlitz, Susi was encouraged not to ask about her past, learned almost nothing of the Holocaust, and was brought up as a Christian; she only uncovered the details of her mother's life and her own heritage in the late 1980s. It was this notion of not knowing the past, or even, as Austerlitz puts it, 'living the wrong life' (298), that drew Sebald to Bechhofer's story.

There are other sources for *Austerlitz* not explicitly mentioned by Sebald, but which stand out within the text itself. These concern texts I have discussed elsewhere in this study. Saul Friedländer's memories, recounted in *When Memory Comes*, are very much like Austerlitz's: they consist of a Jewish infancy in Prague, followed by a Christian childhood; both sets of parents perished in Auschwitz. Each boy had a much-loved nursemaid in pre-war Prague: just as Friedländer met Vlasta again when he returned to the city of his birth in adulthood, so Austerlitz met Vera. Friedländer is struck by the fact that at the moment of utterance he is older than his parents were when they died,[8] and Austerlitz also notes this irony (342).

Similarly, some moments of unreliable memory from Georges Perec's *W or the Memory of Childhood* reappear in *Austerlitz*. Here, however, a subtle alteration takes place. While Perec's *W* is about the difficulty of recall, *Austerlitz* is about the possibility of full remembrance, and the citations are changed accordingly. Again, this suggests a change of emphasis in the shift from autobiographical to intertextual fiction about a child during the Holocaust years. In Sebald's novel, the nursemaid Vera reminds Austerlitz that she bought him a Charlie Chaplin comic to take on the train to Britain in 1939 (245, 308). In Perec's novel, Georges claims that in 1942, when he was a child of six, his mother gave him a comic with Chaplin on the cover to read on his journey into hiding in unoccupied France.[9] However, as David Bellos has argued, Perec's 'memory' must be false, or fictive, as Chaplin's films were banned throughout occupied Europe.[10] By transplanting this detail to the Prague of 1939, Sebald restores a truth to Austerlitz's recovered memory. Sebald adapts a second site of unreliable memory from *W or the Memory of Childhood* by having Austerlitz say that he 'once thought' his six-year-old self in an old photograph might be holding his arm at an angle because it was 'broken or in a splint' (260). Perec too recalls in *W* that he had a broken arm and wore a splint – yet he eventually admits that it was another boy whose arm was broken, although he remembered this injury as if it were his own.[11] Once more, the full force of this unreliability is not reproduced in *Austerlitz*. Indeed, Austerlitz accomplishes a surprisingly full return to the past through locating the nursemaid Vera: his command of Czech returns; he finds a photograph of himself as a child slipped into a book; and, most miraculously of all, he sees a fleeting image of his mother's face in a Nazi documentary about the Czech concentration camp Terezín.

The background material from the different sources I have mentioned is blended seamlessly in the figure of Austerlitz. At the same time, the mixture of material – based not only on Kindertransport accounts but also on texts about children in hiding in Europe – makes *Austerlitz* into a memorial book,[12] a novel about collective as much as individual remembrance of deracination and exile. The child's-eye view of the Holocaust has itself taken on a new form, in which it symbolizes the continuing presence of the past, as Austerlitz says of memory: it is 'as if time did not exist at all, only various spaces interlocking...between which the living and the dead can move back and forth as they like' (261). This insight seems indebted to Friedländer, who emphasizes instead the difficulty of childhood recall: 'The veil between events and me had not been rent...I was destined, therefore, to wander among several worlds, knowing them, understanding them' only partially.[13] *Austerlitz* makes clear that a child's memory of the Holocaust years is paradigmatic of historical memory itself.

Throughout this study, I have argued that special narrative forms are needed to represent the experience of children during the Holocaust years. All the features of recalling a traumatic historical event are present in these texts in extreme form, particularly lost, belated, incoherent and incomprehensible memory. Holocaust narratives by and about children are characterized by their narrator's innocence and inability to understand. In this way, child's-eye-view texts are not unusual but exemplary representations of the event.

Notes

Introduction

1. Binjamin Wilkomirski, *Fragments: Memories of a Childhood, 1939–1948*, trans. Carol Brown Janeway, London: Picador 1996 [1995]. See Stefan Maechler, *The Wilkomirski Affair: A Study in Biographical Truth*, trans. John E. Woods, New York: Schocken 2001 for a full account.
2. In Britain, the controversy was first reported by Philipp Blom, in the *Independent Sunday Review*, 30 September 1998, p. 1.
3. *Scroll of Agony: The Warsaw Diary of Chaim A. Kaplan*, trans. and ed. Abraham I. Katsch, New York: Macmillan 1965.
4. See the 'Literary and cultural criticism' section of the bibliography for other works on children and the Holocaust; most of these concern either texts for a child readership, or include children involved in the war as a whole, not the Holocaust specifically.
5. In practice this means focusing on texts not directed at a child readership, although some of those I discuss have at some point in their publication history also been explicitly aimed at children or young adults. On the notion of 'crossover' texts, see Sandra Beckett, ed., *Transcending Boundaries: Writing for a Dual Audience of Children and Adults*, New York: Garland 1999.
6. This is also Serge Klarsfeld's practice in his *French Children of the Holocaust: A Memorial*, trans. Glorianne Depondt, New York: New York University Press 1996.
7. Johan P. Snapper, essay on Marga Minco in S. Lillian Kremer, ed., *Holocaust Literature: An Encyclopedia of Writers and Their Work*, London and New York: Routledge 2002, p. 850.
8. Hans Keilson, *Sequential Traumatization in Children: A clinical and statistical follow-up of the Jewish war orphans in the Netherlands*, with the collaboration of Herman R. Sarphatie, trans. Yvonne Bearne, Hilary Coleman and Deirdre Winter, Jerusalem: The Magnes Press 1992, p. 37.
9. See Debórah Dwork, *Children with a Star: Jewish Youth in Nazi Europe* (New Haven and London: Yale University Press 1991): '[Children's] death was a matter of automatic procedure' in the death-camps (p. x).
10. Keilson, *Sequential Traumatizaion*, p. 125.
11. The World Movement for the Care of Children (Kindertransport movement) brought around 7400 unaccompanied Jewish children on commissioned trains from occupied Europe to Britain in 1938 and 1939.
12. See for instance, David Storey's *This Sporting Life* (London: Longman 1960), which consists of present-tense, present-time narration alternating with past-tense, past-time narrative.
13. I use 'trauma' in Cathy Caruth's sense: she follows Freud in defining trauma as, 'the response to a sudden or unexpected threat of death that happens too soon to be fully known and is then endlessly repeated in reenactments and nightmares that attempt to relive, but in fact only miss again, the original

event' (*Unclaimed Experience: Trauma, Narrative, and History*, Baltimore and London: Johns Hopkins University Press 1996, p. 139, n. 5).

14. See the 'History' section of the bibliography.

15. See Himmler's speech at Posen to the Gauleiters and Reichsleiters on 6 October 1943: 'Then the question arose: What about the women and children? I decided to find a perfectly clear-cut solution to this too. For I did not feel justified in exterminating the men – that is, to kill them or to have them killed – while allowing the avengers, in the form of their children, to grow up in the midst of our sons and grandsons' (quoted in Gerald Fleming, *Hitler and the Final Solution*, Berkeley, Los Angeles and London: University of California Press, 1984, p. 57).

16. Norman Geras, *The Contract of Mutual Indifference: Political Philosophy after the Holocaust*, London: Verso 1998, p. 81. Peter Novick raises a different, political caveat by contrasting contemporary (American) awareness of the 'indifference' that led to the deaths of over a million children during the Holocaust years, with present-day indifference to the fact that, 'well over *ten times* that many children around the world die of malnutrition and preventable diseases *every year*' (*The Holocaust and Collective Memory: The American Experience*, London: Bloomsbury 2001, p. 255). See Alex Callinicos' discussion of this point in his 'Plumbing the Depths: Marxism and the Holocaust' (*Yale Journal of Criticism* 14(2) 2001: pp. 385–414): he concludes that rather than 'relativiz[ing] the Holocaust out of existence' such comparisons show that 'avoidable, socially caused mass death' of historically specific kinds 'is a chronic feature of the modern world' (p. 411).

17. Gabriel Motola, 'Children of the Holocaust', *TriQuarterly* 105, 1999, pp. 209–32: 212.

18. Motola's description is only at all true of *Fragments* (the article was published before Wilkomirski's unmasking), which he uses to stand metonymically for the other writers' works. Motola concludes his article by inveighing against perpetrators, thus thoroughly confusing history and representation (ibid., p. 231).

19. Lawrence L. Langer, 'Family Dilemmas in Holocaust Literature', *Michigan Quarterly Review*, 26(2) 1987, pp. 387–99: 392.

20. Irving Greenberg, 'Cloud of Smoke, Pillar of Fire', *Holocaust: Religious and Philosophical Implications*, eds John K. Roth and Michael Berenbaum, New York: Paragon House 1989, p. 318.

21. Ibid., p. 323.

22. David Patterson, *Along the Edge of Annihilation: The Collapse and Recovery of Life in the Holocaust Diary*, Seattle and London: University of Washington Press 1999, p. 200.

23. 'Backshadowing' means that past events are seen as inevitable to such an extent that their victims may be blamed for not anticipating them. See Michael André Bernstein, *Foregone Conclusions: Against Apocalyptic History*, Berkeley and London: University of California Press 1994.

24. One might argue that diaries or testimony gathered immediately after the war do represent children's voices in their own terms; however, as I argue in Chapter 7, even the diary cannot completely unite the moment of *énoncé* with that of *énonciation*, although diaries do achieve the closest fit of all between narrator and character – both are children, separated temporally by at most a few days.

25. János Nyiri, *Battlefields and Playgrounds*, trans. William Brandon and János Nyiri, Hanover and London: University Press of New England/Brandeis University Press 1994 [1989].
26. Nyiri, *Battlefields and Playgrounds*, pp. 180, 201.
27. Ibid., p. 367.
28. 'This memoir is the result of an intensely creative collaboration between those who experienced the events it describes and one who attempted to bring their stories...back to life on the page' (prefatory note, Fay Walker and Leo Rosen, with Caren S. Neile, *Hidden: A Sister and Brother in Nazi Poland*, University of Wisconsin Press 2002, p. iii).
29. See Henry Greenspan, *On Listening to Holocaust Survivors: Recounting and Life History*, Westport, CT and London: Prager 1998; and Lawrence Langer, *Holocaust Testimonies: The Ruins of Memory*, New Haven and London: Yale University Press 1991.
30. Mikhail Bakhtin, *Problems of Dostoevsky's Poetics*, trans. Caryl Emerson, Minneapolis: University of Minnesota Press 1984, p. 8.
31. Ibid., p. 191.
32. Walker and Rosen, *Hidden*, pp. 9–10.
33. See Mikhail Bakhtin, 'Discourse in the Novel', *The Dialogic Imagination: Four Essays*, trans. Caryl Emerson and Michael Holquist, Austin: University of Texas Press 1981, p. 366.
34. Leah Iglinski-Goodman, *For Love of Life*, London: Vallentine Mitchell 2002, p. 1.
35. Martin Gilbert, 'Foreword' to ibid., p. iii.
36. Cordelia Edvardson, *The Burned Child Seeks the Fire: A Memoir*, trans. Joel Agee, Boston: Beacon Press 1997 [1984] (thanks to Joan Michelson for bringing this text to my attention); Karen Gershon, *A Lesser Child: An Autobiography*, trans. unnamed, London: Peter Owen 1992. Gershon wrote her memoir in German, despite having lived in Britain since 1938, as another narrative means of conveying the distinction between past and present.
37. 'Gershon', Paul Loewenthal's Hebrew name, is the author's *nom de plume*; it means 'stranger in a strange land' (Peter Lawson, essay on Gershon in Kremer, ed., *Holocaust Literature*, p. 416).
38. Gershon, *A Lesser Child*, p. 102.
39. Dominick LaCapra, *History and Memory after Auschwitz*, Ithaca, NY: Cornell University Press 1998, p. 47.
40. See Carmel Finnan, 'Autobiography, Memory and the Shoah: German-Jewish Identity in Autobiographical Writings by Ruth Klüger, Cordelia Edvardson and Laura Waco', in Pól O'Dochartaigh, ed., *Jews in German Literature Since 1945: German-Jewish Literature*, Amsterdam and Atlanta: Rodopi 2000, p. 451.
41. Edvardson, *The Burned Child Seeks the Fire*, p. 18.
42. Ibid., p. 19.
43. 'Translator's Note', Bogdan Wojdowski, *Bread for the Departed*, trans. Madeline G. Levine, Evanston, Illinois: Northwestern University Press 1997 [1971], p. xi.
44. Bakhtin, *Problems of Dostoevsky's Poetics*, pp. 6, 15, italics in original.
45. See the Foreword by Henryk Grynberg to Wojdowski, *Bread for the Departed*, p. ix. The one voice not represented among the text's polyphony is that of the

Nazi Sturmbannfürher Höfle, who makes a speech (352–8); instead, we hear the audience's responses to it.

46. Levine mentions the 'ingenious blend of standard Polish, Warsaw dialect, thieves' argot, Yiddish and Hebrew words or phonemes', alongside passages of German, in the original ('Translator's Note', p. xi).

47. Wojdowski, *Bread for the Departed*, p. 240.

48. Ruth Kluger, *Landscapes of Memory: A Holocaust Girlhood Remembered*, London: Bloomsbury 2003.

49. See Andrea Hammel, 'Gender, Individualism and Dialogue: Jakov Lind's *Counting My Steps* and Ruth Klüger's *weiter leben*', in Silke Hassler and Edward Timms, eds, *Writing after Hitler: The Work of Jakov Lind*, Cardiff: University of Wales Press 2001, p. 189. In her memoir of life in hiding in wartime Budapest, Magda Denes uses a similar technique to comic effect; the adult narrator supplies the commentary and ripostes that the child could not (*Castles Burning: A Child's Life in War*, London: Anchor 1997).

50. The title of the American edition is *Still Alive*, New York: Feminist Press at CUNY 2003.

51. See also Aharon Appelfeld's novels, in which the death and suffering of the Holocaust take place outside the narrative world, and historical details are not supplied; while some of Appelfeld's novels have a child protagonist or focalizer (*To the Land of the Reeds*, trans. Jeffrey M. Green, London: Quartet 1994 [1986], *Tzili: The Story of a Life*, trans. Dalya Bilu, New York: Penguin 1984), others retain a narrative voice of childlike naiveté to convey historical ignorance in a fabular manner (*Badenheim 1939*, trans. unnamed, New York: Washington Square Press 1981 [1980]). See Philip Roth, 'Conversation in Jerusalem with Aharon Appelfeld', *Shop Talk*, London: Vintage 2000, p. 25, on the notion of a child's viewpoint without such a character.

52. Norman Manea, *October Eight O'Clock*, trans. Cornelia Golna *et al.*, London: Quartet 1993, p. 8.

53. Ibid., p. 3.

54. Ibid., pp. 11–12.

55. Ibid., p. 15.

56. This line seems to echo Shakespeare's Hamlet on historical transgression: 'The time is out of joint' (*Hamlet*, I.v.189).

57. Louis Begley, 'Introduction' to *October Eight O'Clock*, p. viii.

Split narration

1. Saul Friedländer, *When Memory Comes*, trans. Helen R. Lane, New York: Farrar, Straus Giroux 1979; Shlomo Breznitz, *Memory Fields: The Legacy of a Wartime Childhood in Czechoslovakia*, New York: Alfred A. Knopf 1993; Georges Perec, *W or the Memory of Childhood*, trans. David Bellos, London: Harvill 1988 [1975]. All page references are in the text.

2. See Dan Stone, 'Holocaust Testimony and the Challenge to the Philosophy of History', in Robert Fine and Charles Turner, eds, *Social Theory after the Holocaust*, Liverpool University Press 2000, p. 221.

3. By contrast Louis Begley and Ida Fink represent only the past in their novels, although the present is implied in both *Wartime Lies* (London: Picador 1991)

and *The Journey* (trans. Joanna Wechsler, Harmondsworth: Penguin 1992). See also Stone's claim that this kind of 'testimony' shows textually 'the radical challenge of the Holocaust to historiography' and its insistence on linear, cause and effect relations, 'Holocaust Testimony', p. 223.

4. Binjamin Wilkomirski, *Fragments: Memories of a Childhood, 1939–1948*, trans. Carol Brown Janeway, London: Picador 1996, p. 68. All further page references are in the text.

5. Naomi Samson, *Hide: A Child's View of the Holocaust*, Lincoln and London: Nebraska University Press 2000.

6. Sidra DeKoven Ezrahi points out that the young Saul changes his name five times: 'from Pavel in Prague to Paul in France to Paul-Henri Ferland in the world of his Catholic refuge to Shaul in Israel and Saul in the international scholarly community' ('See Under: Memory: Reflections on *When Memory Comes*', *History and Memory* 9(1/2), Fall 1997, pp. 364–75: 371).

7. Saul wonders, for instance, if he was sent to boarding school by his parents in anticipation of fleeing, or because of German edicts; his attempts at reconstruction fail, however: 'I cannot say' (26).

8. See Michael André Bernstein, *Foregone Conclusions: Against Apocalyptic History*, Berkeley and London: University of California Press 1994.

9. See Sigmund Freud, 'From the History of an Infantile Neurosis', Pelican Freud Library Vol. 9: Case Histories II: 'Rat Man', Schreber, 'Wolf Man', Female Homosexuality, Harmondsworth: Penguin 1979.

10. Jean Laplanche discusses why human sexuality in particular is subject to belated activation, and suggests that it 'alone' is available to 'action in two phases' because of its constitution out of a 'complex and endlessly repeated atemporal succession of missed occasions – of "too early" [from the world of adults] and "too late" [in one's own puberty]' (*Life and Death in Psychoanalysis*, trans. Jeffrey Mehlman, Baltimore: Johns Hopkins University Press 1976, p. 43). We might add that the same logic characterizes someone, like Saul, subject to historical calamity: events from the adult world occur too early; one's own understanding comes too late.

11. Jean-François Lyotard, *Heidegger and 'the Jews'*, trans. Andreas Michel, Minneapolis: University of Minnesota Press 1990, p. 16.

12. The opposition between memory and knowledge is also a generic one, marking the text's hesitation between the techniques of fiction (memory) and those of epic or history (knowledge); see Mikhail Bakhtin, 'Epic and Novel', in *The Dialogic Imagination: Four Essays*, ed. Michael Holquist, trans. Caryl Emerson and Michael Holquist, Austin: University of Texas Press 1981, p. 15.

13. Referring to oneself in the third person in this manner need not always have such a divisive effect, but see James Kelman's novel *How Late It Was, How Late* (1998) for another instance of splitting self-reference.

14. Jean Laplanche and J.-B. Pontalis point out that, unlike repression, suppression can be a conscious act; suppression of affect can lead to its abolition rather than its transposition into the unconscious, as in Saul's case (*The Language of Psychoanalysis*, trans. Donald Nicholson-Smith, London: Karnac 1988, pp. 438–9).

15. Versions of the 'memory' versus 'knowledge' dichotomy persist in Saul Friedländer's historical writings. For instance, in *Memory, History and the Extermination of the Jews of Europe* Friedländer explicitly questions the division

of memory from history (Bloomington and London: Indiana University Press 1993, pp. vii–viii), and describes the historian's unease at the non-congruence between 'intellectual probing' and 'the blocking of intuitive comprehension' where the Holocaust is concerned (111).

16. Shirley Jucovy, review of *When Memory Comes*, *Psychoanalytic Review* 75(4), Winter 1988, pp. 653–5: 655.

17. Laplanche and Pontalis, *The Language of Psychoanalysis*, p. 1.

18. By contrast, Alan Astro speaks of the 'completion of mourning' shown by Perec's linguistic playfulness ('Allegory in Georges Perec's *W ou le souvenir d'enfance*', *Modern Language Notes* 102(4), September 1987, pp. 867–76: 873) – in other words, by the *fictiveness* of *W*.

19. These are often of the kind used by Virginia Woolf in *To the Lighthouse*: although conventionally used to bracket off extra-textual information, in Woolf's novel they convey, in an ironic reversal, significant events such as the deaths of the central characters.

20. Paul Valent, 'Child Survivors: A Review', in Judith S. Kestenberg and Charlotte Kahn, eds, *Children Surviving Persecution: An International Study of Trauma and Healing*, Praeger: Westport, CT and London 1998, p. 112.

21. Shlomo Breznitz is Professor of Psychology at the New School for Social Reseach in New York and the University of Haifa.

22. Perec referred to *W* as being in the 'autobiographical mode', a typically ambiguous phrase, in his 'Statement of Intent', *Review of Contemporary Fiction* 13(1), 1993, p. 21.

23. Warren F. Motte gives a tripartite diagram of *W*'s structure (107); Paul Schwartz's diagram is divided into four but the two autobiographical parts are taken to be the same (*Georges Perec: Traces of His Passage*, Birmingham, Alabama: Summa Publishers, 1988, p. 48).

24. Perec said of the *'points de suspension'* that they were 'the original site from which this book emerged' (my translation of a comment quoted in Schwartz, *Georges Perec*, p. 51). Schwartz points out that the same device is used by Victor Hugo in a volume of poetry to signify the death of his daughter which was the origin of the poems (52), as his mother's death was for Georges.

25. Or allegorical, in Astro's formulation in his 'Allegory in Georges Perec's *W ou le souvenir d'enfance*'.

26. Philippe Lejeune, 'W or the Memory of Childhood', *Review of Contemporary Fiction* 13(1) 1993, p. 92.

27. Lejeune points out that, biographically speaking, *W* 'actually "evades" the question of links between the two tales' (ibid., p. 90); and it is true that in neither part of the text are childhood memories reliably represented.

28. Interestingly, the W half was published first and alone as a serial called 'W' starting in 1969, and, without the childhood context that made its horror 'bearable' [*sic*], it baffled and upset many readers (see Lejeune, 'W or the Memory of Childhood', pp. 88, 93).

29. See Rosemarie Scullion, 'Georges Perec, *W*, and the Memory of Vichy France', *SubStance* 87, 1998, pp. 107–29; Nicola King mentions Leni Riefensthal's film of the Berlin Olympics (*Memory, Narrative, Identity: Remembering the Self*, Edinburgh: Edinburgh University Press 2000, p. 130).

30. Robert Gordon argues that Roberto Benigni's film *Life is Beautiful* (1997) continues this idea in the conceit of a father saving his son in Auschwitz by

pretending they are playing an elaborate game ('Fable, satire, fantasy: playing games with history in *La vita è bella*', unpublished paper).

31. The word 'fils' is used each time in French (Paris: Denoel 1975), respectively on the back cover and pp. 22, 77; it is hard not to detect wordplay here on the two meanings of 'fils': 'thread' and 'son'. Wilkomirski's term in German is 'Faden' (*Bruchstücke*, Berlin: Suhrkamp Verlag 1995, p. 64).

32. The name itself is reminiscent of, for example, the infamous Ninth Fort just outside Kaunas in Lithuania where the Nazis murdered over 30,000 Jews. Other 'trigger' signifiers include the phrases 'training camps', 'selections' (77) used ostensibly to describe the infrastructure of W; the punning use of the word 'Race' (153); and elements of the diegesis, such as the food deprivation suffered by athletes at W (91), the replacement of their names with serial numbers (99), white triangles on their clothes (99) and the maltreatment of failed athletes (139).

33. Astro argues that the text's parallel tracks crossover at this point: 'the autobiographical text functions allegorically and the fantastic text beomes real' ('Allegory', p. 869).

34. This is a typically dual reference: historically, to those who have no childhood memories of the Holocaust because of their youth, and psychoanalytically, to those who have no access to their earliest life.

35. David Bellos details Perec's interest in Resnais' films and in the author of the voiceover to *Night and Fog*, the poet Jean Cayrol (*Georges Perec: A Life in Words*, London: Harvill 1993, pp. 238, 439).

36. Magné Bernard argues for a Perecian as opposed to Lacanian notion of suture in his analysis of the the the 'traces' connecting W's two parts ('Les Sutures dans W', *Cahiers Georges Perec* (2) 1988, 34–44: 40).

37. Schwartz points out that the ellipses follow the death of both mothers, Caecilia Winckler and Cyrla Perec, *Georges Perec*, p. 50.

Choral narration

1. The term is from the blurb on the back cover of Henryk Grynberg, ed., *Children of Zion* (trans. Jacqueline Mitchell, Evanston, ILL: Northwestern University Press 1997; all further page references are in the text). It is also used in the blurb of Karen Gershon's *Postscript: A Collective Account of the Lives of Jews in West Germany since the Second World War*, London: Victor Gollancz 1969, the constituent voices of which are described as 'a many-voiced choir bearing witness'.

2. Claudine Vegh, ed., *I Didn't Say Goodbye*, trans. Ros Schwartz, London: Caliban Books 1984.

3. Clara Asscher-Pinkhof, *Star Children*, trans. Terese Edelstein and Inez Smith, Detroit: Wayne State University Press 1986 [1946]. All page references are in the text.

4. See Joanne Reilly, *Belsen: The Liberation of a Concentration Camp*, London: Routledge 1998, pp. 13–18.

5. Gillian Lathey points out that books of this kind may be categorized differently at various points in their production or reception (*The Impossible Legacy: Identity and Purpose in Autobiographical Children's Literature Set in the Third Reich and the Second World War*, Berne: Peter Lang 1999, p. 31), so my commentary will assume an adult reader of Asscher-Pinkhof's text.

6. Hans Keilson, *Sequential Traumatization in Children: A clinical and statistical follow-up of the Jewish war orphans in the Netherlands*, with the collaboration of Herman R. Sarphatie, trans. Yvonne Bearne, Hilary Coleman and Deirdre Winter, Jerusalem: The Magnes Press 1992, p. 53.

7. Christine Lattek, 'Bergen-Belsen: From "Privileged" Camp to Death Camp', *Journal of Holocaust Education* 5(2&3) Autumn/Winter 1996, Special Issue: Belsen in History and Memory, pp. 37–71: 46.

8. See Mikhail Bakhtin, 'Forms of Time and Chronotope in the Novel', in *The Dialogic Imagination: Four Essays*, trans. Caryl Emerson and Michael Holquist, Austin, Texas: University of Austin Press 1981.

9. An exception to this is the series of stories set in 'Star Hell' which is a part of its ultimately redemptive plot: a woman adopts, is separated from, then reunited with a little girl whom she hopes to take to the child's parents in Palestine (the episode, like the text as a whole, is a fictionalized version of Asscher-Pinkhof's own experiences, 'About the Author', *Star Children*, p. 19).

10. Lattek, 'Bergen-Belsen', p. 46; she points out that the majority of the 4000 'exchange Jews' housed in the camp by July 1944 were never exchanged.

11. The Gruene Polizei (Green Police) were the German *ordnungspolizei* who operated mainly in the big cities of the Netherlands. They were used to augment the Dutch police and also to carry out tasks for the Gestapo and SD.

12. Free indirect discourse is not omnipresent: one story, 'Little White Bundle' (140–1), is in the first person.

13. Cargas, in his Foreword to *Star Children*, ascribes this atypicality to the text's setting in the Netherlands (13), but it is rather the exchange which makes it so.

14. See also Dominic Head's argument that many of James Joyce's stories in *Dubliners* have an apparent and a less obvious epiphanic moment, *The Modernist Short Story: A Study in Theory and Practice*, Cambridge: Cambridge University Press, 1992.

15. See for instance Shimon Redlich, 'The Jews in the Soviet Annexed Territories, 1939–1941', *Soviet Jewish Affairs* (1) 1971, pp. 81–90.

16. Irena Grudzinska-Gross and Jan Tomasz Gross discuss the difficulty of ascertaining the numbers involved; Polish authorities estimate that 1.2 million people were resettled in the Soviet Union from south-eastern Poland in the first two years of the war, of whom 8,80,000 were forcibly sent to Russia between 1940 and 1941; about 4,40,000 people were 'dumped into settlements (*posëlki*)' of whom a quarter were children below fourteen (Irena Grudzinska-Gross and Jan Tomasz Gross, eds and compilers, *War Through Children's Eyes: The Soviet Occupation of Poland and the Deportations, 1939–1941*, trans. Ronald Strom and Dan Rivers, Stanford: Hoover Institution Press 1981, pp. xxii–xxiii).

17. The estimated total number of Polish children deported is between twelve and twenty thousand, and Jewish children constituted between 30 and 50 per cent of these, so, as Grynberg points out, 871 represents a very small proportion.

18. The 73 interviewees Grynberg quotes are identified by name, parents' names and town of origin in an appendix, pp. 167–73. Grynberg notes that the children's ages range from 11 to 18, although the majority were 14 or 15 in 1943 (x).

19. Irena Wasilewska, *Suffer Little Children*, London: Maxlove Publishing 1946, pp. 6–8.

20. As the title of Wasilewska's text makes clear – the full quotation from St Matthew is the book's epigraph – her concern is with Catholic Polish children, although she mentions the deportation of 'Polish, Jewish, Byelorussian and Ukrainian children' (ibid., p. 15).

21. Ibid., pp. 6, 8.

22. Ibid., p. 15.

23. There is no direct evidence that Grynberg is offering a polemical response to Wasilewska in the way he does to the de-judaized compilation of Irena Grudzinska-Gross and Jan Tomasz Gross; but although Grynberg does not mention *Suffer Little Children*, it is cited in *War Through Children's Eyes*, which he has read.

24. According to Grynberg, the correct proportion would have been 30–50 per cent (x).

25. Irena Grudzinska-Gross and Jan Tomasz Gross discuss the 'repetitive' nature of Polish children's accounts of deportation and forced labour, precisely because of the historical calamity they shared: 'Clearly the Soviet domination adversely affected the *entire* society' (xxviii).

26. Michael Bernard-Donals, 'The Rhetoric of Disaster and the Imperative of Writing', *Rhetoric Society Quarterly*, Winter 2001, pp. 49–94: 82

27. The narrators occasionally refer to what they have done specifically as children, for instance winning over Russian guards on the train to Siberia (80); digging their own latrine hole in the train floor (81); picking blueberries and mushrooms, which only those with children could get, to help their families survive in the penal colonies (100, 106).

28. Bernard-Donals, 'The Rhetoric of Disaster', p. 82, citing Hayden White.

29. Elie Wiesel, *Night*, trans. Stella Rodway, Harmondsworth: Penguin 1981 [1958], p. 80; Art Spiegelman, *Maus I: A Survivor's Tale*, Harmondsworth: Penguin 1987, p. 28.

30. Redlich points out that the Jews from the 'acquired territories' constituted a 'reservoir of Jewish national and religious consciousness' within the largely assimilated Soviet Jewish population; however, the war and the Holocaust put paid to this potential ('The Jews in the Soviet Annexed Territories', p. 90).

31. In Gerhard Durlacher's *The Search: The Birkenau Boys* (trans. Susan Massotty, London: Serpent's Tail 1998) Gerhard is a character in his own text rather than simply its narrator, as his responses to the adult boys' reactions to their experiences frequently show: he is 'taken aback' (69), envious of those whose parents survived (75), weeps (92) and he refers to 'our past' (22).

32. Mikhail Bakhtin, 'Epic and Novel', in *The Dialogic Imagination: Four Essays*, ed. Michael Holquist, trans. Caryl Emerson and Michael Holquist, Austin: University of Texas Press 1981, p. 13. See Rachel Falconer's discussion of this essay, 'Bakhtin and the Epic Chronotope', in Carol Adlam *et al.*, eds, *Face to Face: Bakhtin in Russia and the West*, Sheffield: Sheffield Academic Press 1997.

33. This contrasts with Irena Wasilewska, whose lack of distance from her subject would, according to Bakhtin, disqualify *Suffer Little Children* from epic status.

34. Bakhtin would prefer it to be a dialogic epic; his account of what defines epic is a negative one.

35. Bakhtin, 'Epic and Novel', pp. 16, 18.

36. 'Forms of Time and Chronotope in the Novel', in *The Dialogic Imagination: Four Essays*, ed. Michael Holquist, trans. Caryl Emerson and Michael Holquist,

Austin: University of Texas Press 1981, p. 218. Bakhtin's emphasis here is a positive one, while Grynberg is aware of the 'tragic' status of the 'anonymous and helpless' (ix) victims whose testimonies he presents.

37. Karen Gershon, ed., *We Came as Children: A Collective Autobiography*, New York: Harcourt, Brace and World 1966, p. 28; all further page references are in the text. Although the Movement for the Care of Children, founded in November 1938 after Kristallnacht to bring unaccompanied children under 17 to Britain, was only briefly known as the Children's Transports, the German term *Kindertransport* is widely used in English.

38. Gershon contacted three hundred people via the national press in Britain; she 'selected from' material in the 'outline of their refugee lives' that she asked each correspondent to submit, supplemented with interviews of thirty people (iv).

39. When the war broke out 9354 children had arrived in Britain, mainly from German, Austria and Czechoslovakia, under the auspices of the World Movement for the Care of Children from Germany (later named the Refugee Care Movement), of whom 7482 were Jewish (21). Gershon estimates that a further thousand children came to Britain as domestic servants or with their parents (iv).

40. No record exists of how many children stayed permanently in Britain, but many of those who did had no remaining families; others left to join survivors in the USA, Canada or Israel.

41. Vera Gissing, *Pearls of Childhood: The poignant true wartime story of a young girl growing up in an adopted land* (London: Robson Books 1994).

42. Marion Berghahn, *Continental Britons: German-Jewish Refugees from Nazi Germany*, Oxford: Berg Publishers 1988, pp. 110–11. She explicitly contrasts her conclusions with Gershon's possibly 'too rosy' picture of how the children settled down with their foster-families (ibid., p. 150). Rather, the picture of British generosity towards and acceptance of the refugees is 'rosiest' in the compilation *I Came Alone* (Bertha Leverton and Shmuel Lowensohn, eds, *I Came Alone: The Stories of the Kindertransports*, Sussex, England: The Book Guild 1996).

43. Karen Gershon, ed. and trans., *Postscript: A Collective Account of the Lives of Jews in West Germany since the Second World War*, London: Victor Gollancz 1969, p. xv.

44. Mark Jonathan Harris and Deborah Oppenheimer, eds, *Into the Arms of Strangers: Stories of the Kindertransport*, London: Bloomsbury 2000.

45. Harris and Oppenheimer note that 'in selecting the witnesses who speak here, we have tried to represent what we consider the most essential aspects of the Kindertransport'; the editors chose those who showed the most 'willingness to confront the pain and trauma of their childhood' and 'diversity' (p. 274).

46. The title of Gershon's text points most clearly to the communal aspect of the Kindertransport experience; Leverton and Lowensohn's to the subjective; Harris and Oppenheimer's to the work of rescue.

47. Berghahn argues that the foundation of the 'Thank-you Britain Fund' in the 1960s by former German and Austrian refugees was at least partly 'an unconscious response to British antisemitism' or at least to the continued expectation of gratitude (*Continental Britons*, p. 144).

48. With even greater irony, Wasilewska describes the fleeing of Polish exiles after their release from Soviet penal colonies to the southern republics of Central Asia as, 'that modern journey to the Promised Land' (*Suffer Little Children*, p. 82).
49. Not all the refugees were Jewish, although Bernard Wasserstein puts the figure at 90 per cent (*Britain and the Jews of Europe 1939–1945*, London: Institute of Jewish Affairs/Oxford: Clarendon Press 1979, p. 10); Gershon includes accounts from the children of Lutherans (*We Came as Children*, pp. 45, 61).
50. Berghahn, *Continental Britons*, pp. 216–17.
51. See the Preface to Norman Bentwich, *They Found Refuge: An account of British Jewry's work for victims of Nazi oppression*, London: The Cresset Press 1956, pp. vii–viii. Turner's *And the Policeman Smiled*, as its apocryphal title suggests, is on the whole a tale of rescue and success.
52. Keilson, *Sequential Traumatization*, p. 3. Like Grynberg and (partly) Gershon, Keilson relies largely on textual information for his study rather than interviews (p. 5).
53. Endelman gives assimilation before emigration as the reason the 50,000 – adult and child – refugees from Germany and Austria 'have not served as a significant demographic reinforcement to counter the impact of widespread disaffiliation' among the Jews of Britain (*Radical Assimilation*, p. 204). This goes counter to Bentwich's prediction, written fifty years earlier, that the refugees constituted 'an addition of almost a quarter to the [Jewish] community' (*They Found Refuge*, p. 204).
54. Alan L. Berger, 'Jewish Identity and Jewish Destiny, the Holocaust in Refugee Writing: Lore Segal and Karen Gershon', *Studies in American Jewish Literature* 11(1) 1992, pp. 83–95: 83. His concluding remark – 'Yet through their writings, refugee children witness to the world both their pain and their espousal of Jewish identity after Auschwitz' (p. 93) – is true only ironically of *We Came as Children*.
55. Endelman, *Radical Assimilation*, p. 173.
56. See Keilson, *Sequential Traumatization*: 'It is not merely a question of individuals who were persecuted and by coincidence were also Jews; the Jews as a group were the target' (p. 53).

Lost memories

1. Ingrid Kisliuk, *Unveiled Shadows: The Witness of a Child*, Newton, MA: Nanomir Press 1998; Claude Morhange-Bégué, *Chamberet: Recollections from an Ordinary Childhood*, trans. Austryn Wainhouse, Evanston, Illinois: North-western University Press 2000 [1987]; Raymond Federman, *The Voice in the Closet/La Voix dans le Cabinet de Débarras*, Madison: Coda Press 1979, unnumbered pages; all page references are in the text.
2. Ingrid's original name is withheld until p. 171; she describes her first name only as 'totally foreign-sounding' on p. 110.
3. Serge Klarsfeld and Maxime Steinberg, *Mémorial de la Déportation des Juifs de Belgique*, New York: Beate Klarsfeld Foundation 1982.
4. By contrast, the narrator of Miriam Winter's *Trains* experiences writing as the flight of memory: 'as soon as I try to catch [images of my parents], as

soon as I stop to jot down what I see, they flit back into the dark corners of nowhere, and my memory is blank again' (Miriam Winter, *Trains: A Memoir of a Hidden Childhood Before and After World War II*, Jackson, Michigan: Kelton Press 1997, p. 23; all further page references in the text).

5. This phrase is repeated when the arrival of Herta's postcard is narrated chronologically; as in Ida Fink's *The Journey*, repetition conveys the presentness of past trauma.

6. However, Irène continued to maintain 'a double life' and 'a double personality' after the war in Belgium (149).

7. Ellen S. Fine argues that the narrator of *Chamberet* (who she calls 'author-narrator' or simply 'author') is especially preoccupied with the 'absence of written testimony' about her mother's experiences, hence her own act of writing ('Transmission of Memory: The Post-Holocaust Generation in the Diaspora', in Efraim Sicher, ed., *Breaking the Crystal: Writing and Memory after Auschwitz*, Urbana and Chicago: University of Illinois Press 1998, p. 197).

8. Patrick Modiano, *Dora Bruder*, trans. Joanne Kilmartin, Berkeley and London: University of California Press 1999; Pierre Pachet, *Autobiographie de mon père* (Paris: Belin 1987); Miriam Akavia, *An End to Childhood*, from her brother's viewpoint. Froma Zeitlin discusses 'acquired or vicarious testimony' in novels by Henri Raczymow and Jaroslaw Rymkiewicz in 'The Vicarious Witness: Belated Memory and Authorial Presence in Recent Holocaust Literature', *History and Memory* 10(2), Fall 1998, pp. 5–42.

9. As in Ingrid's case in *Unveiled Shadows*, Claude's memory is provoked in the act of writing: uncertainty about her mother's reassurances is revived 'now, as I write' (30; and 59, 84).

10. Mikhail Bakhtin, 'Forms of Time and the Chronotope', p. 97.

11. *The Voice in the Closet / La Voix dans le Cabinet de Débarras* is a 'reversible' book, its French and English versions separated by '*Echos (à RF)*', a prose piece in French by Maurice Roche (for publishing history, see Larry McCaffery *et al.*, eds, *Federman A to X-X-X-X: A Recyclopedic Narrative*, San Diego: San Diego University Press 1999, pp. 36, 373–4). The edition cited here is Evamaria Erdpohl, *Criteria of Identity: A Comparative Analysis of Raymond Federman's 'The Voice in the Closet' and Selected Works by Jasper Johns*, together with the original text of Raymond Federman's 'The Voice in the Closet' and an introduction by Richard Martin, Frankfurt: Peter Lang 1992; all page references are in the text. See Erdpohl, *Criteria of Identity*, for a discussion of the book's closet-like visual design, pp. 81–4.

12. Erdpohl, for instance, claims that the text 'exposes *nothing* but its own fictionality', *Criteria of Identity*, p. 87, my italics; one of the anonymous readers who recommended part of *The Voice* for publication in the *Chicago Review* in 1978 says that the novel is about 'that fear and resentment of our own mortality, of time, which is not tied to a specific event [. . .] it is not so much the Nazi experience [the youth] cannot explain, but the inevitability of death itself' (quoted in McCaffery *et al.*, *Federman*, p. 381).

13. Interview with Raymond Federman in Tom LeClair and Larry McCaffery (eds), *Anything Can Happen: Interviews with Contemporary American Novelists*, Urbana: University of Illinois Press 1983, pp. 143–4.

14. Even here the writer seems to intrude onto the ambiguous 'now', which refers as much to the writer's as to the boy's present: to follow the latter's tenses here, the correct word would be 'then'.

15. Erdpohl describes how Federman originally composed *The Voice* with two voices speaking at once, the boy in fragmented discourse, the writer coherently, using 'two different selectric balls'; eventually he abandoned typographical distinctions between the voices and allowed much greater intermingling (*Criteria of Identity*, p. 89).

16. Martin, 'Introduction', p. 19.

17. According to McCaffery *et al.*, Federman began the English version of *The Voice* in October 1975, the French one in 1977 (*Federman*, p. 373).

18. See Martin's introduction to Erdpohl, *Criteria of Identity*, p. 14.

19. As with any temporal relativity in *The Voice*, this utterance is ambiguous. 'The present' could mean the boy's day in the closet, which can only be (mis)remembered in the light of what came next ('the coming future'); or 'the present' could be that of the writer, who equally depends on what happened next to his boyhood self – 'the coming future' – but which he has not yet related.

20. McCaffery *et al.*, *Federman*, p. 382, quoting an anonymous reader; the latter adds that this 'omission' has not taken place, 'despite [Federman's] cover letter [to the *Chicago Review*], to avoid sentimentality but it implies that the feelings RF associates with these words are too much for him to bear'. This comment takes for granted the identity of boy and adult that *The Voice* questions; rather, it seems to me that the construction of the text explains the words' absence – a young boy in 1942 would not naturally use them.

21. See especially Federman's bilingual collection of poetry, *Among the Beasts/ Parmi les Monstres*, Paris: Millas and Martin 1967; and the autobiographical novels *Double or Nothing* (Chicago: Swallow Press 1971), *Take It or Leave It* (New York: Fiction Collective 1976), *The Twofold Vibration (1982)*. *The Voice* was originally a part of the latter (McCaffery *et al.*, *Federman*, pp. 361–2).

22. Bakhtin, 'Forms of Time', 248.

23. Ibid., p. 255.

24. *The Voice* is dedicated to Simon, Marguerite, Sarah and Jacqueline – Federman's parents and sisters respectively. Joyce's *Portrait* has no dedication, but an epigraph predicting Stephen's future as a writer: 'Et ignotas animum dimittit in artes' (Ovid, *Metamorphoses*, VIII, 188), that is, 'Then to unimagined arts he set his mind.'

Hidden children

1. Gunnar Paulsson, *Secret City: The Hidden Jews of Warsaw 1940–1945*, New Haven and London: Yale University Press 2002, pp. 14–15. He argues that historical study of Jews during the Holocaust who, by taking efforts to save themselves 'without taking up arms, were at least to some extent masters of their own fate – virtually does not exist' (ibid., p. 7): hidden children were unwittingly partial 'masters of their own fate'.

2. 'German preoccupation with the destruction of hidden children suggests that most of the child survivors were hidden children and that the survival

rate of 7 per cent among Jewish children during the war lags behind the general survival rate of 33 per cent' (Nechama Tec, 'Historical Perspective: Tracing the History of the Hidden-Child Experience', in Jane Marks, *The Hidden Children: The Secret Survivors of the Holocaust*, London: Bantam 1995, p. 273).

3. Eva Fogelman, in Marks, ed., *The Hidden Children*: Fogelman distinguishes ' "active" ' from the ' "passive hiding" ' of children being hidden by others (p. 293), although in practice the two often overlapped; Lawrence L. Langer, 'Damaged Childhood in Holocaust Fact and Fiction', in Michael A. Signer, ed., *Humanity at the Limit: The Impact of the Holocaust Experience on Jews and Christians*, Bloomington and London: Indiana University Press 2000, p. 330: later he amends the opposition simply to 'hiding or passing' (335); Paulsson, *Secret City*, pp. 106 ff.

4. Ibid., p. 294.

5. Louis Begley, *Wartime Lies*, London: Picador 1991, all page references are in the text; Henryk Grynberg, *Child of the Shadows*, trans. Celina Wieniewska, London: Vallentine Mitchell 1969, reissued 2001 as *The Jewish War*, trans. Celina Wieniewska and Richard Lourie, Evanston, Illinois: Northwestern University Press: all references in the text are to the original English edition.

6. Despite the fact that it is published as fiction and has been awarded literary prizes on that basis, critics seem unwilling to give up speculation on the autobiographical point. Begley claims that 'without exception, journalists who have interviewed me about *Wartime Lies* have assumed that it is autobiographical' (Louis Begley, 'Who the Novelist Really Is', *New York Times Book Review*, 16 August 1992, p. 2).

7. This is a free translation of the song (courtesy of Teresa Bela):

> Maciek is dead, is dead;
> He is lying on the board (i.e. a bier),
> If they had played music to him,
> He still would have danced
> Because a Mazurian soul is like this:
> Although he dies, he can still move around.
> Oy dana, dana, dana, dana.

Like the Maciek of the song, the protagonist of *Wartime Lies* 'dies' but continues to dance on command.

8. Peter Quartermaine, for instance, casting doubt on the accuracy of dialogue in Thomas Keneally's *Schindler's List*, observes that this is 'hardly the form in which most records tend to be kept' (*Thomas Keneally*, London: Arnold 1991, p. 64) – and, one might add, hardly the way in which memory works.

9. Christoph Ribbat argues that Maciek's childhood is fabricated, not real, 'for want of one [the grown-up narrator] truly remembers as being a part of his self' ('Shiny Silk Blouses: Luxury and Memory in the Novels of Louis Begley', *Zeitschrift für Anglistik und Amerikanistik* 46(3) 1998, pp. 243–52: 247). Thus the novel's title refers not only to lies told *during* wartime but *about* wartime. Lawrence Douglas asks the same question of the novel's final chapter: 'was Maciek himself an invention?' ('Wartime Lies: Securing the Holocaust in Law and Literature', *Yale Journal of Law & the Humanities* 7(45), pp. 45–73: 63).

10. *Pace* Allan Hepburn's statement that 'the older man [is] named Maciek' ('Lost Time: Trauma and Belatedness in Louis Begley's *The Man Who Was Late*', *Contemporary Literature* 39(3) 1998, pp. 380–44: 381): this seems to be a misreading of the narrator's observation that Maciek 'died' and a 'man who bears one of the names Maciek used has replaced him' (198). Janet Malcolm also claims that the narrator is 'the adult the child has become' ('A Matter of Life and Death: Louis Begley, *Wartime Lies*', *New York Review of Books*, 13 June 1991, pp. 16–17: 16).

11. See Douglas, 'Wartime Lies'. Interestingly, although Douglas argues that an impression of veracity is given to *Wartime Lies* by the inclusion of extraneous details and stories, Begley suggests that such moments on the contrary give an impression of fictionality ('Who the Novelist Really Is', 23). He gives the example of transforming his account of the characters' time in a cellar during the Warsaw Uprising from reading like 'history' by adding to it the character of the friendly woman lawyer: 'I have no idea why this woman appeared at that particular time or from where. There certainly was no such person in any cellar I have frequented' (ibid.).

12. The narrator says of a fellow lodger at Pani Dumont's, 'I still sing Pan Stasiek's tunes; almost everything else about him has faded from my memory' (104). Usually it is simply the adult narrator's linguistic ability and overview of events which signify his place in the future.

13. Henry James, *What Maisie Knew*, Harmondsworth: Penguin 1966 [1897], p. 24.

14. See Mikhail Bakhtin, *Problems of Dostoevsky's Poetics*, trans. Caryl Emerson, Minneapolis: University of Minnesota Press 1984.

15. Tania's discourse here is already double-voiced; she is repeating the epithets of others.

16. Sigmund Freud, 'From the History of an Infantile Neurosis', *Pelican Freud Library vol. 9: Case Histories II: 'Rat Man', Schreber, 'Wolf Man', Female Homosexuality*, Harmondsworth: Penguin 1979.

17. Sander L. Gilman, *Freud, Race, and Gender*, Princeton, NJ: Princeton University Press 1993, p. 76.

18. Hepburn oddly follows this notion in describing *Wartime Lies* as the record of '*avoidance* of the concentration camps' ('Lost Time' p. 381, my italics), implying this was an experience that should have been faced; rather, it is surely the record of people trying to save their lives in whatever way they can. Gabriele Rosenthal, for example, draws a greater distinction between survivors who were able to emigrate, not those in hiding, and those who went through the camps (Rosenthal, Gabriele, *The Holocaust in Three Generations: Families of Victims and Perpetrators of the Nazi Regime*, London: Cassell 1998, p. 6).

19. Freud, 'From the History of an Infantile Neurosis', p. 278, n. 2.

20. Ibid., p. 284.

21. Hal Espen, 'The Lives of Louis Begley', *New Yorker*, 30 May 1994, pp. 38–46: 44.

22. Freud, 'From the History of an Infantile Neurosis', p. 293.

23. Lawrence Douglas sees this moment as a staging of the novel's 'crisis of representation', since it 'claims to offer credible eyewitness testimony at the same time that the witness portrays himself as a liar' ('Wartime Lies: Securing the Holocaust in Law and Literature', *Yale Journal of Law & the Humanities* 7(45), pp. 45–73: 60). Douglas sees in this combination the potential for

'truth' to be uttered by a 'dissembler' (73). In my view, such a 'crisis' as this moment in Maciek's boyhood is also an *enabling* moment: the combination of unreliability and an impression of testimony is precisely what makes up the novel's autobiographical illusion.

24. Begley describes the phrase 'living on Aryan papers' as a 'bizarre and shameful expression' referring to 'shedding of one's Jewish identity' ('Who the Novelist Really Is', p. 22).

25. Begley here echoes Jaroslaw Rymkiewicz's novel about the Holocaust in Poland, *The Final Station: Umschlagplatz* (trans. Nina Taylor, New York: Farrar Straus Giroux 1994), which was originally published in Polish in 1988. In *The Final Station*, the fictional narrator, who bears the same name as the author, notes wryly that in post-war Poland he was often mistaken for a Jew. He recounts an encounter with an 'elderly gentleman' who asked which branch of the Rymkiewicz family Jaroslaw was from: 'his smile made it patently clear that I was neither a wellborn Rymkiewicz nor any kind of Rymkiewicz, but a Rozenkranz, Rozenfeld, or Rozenduft. The sickly smell of roses, the sickly smell of anti-Semitism' (p. 152).

26. Eric Santner, 'History beyond the Pleasure Principle: Some Thoughts on the Representation of Trauma', in Saul Friedländer, ed., *Probing the Limits of Representation: Nazism and the 'Final Solution'*, Cambridge, MA: Harvard University Press 1992, p. 144.

27. See for instance Yitzhak Arad, *Belzec, Sobibor, Treblinka: The Operation Reinhard Death Camps*, Bloomington: Indiana University Press 1987, p. 189, and Martin Gilbert, *The Holocaust: The Jewish Tragedy*, p. 432: both mention the dog 'Barry'.

28. Helen Darville, *The Hand that Signed the Paper*, Sydney: Allen & Unwin, p. 103. See Ian MacMillan's novel, *A Village of Spirits*, p. 99, also on 'Barry'. It seems that Darville, notorious for her wholesale literary borrowings, has read *Wartime Lies*. In her novel the Ukrainian SS adopt Polish antisemitic epithets: 'They called Jews *kurwamac* and *kurwysyn*, which meant mother and son of menstrual blood' (113). This is almost identical to Begley's sentence: 'The worst insult was to call someone *kurwamac* or *kurwysyn*. That was mother or son of that blood' (41). In fact, Darville just repeats Maciek's error: '*kurwamac*' means 'son of a whore'.

29. Jean-François Steiner, *Treblinka*, London: Corgi 1969, p. 178.

30. In the Foreword to Grynberg's *The Victory* (trans. Richard Lourie, Evanston, ILL: Northwestern University Press 1993 [1969]), the translator notes that Grynberg's works are 'autobiography and history told as fiction' (p. viii).

31. *Child of the Shadows*, pp. 110–12; *Wartime Lies*, pp. 115–16.

Convent children

1. Flora Hogman, 'The Experience of Catholicism for Jewish Children During World War II', *Psychoanalytic Review* 75(4), Winter 1988, pp. 511–32: 511; all further references are in the text.

2. Frida Scheps Weinstein, *A Hidden Childhood: A Jewish Girl's Sanctuary in a French Convent, 1942–1945*, trans. Barbara Loeb Kennedy, New York: Hill and Wang 1985, p. 108; Renée Roth-Hano, *Touch Wood: A Girlhood in Occupied France*, New York: Four Winds Press 1988; Elisabeth Gille, *Shadows of a Childhood:*

A Novel of War and Friendship, trans. Linda Coverdale, New York: New Press 1996; all page references are in the text.

3. Hogman, 'The Experience of Catholicism for Jewish Children During World War II', p. 511.

4. Both Weinstein's and Roth-Hano's novels are discussed in ibid., which also relies on interviews; interviews with Weinstein and her novel are used interchangeably in Margrit Wreschner Rustow, 'From Jew to Catholic – and Back: Psychodynamics of Child Survivors' (in Paul Marcus and Alan Rosenberg, eds, *Healing Their Wounds: Psychotherapy with Holocaust Survivors and Their Families*, New York, Westport and London: Praeger 1989); Rustow also discusses the cases of Renée Fersen-Osten, using a pseudonym, and Saul Friedländer. Again, no distinction is made between Weinstein's novel and her case history in Judith S. Kestenberg, Flora Hogman, Milton Kestenberg and Eva Fogelman, 'Jewish-Christian Relationships as Seen Through the Eyes of Children, Before, During and After the Holocaust' (in *Remembering for the Future: Working Papers and Addenda. Volume 1. Jews and Christians During and After the Holocaust*, eds Yehuda Bauer *et al.*, Oxford: Pergamon 1989). Despite being published a year after Roth-Hano's novel and Hogman's 'The Experience of Catholicism for Jewish Children During World War II', this article was written during, and in the knowledge of, *Touch Wood*'s composition: Hogman wrote the section in which *A Hidden Childhood* and Renée – under a pseudonym – are cited (625–8). Hogman confirms that Roth-Hano was a long-term friend rather than a patient, whose story was well known to her (personal communication, 30 August 2002).

5. Gunnar Paulsson, *Secret City: The Hidden Jews of Warsaw 1940–1945*, London and New Haven: Yale University Press 2002, pp. 124–5.

6. Roth-Hano, *Touch Wood*, p. 161.

7. Saul Friedländer, *When Memory Comes*, trans. Helen R. Lane, New York: Farrar Straus Giroux 1979, p. 79.

8. Nor are they accounts of the 'imposition', in André Stein's term, of Christian faith by rescuers (*Hidden Children: Forgotten Survivors of the Holocaust*, Toronto: Viking 1993, p. 268). Nechama Tec points out that priests were often reluctant to baptise Jewish children without their parents' consent (Nechama Tec, 'A Historical Perspective: Tracing the History of the Hidden-Child Experience', in Jane Marks, *The Hidden Children: The Secret Survivors of the Holocaust*, London: Bantam 1995, p. 289) – although Paul's gave consent in *When Memory Comes*, the impossibility of gaining consent and therefore of being baptised was a source of torment to Marysia in *Trains*. Pace Sarah Moskovitz's account of the perils for small children of being hidden in Catholic institutions – she claims that their conformity was the result of fear of attracting 'displeasure, rejection and annihilation' ('Making Sense of Survival: A Journey with Child Survivors of the Holocaust', in Robert Krell, ed., *Messages and Memories: Reflections on Child Survivors of the Holocaust*, Vancouver: Memory Press 1999, p. 14) – both F. in *A Hidden Childhood* and Renée in *Touch Wood* develop ambivalence precisely because their experience was positive.

9. Stephen J. Dubner, *Turbulent Souls: A Catholic Son's Return to His Jewish Family*, New York: Avon Books 1998.

10. Janina David, *A Square of Sky: Memoirs of a Wartime Childhood*, London: Eland 1992 [1964], p. 57.

11. Miriam Winter, *Trains: A Memoir of a Hidden Childhood Before and After World War II*, Jackson, Michigan: Kelton Press 1997, p. 62.
12. Henryk Grynberg, *Child of the Shadows*, trans. Celina Wieniewska, London: Vallentine Mitchell 1969, p. 115.
13. Ibid.
14. Ibid., p. 113.
15. Louis Begley, *Wartime Lies*, London: Picador 1991, p. 117.
16. Ibid., pp. 76–7.
17. Ibid., *Wartime Lies*, p. 115.
18. Grynberg, *Child of the Shadows*, p. 110.
19. Kestenberg *et al.*, 'Jewish-Christian Relationships as Seen Through the Eyes of Children', p. 625.
20. See Mortimer Ostow, 'The Psychological Determinants of Jewish Identity', in Mortimer Ostow, ed., *Judaism and Psychoanalysis*, New York: KTAV 1982.
21. Anne Frank, *The Diary of a Young Girl: The Definitive Edition*, trans. Susan Massotty, eds Otto H. Frank and Mirjam Pressler, New York: Bantam Books 1995 [1947], p. 148, entry for Monday, 6 December 1943.
22. Gerhard Durlacher, *Drowning: Growing Up in the Third Reich*, trans. Susan Massotty, London: Serpent's Tail 1993.
23. Begley, *Wartime Lies*, p. 14.
24. André Stein, *Broken Silence: Dialogues from the Edge*, Toronto: Lester and Orpen Dennys 1984, p. 1.
25. Ostow, 'The Psychological Determinants of Jewish Identity', p. 163.
26. Sarah Kofman, *Rue Ordener, Rue Labat*, trans. Ann Smock, Lincoln and London: University of Nebraska Press 1996, p. 44.
27. Kestenberg *et al.*, 'Jewish-Christian Relationships as Seen Through the Eyes of Children', p. 626.
28. Kofman, *Rue Ordener, Rue Labat*, pp.15, 27, 47.
29. Ibid., p. 80.
30. Ostow, 'The Psychological Determinants of Jewish Identity', p. 169.
31. Grynberg, *Child of the Shadows*, p. 80. As Grynberg was born in 1936 and spent the years 1942–1944 in hiding on Aryan papers, we can assume that at this point Henryk – Grynberg's fictional alter ego – is about six.
32. Stein, *Broken Silence*, p. 1.
33. Ostow, 'The Psychological Determinants of Jewish Identity', p. 164.
34. Ibid., p. 185.
35. Ibid., p. 169.
36. Ibid., p. 185.
37. Ibid., p. 167.
38. Winter, *Trains*, p. 19.
39. That is, a name 'characteristic of the surrounding culture'.
40. Friedländer, *When Memory Comes*, p. 122.
41. Sigmund Freud, *Standard Edition of the Complete Psychological Works of Sigmund Freud*, trans. James Strachey, London: Hogarth Press 1953, Vol. XVIII, 'Two Artificial Groups: The Church and the Army' (1921), pp. 94–5.
42. Friedländer, *When Memory Comes*, p. 120.
43. Ibid., p. 121. Similarly, after the war Henryk thinks his Jewishness and the loss of his family make him better suited to be Catholic than any of the

other boys (Henryk Grynberg, *The Victory*, trans. Richard Lourie, Evanston, Illinois: Northwestern University Press 193 [1969], p. 50).

44. Tec, 'A Historical Perspective', p. 288.
45. Gille, *Shadows of a Childhood*, p. 31.
46. Anita Lobel, *No Pretty Pictures: A Child of War*, New York: Greenwillow Books 1998, p. 61.
47. Rustow, 'From Jew to Catholic – and Back', p. 281.
48. Renée Fersen-Osten, *Don't They Know the World Stopped Breathing? Reminiscences of a French Child During the Holocaust Years*, New York: Shapolsky 1991, p. 43.
49. Ibid., pp. 48–9.
50. Ibid., p. 282.
51. Friedländer, *When Memory Comes*, p. 122. Paul was clearly intoxicated by the beauty of the words for Catholic vestments and objects here as well – see also Jerzy Kosinski, *The Painted Bird*, New York: Bantam 1978, p. 126.
52. Rustow, 'From Jew to Catholic – and Back', p. 278.
53. Ibid., p. 282.
54. Winter, *Trains*, p. 87.
55. Lobel, *No Pretty Pictures*, p. 6.
56. Stein, *Broken Silence*, p. 3.
57. Roth-Hano, *Touch Wood*, p. 31.
58. Weinstein, *A Hidden Childhood*, p. 108.
59. Winter, *Trains*, p. 48.
60. Grynberg, *The Victory*, p. 49: this novel is the post-war sequel to *Child of the Shadows*.
61. Winter, *Trains*, pp. 36–7.
62. Ibid., p. 217.
63. Julia Kristeva, *Powers of Horror: An Essay on Abjection*, trans. Leon L. Roudiez, New York: Columbia University Press 1984, p. 127. The distinction Kristeva draws here between material and spiritual transgression is overly polarized. Many commentators point out the specifically religious nature of the Levitical laws.
64. Ibid., p. 130.
65. Ibid., p. 131.
66. Ibid., pp. 2–3.
67. Ibid., pp. 119, 129.
68. Ibid., p. 3.
69. One could argue that a second transgression is added to the first as F. tries to drink milk having eaten meat; Kristeva discusses the Levitical prohibition to eat milk and meat together as another Oedipal anxiety (*Powers of Horror*, pp. 105–6).
70. Ibid., p. 119.
71. Fersen-Osten, *Don't They Know the World Stopped Breathing?*, p. 47.
72. The title of the original French edition, *Paysage de cendres* (Landscape of ashes), Paris: Seuil 1996, emphasizes the Holocaust deaths of Léa's parents, but 'ashes' become a trope for an existential withdrawal and meaninglessness, as Léa's reaction to Benedicte's death, also the last line of the novel, shows: she feels herself covered in a 'rain of ashes [...] that finally deadened all sound' (*Shadows* p. 138; the word *'cendres'* is also used in the French original at this point, *Paysage* p. 201).

73. Unlike Léa, who was hidden in a convent, Gille was hidden in the French countryside with her sister; very little detail is given about Léa's parents in *Shadows*, but Gille's mother, Irène Nemirovsky, was a well-known Russian writer.
74. Gille, *Shadows of a Childhood*, p. 4.
75. Ibid., p. 95.
76. Ibid., p. 32.
77. Ibid., p. 89.
78. Eva Fogelman, 'Between Two Religions: Religious Transformation and Continuity', http://www.adl.org/hidden/between_religions/between_religions_toc.asp, visited 5 July 2002.
79. The original French title is *J'habitais rue des Jardins Saint-Paul*, referring to a recognizably Jewish district of Paris. The English title has substituted an apparently more simplistic and descriptive title, which nonetheless has its own ambiguity: not only did a child live in hiding, but the childhood itself is 'hidden'.
80. The child learns, in a matter of pages, who is the 'naked man on the cross' (20); what the 'signs' are that Catholics make with their hands (21); what praying is ('telling secrets', 21); what the 'little white disks' (26) are for.
81. Yolanda Gampel, 'Facing War, Murder, Torture, and Death in Latency', *Psychoanalytic Review* 75(4), Winter 1988, pp. 499–510: 499–500.
82. Mikhail Bakhtin, *Problems of Dostoevsky's Poetics*, trans. Caryl Emerson, Minneapolis: University of Minnesota Press 1984, p. 193.
83. Ibid., p. 227.
84. Later the narrator notes, 'I'm thinking about all the things in Jerusalem and the Holy Land' (122): F. sees this as a sign of her Catholic piety, but it is also a suppressed memory of her Jewish father, one of the 'things' to be found in Jerusalem. As part of her return to the past, F. asks herself 'whether the Palestine where [my father] lives is the same as the one Jesus Christ lived in' (129). While her mother is identified with a Pharisee – an imperfect Jew – F.'s father is identified with Christ himself: 'Every time I'm in trouble my father does something to save me' (128; see Hogman on the 'familial designations of the divine figures' adopted by Jewish children hiding in Catholic settings, 'Jewish Children's Experience of Catholicism', p. 520).
85. See Maciek's analogous battle with bedbugs in *Wartime Lies*, a 'war game' which allows him to act out Nazi brutality against partisans and Jews (93).
86. Hogman drew on interviews for her analysis of four Jewish girls hidden in Catholic environments, although she does refer to Weinstein's and Roth-Hano's novels.
87. Ibid., p. 528. Hogman describes other features of Frida's story which do not appear in Weinstein's novel: for instance, that Frida suspected her mother sent her to the convent because she was a 'difficult' child (514) who would impede the mother's escape plans, thus accidentally ensuring the child's survival. Although the reader of *A Hidden Childhood* does see that F. 'confused' her relationship with her mother with 'negative feelings about Judaism', as Hogman puts it (520), it is not clear *in the novel* that the familial relationship was especially 'conflictual' (ibid.) – thus Weinstein's version places more emphasis than Hogman's on the shortcomings of Judaism and the naturalness in the circumstances of rejecting the Jewish mother.

88. Kestenberg *et al.*, 'Jewish-Christian Relationships as Seen Through the Eyes of Children', p. 628,
89. Although originally published for adults, Roth's *Touch Wood* has become a crossover text: it was reissued in 1989 in paperback as a Puffin book for teenagers. Its sequel, about Renée's post-war life in the USA, is *Safe Harbors*, New York: Four Winds Press 1993.
90. Wreschner Rustow, 'From Jew to Catholic – and Back', p. 281.
91. As well as the elements I discuss, Renée – like F. – envies the French their Gallic past (*Touch Wood* 73; *Hidden Childhood* 66); she has a beloved object, a doll Jackie who is 'all I have left of Mulhouse' (171), just as F. has her brown skirt; and mistakes Pétain for a benevolent, paternal figure (*Touch Wood* 71; *Hidden Childhood* 121). It is not that Roth-Hano is inventing or appropriating these details, but it seems that their appearance in her novel owes a debt to Weinstein's, and to Hogman's, analysis.
92. As in many child's-eye-view Holocaust texts, historical and developmental issues overlap in these instances as youthful concern with appearance is inflected by Nazi racial categories. At times it is unclear on what grounds Renée is lamenting the details of her appearance, such as her 'uneven front teeth and big lips' (170), so imbricated have the 'racial' and the personal become. Elsewhere, Renée conflates her own infancy with pre-war life: 'I want to be little again, I want to go back to that day in September in Villers-sur-Thur with the Peterses – I don't want war to have broken out!' (102).
93. Renée also mentions her new-found ability, as a Catholic, to address God or at least 'St Antoine' directly in prayer; identification with Christ's suffering (109); and guilt at abandoning to hell unbaptised parents (230), all of which are mentioned by Hogman in relation to 'Renée' (521, 524, 526, respectively).
94. Stein sees this shift of allegiance in a starker light: 'Since the God of Christians – unlike the God of Israel – protected [hidden children] in their need, they wanted to be Christians' (*Hidden Children*, p. 269).

Masquerading as gentile

1. Ida Fink, *The Journey*, trans. Joanna Wechsler and Francine Prose, Harmondsworth, Penguin: 1992; Solomon Perel, *Europa, Europa*, trans. Margot Bettauer Dembo, New York: John Wiley, 1997. All page references are in the text. (Thanks to Eugenie Georgaca and Sean Homer for their help with this chapter.)
2. Gunnar S. Paulsson, *Secret City: The Hidden Jews of Warsaw 1940–1945*, London and New Haven: Yale University Press 2002, p. 106, quoting Emanuel Ringelblum.
3. Theresa I. Cahn, 'The Diary of an Adolescent Girl in the Ghetto: A Study of Age-Specific Reactions to the Holocaust', *Psychoanalytic Review* 75(4), Winter 1988, pp. 589–617: 593. Eva's diary stops abruptly in May 1941, otherwise the relation of her adolescent concerns to those of her circumstances would inevitably have changed; her fate is unknown.
4. I have borrowed this phrase from Joan Riviere's article 'Womanliness as a Masquerade', *International Journal of Psychoanalysis* X, 1929, reprinted in H. Ruitenbeeck, ed., *Female Sexuality*, New Haven: College and UP 1963.

5. See for instance Sander L. Gilman, *The Jew's Body*, London and New York: Routledge 1991; Ann Pellegrini, *Performance Anxieties: Staging Psychoanalysis, Staging Race*, London and New York: Routledge 1997; Miriam Peskowitz and Laura Levitt, eds, *Judaism Since Gender*, London and New York: Routledge 1997.

6. Louis Begley, *Wartime Lies*, London: Picador 1992, p. 54. This remark (the protagonist Maciek's grandfather is ventriloquizing a Polish speaker) is preceded by the observation that, by contrast, a woman might get rid of a blackmailer by insisting on the impeccable credentials of her Polish surname.

7. Other works in this category include Begley's *Wartime Lies*, and Arnost Lustig's *Children of the Holocaust*, trans. Jan Nemcova and George Theiner, Evanston, ILL: Northwestern University Press 1984. See also Lawrence Douglas's discussion of fact and fiction intersecting in his 'Wartime Lies: Securing the Holocaust in Law and Literature', *Yale Journal of Law & the Humanities* 1995, 7(45), pp. 45–73.

8. Sara R. Horowitz, *Voicing the Void: Muteness and Memory in Holocaust Fiction*, Albany: State University of New York Press 1997, p. 8. See also Marek Wilczynski, 'Trusting the Words: Paradoxes of Ida Fink' (*Modern Language Studies* 24(4), Fall 1994, pp. 25–38) who translates Fink's comment from an interview published in the Polish journal *Gazeta Wyborcza*: 'Everything I write is a reconstruction of the events excavated from memory' (p. 26).

9. Ida Fink, *A Scrap of Time and Other Stories*, trans. Madeline Levine and Francine Prose, Harmondsworth: Penguin 1989; *Traces: Stories*, trans. Philip Boehm and Francine Prose, New York: Metropolitan Books 1997.

10. The literal and symbolic senses of 'hiding' are summed up neatly in Miriam Winter's memoir, in which the older Miriam says of her younger self, ' "I was still hiding after the war" ' (*Trains: A Memoir of a Hidden Childhood Before and After World War II*, Jackson, Michigan: Kelton Press 1997, p. 22).

11. Michael Burleigh describes how a 'centralised labour procurement programme was established under the ex-merchant seaman Fritz Sauckel in March 1942, which combed western and eastern Europe in search of a workforce. The ruthless tactics used in Poland were repeated in the occupied parts of the Soviet Union' (*The Third Reich*, London: Pan Books 2001, p. 479; see also Ulrich Herts, *Hitler's Foreign Workers: Enforced Foreign Labor in Germany under the Third Reich*, trans. William Templer, Cambridge: Cambridge University Press 1997).

12. Josey Fisher, ed., *The Persistence of Youth: Oral Testimonies of the Holocaust*, New York: Greenwood Press 1991, p. x.

13. The protagonist must be at least in her late teens, although the girls' developmental age is a matter of debate within the novel itself. Halinka, who offers a hiding-place to only one of the sisters, inflates Elzbieta's age to make abandoning her seem a possibility: ' "She's not a child. She's sixteen years old" ' (46); while the warmer Fräulein Hedwig, who gives them money, reduces Elzbieta to tears by greeting the sisters with, ' "Come in, children" ' (48).

14. Nonetheless, as Nechama Tec points out, 'In eastern Europe Jewish women seem to have had certain advantages' over men trying to hide or pass as gentile; as well as noting that women were exempt from the 'special vulnerability' of circumcision, Tec notes the greater likelihood that women would have had access to a secular eduction including knowledge of local languages and culture; and that 'stricter laws' were applied by the Nazis to both Jewish and

gentile men (*Resilience and Courage: Women, Men, and the Holocaust*, New Haven and London: Yale University Press 2003, pp. 216–17, 223).

15. Begley, *Wartime Lies*, p. 97. Neither of these features is gender-specific, however, while for men the racial signifier *par excellence* is also a gendered one.

16. On one occasion the protagonist claims to have a husband who is a German soldier at the front (198), as a ruse both to explain the absence of a male partner and to authenticate her and her sister's national and racial status.

17. Daniel Boyarin, 'What Does a Jew Want?; or, The Political Meaning of the Phallus', in Christopher Lane, ed., *The Psychoanalysis of Race*, New York: Columbia University Press 1998, p. 212, speaking of Freud.

18. Jacques Lacan, *The Seminar. Book 1. Freud's Papers on Technique, 1953–54*, trans. John Forrester, Cambridge: Cambridge University Press 1988, p. 167.

19. Jacques Lacan, *Écrits*, Paris: Seuil, p. 165, quoted in Dylan Evans, *An Introductory Dictionary of Lacanian Psychoanalysis*, London: Routledge 1996, p. 109.

20. Riviere, 'Womanliness as a Masquerade', pp. 217–18.

21. See ibid., for instance p. 212.

22. Jacques Lacan, 'The mirror stage as formative of the function of the I', *Écrits: A Selection*, trans. Alan Sheridan, London: Tavistock 1977, p. 2.

23. Riviere, 'Womanliness as a Masquerade', p. 210.

24. 'The reader may now ask how I define womanliness or where I draw the line between genuine womanliness and the "masquerade". My suggestion is not, however, that there is any such difference; whether radical or superficial, they are the same thing' (ibid., p. 213).

25. Judith Butler, *Gender Trouble: Feminism and the Subversion of Identity*, London and New York: Routledge 1990, p. 31.

26. See for instance the scene of shedding of glasses and other 'undesirable' features such as a bun and lace-up shoes by Bette Davis's character in *Now Voyager* (1942), discussed by Mary Ann Doane, 'Film and the Masquerade', in *Femmes Fatales: Feminism, Film Theory, Psychoanalysis*, London: Routledge 1991, pp. 26–7.

27. At another moment the protagonist's masquerade supersedes official evidence of identity: she throws down documents on the table during an interrogation in a performance of fury, and this helps her cause more than 'the best identity card and rubber stamps' (*The Journey*, 60).

28. Barbara Brook, *Feminist Perspectives on the Body*, Harlow: Longman 1999, p. 115.

29. Riviere, 'Womanliness as a Masquerade', pp. 212–13. See Pellegrini, *Performance Anxieties*, pp. 136–40, and Stephen Heath, 'Joan Riviere and the Masquerade', *Formations of Fantasy*, eds Victor Burgin *et al.*, London: Methuen 1986.

30. See Pellegrini, *Performance Anxieties*, p. 34. In his Holocaust cartoon *Maus* Art Spiegelman appears to try and evade both 'racial' and gendered stereotypes in drawing Jews as mice, and the character Anja's 'Jewish looks' are represented by a very long mouse-tail; but the tail's phallicism reveals the image's implicit reliance on gender signification and the male nature of Jewishness (Art Spiegelman, *Maus: A Survivor's Tale. My Father Bleeds History*, New York: Pantheon 1986, p. 136).

31. Sigmund Freud, *New Introductory Lectures on Psycho-analysis. The Standard Edition of the Complete Psychological Works of Sigmund Freud*, ed. James Strachey, London: Hogarth Press 1964, vol. XXII, p. 113.

32. Ludwig Hirschfeld, *Was nicht in Baedeker steht: Wien und Budapest* (Munich: Piper, 1927), quoted in Sander L. Gilman, *Freud, Race, and Gender*, Princeton, NJ: Princeton University Press 1993, p. 44.

33. Michael Rothberg, ' "We Were Talking Jewish": Art Spiegelman's *Maus* as "Holocaust" Production', *Contemporary Literature* 35(4), Winter 1994, pp. 661–87: 677. Gilman mentions the character Rebecka in Mynona's (Salomo Friedlaender) 1922 short story 'The Operated Goy', whose red-blond wig conceals the dark hair of true difference, both gendered and racial (*The Case of Sigmund Freud: Medicine and Identity at the Fin de Siècle*, Baltimore and London: Johns Hopkins University Press 1993, p. 41).

34. Andrzej Szczypiorski, *The Beautiful Mrs Seidenman*, trans. Klara Glowczewska, London: Orion Books 1996 [1986].

35. Ira Nadel, *Joyce and the Jews*, Basingstoke: Macmillan Press 1989, pp. 159, 160, 162, 168, 170, 171, and Bryan Cheyette, on the same and other episodes from James Joyce's work and life, *Constructions of 'The Jew' in English Literature and Society: Racial Representations, 1875–1945*, Cambridge: Cambridge University Press 1993, pp. 214–15, 226, 230–1. Many of the authors cited in Livia Bitton Jackson's *Madonna or Courtesan? The Jewish Woman in Christian Literature* (New York: Seabury Press 1982) mention Jewish women's eyes, see for instance pp. 23, 60, 81, 90, 94, 98, 115.

36. Cheyette quotes two extracts from George Bernard Shaw's novels, one on Jewish woman's eyes, one on a Jewish man's (*Constructions of 'The Jew'*, pp. 96, 97).

37. Gilman, *Freud, Race and Gender*, p. 74; see also Gilman on the 'gaze of the Jew', *The Case of Sigmund Freud*, pp. 42–64.

38. Nechama Tec, 'How Did We Survive?', in Alice L. Eckhardt, ed., *Burning Memory: Times of Testing and Reckoning*, Oxford: Pergamon Press 1993, p. 114. The mention of 'eyes' here is presumably synecdochic, or was seen so by those who did the 'recognizing', signifying what could only be *Jewish* sorrow. This is not to suggest that such synecdoche did not become infused with real meaning; Paulsson mentions Ringelblum's examples of 'cures' for sad eyes: 'one man …darted angry glances at everyone; others wore sunglasses' (*Secret City* p. 109).

39. Gilman, *The Case of Sigmund Freud*, p. 44.

40. Amy-Jill Levine argues that the term 'Jewess', as opposed to 'Jewish mother' or 'Jewish woman', suggests 'sexual desirability' and thus a 'sexual threat', and that the epithet 'exotic' used of her may shade into 'the primitive, and the atavistic' ('A Jewess, More and/or Less', in Peskowitz and Levitt, eds, *Judaism Since Gender*, p. 151). In *The Journey* the young women are precisely, to follow Rahel Levin Varnhagen's distinction about herself, Jewesses rather than Jewish (Levin Varnhagen says she was born a Jewess (*ein Jüdin*) rather than Jewish (*jüdisch*): quoted in Jay Geller, 'Circumcision and Jewish Women's Identity: The Failed Assimilation of Amy Levin Varnhagen', in Peskowitz and Levitt, eds, *Judaism Since Gender*, p. 175); this is not primarily for the sexualized reasons Levine cites, but because in *The Journey* the sisters' 'racial' identity is entirely inflected by their gender.

41. Sara Horowitz, 'Mengele, the Gynecologist, and Other Stories of Women's Survival', in Peskowitz and Levitt, eds, *Judaism Since Gender*, p. 208.

42. Levine, 'A Jewess, More and/or Less', p. 151; see also Julia Reinhard Lupton, '*Ethnos* and Circumcision in the Pauline Tradition: A Psychoanalytic Exegesis', in Lane, ed., *The Psychoanalysis of Race*, p. 195.

43. Gilman discusses 'the long history of describing the male Jew as having been born circumcised', *Freud, Race and Gender*, pp. 52–6; and notes that this sign of Jewish male difference is present 'even when the Jew is uncircumcised!', p. 74.

44. Paulsson, *Secret City*, p. 105.

45. Spiegelman, *Maus*, p. 140.

46. For instance, Solomon himself comments on the fact that his wanting to stay in touch with men of the Panzer Division he had known on the eastern front in 1941 could appear 'incomprehensible to someone who sees things from a one-dimensional perspective' (85). The two 'dimensions' which would avoid such a limited view are precisely those of Holocaust memoir and picaresque novel, as I will argue.

47. Mikhail Bakhtin, 'Forms of Time and Chronotope in the Novel', in *The Dialogic Imagination: Four Essays*, trans. Caryl Emerson and Michael Holquist, Austin: University of Texas Press 1981, p. 86.

48. Ibid., p. 85.

49. Karl Aloys Schenzinger, *Der Hitlerjunge Quex: Roman*, Berlin 1932.

50. Interestingly, in neither of his sexual encounters with women does Solomon mention fear of racial discovery. The Nazi woman who escorts him away from the eastern front ironically finds sexually alluring the signs of racial difference: 'she found my "beautiful pitch-black hair" especially seductive' (57). Solomon's girlfriend Leni remained in ignorance of his true identity until after the war (118), and no mention is made of particular ways in which she might have found it out. It is as if only transgressive sexuality threatens to reveal the racial truth.

51. There are of course also ways in which it does not fit Bakhtin's template, for instance in not involving a significant romantic element (see Bakhtin, 'Forms of Time and the Chronotope', pp. 87–8).

52. Ibid., p. 92, his italics.

53. Ibid., p. 93.

54. Ibid., p. 95.

55. 'The Jew Solly', as he calls himself (215), is the text's narrator in the present; usually, however, in this memoir it is the synchronic distinctions between Solomon and Jupp that are significant, rather than the diachronic ones between the teenage protagonist Solomon and the adult narrator Solly.

56. Bakhtin, 'Forms of Time and the Chronotope', p. 97.

57. Ibid., p. 97.

58. Jacques Lacan, 'Seminar on "The Purloined Letter" ', quoted in Sue Vice, ed., *Psychoanalytic Criticism: A Reader*, Cambridge: Polity Press 1996, p. 86.

59. Paulsson quotes examples of this phenomenon at opposite extremes: on the one hand, 'camouflage could backfire' in occupied Warsaw, according to a 'ghetto joke' quoted by Emanuel Ringelblum: ' "A Jew on the Aryan side can be recognized by a moustache, high boots, and a *Kennkarte*" ' (all signs of legitimate non-German identity); while on the other hand, a man who ' "looked like a whole synagogue" ' went about freely, apparently reasoning that 'no *smalcownik* [blackmailer] or police agent would believe that such a Jewish-looking Jew would dare to show his face' (*Secret City* p. 107).

60. See Barbara Johnson, 'The Frame of Reference: Poe, Lacan, Derrida', quoted in Vice, ed., *Psychoanalytic Criticism*, p. 87.

Present-time narration: the diaries of children and teenagers

1. There are some older studies (see P.A. Spalding, *Self-Harvest: A Study of Diaries and the Diarist*, London: Independent Press 1949; Alain Girard, *Le journal intime*, Paris: Presses Universitaires de France, 1963) and historically or generically specific ones (Harriet Blodgett, *Centuries of Female Days: Englishwomen's Private Diaries*, New Brunswick: Rutgers University Press 1988; Judy Simons, *Diaries and Journals of Literary Women from Fanny Burney to Virginia Woolf*, London: Macmillan 1990; and Ross Chambers, *Facing It: AIDS Diaries and the Death of the Author*, Ann Arbor: University of Michigan Press 1998 – thanks to Richard Canning for this reference).

2. See Valerie Raoul, *The French Fictional Journal: Fictional Narcissism/Narcissistic Fiction*, Toronto and London: University of Toronto Press 1980.

3. Philippe Lejeune observes that over fifteen years he published seven works on autobiography 'without ever paying the least attention to the genre of the journal' ('The Practice of the Private Journal', in Rachel Langford and Russell West, eds, *Marginal Voices, Marginal Forms: Diaries in European Literature and History*, Rodopi: Amsterdam and Atlanta, GA, 1999, p. 185).

4. Girard, *Le journal intime*, pp. 3–5, 7–13.

5. 'Introduction', Langford and West, eds, *Marginal Voices, Marginal Forms*, p. 6. Although Gerald Prince gives a list of the diary-novel's features, including 'intercalated narration' (incidents take place between entries) and an uncertain narratee, he argues that the only defining feature of the form is thematic: that of 'writing a diary and its concomitant themes and motifs', thus emphasizing the very practice of writing ('The Diary Novel: Notes for the Definition of a Sub-Genre', *Neophilologus* 59, 1975, pp. 477–81: 479).

6. Lawrence L. Langer, ed., *Art from the Ashes*, New York and Oxford: Oxford University Press 1995, p. 153.

7. Susan Rubin Suleiman, 'Diary as Narrative: Theory and Practice', in *The Search for a New Alphabet: Literary Studies in a Changing World, In Honor of Douwe Fokkema*, Amsterdam/Philadelphia: John Benjamins 1996, pp. 235–6, my italics.

8. Michael André Bernstein, *Foregone Conclusions: Against Apocalyptic History*, Berkeley and London: University of California Press 1994.

9. This does not stop later readers, including editors, viewing diaries with a backshadowing eye. Adelson does this in relation to Dawid Sierakowiak's treatment of the Nazi invasion of the Soviet Union (see n. 84), and cannot resist adding such a note to Dawid's entry for Tisha b'Av (24 July) 1939, on which he gave a talk in Hebrew on the Destruction of the First and Second Temples in Jerusalem: 'Four months after Dawid's campfire talk, the two monumental synagogues in his home city [Lódz] would be burned to rubble by the Nazis' (*The Diary of Dawid Sierakowiak: Five Notebooks from the Lódz Ghetto*, trans. Kamil Turowski, London: Bloomsbury 1997, p. 25; all further page references are in the text).

10. Ana Novac, *The Beautiful Days of My Youth: My Six Months in Auschwitz and Plaszow*, trans. George L. Newman, New York: Henry Holt 1997. All page references are in the text.

11. Hanno Loewy and Andrjez Bodek, eds, *'Les Vrais Riches' – Notizen am Rand: Ein Tagebuch aus dem Ghetto Lódz (Mai bis August 1944)*, trans. Esther Alexander-Ihme *et al.*, Leipzig: Reclam 1997; this German translation includes

a reproduction of the original handwritten text. I have transcribed here English-language entries with date of composition given in the text; translations from Hebrew, Yiddish and Polish entries are from Alexandra Zapruder, ed., *Salvaged Pages: Young Writers' Diaries of the Holocaust*, New Haven and London: Yale University Press 2002. I have transcribed the English-language entries in their original form wherever possible to preserve idiosyncratic grammar, spelling and punctuation.

12. Young argues that 'the [Holocaust] diarists' figures and narrative mythoi functioned as agents in their daily lives', not simply as means of recording fact (James E. Young, *Writing and Rewriting the Holocaust*, Bloomington and Indianapolis: Indiana University Press 1990, p. 36).

13. Exceptions include a chapter of Young's *Writing and Rewriting the Holocaust*; David Patterson's idiosyncratic study *Along the Edge of Annihilation: The Collapse and Recovery of Life in the Holocaust Diary*, Seattle and London: University of Washington Press 1999; and some contributions to Robert Moses Shapiro, ed., *Holocaust Chronicles: Individualizing the Holocaust through Diaries and Other Contemporaneous Personal Accounts*, New York: KTAV 1999.

14. Dina Porat estimates that there are extant 400 diaries, of which half are Polish ('Diaries of the Vilna Ghetto', in Shapiro, ed., *Holocaust Chronicles*, pp. 157–8); Daniel Grinberg mentions 300 diaries held in Warsaw ('Unpublished Diaries and Memoirs in the Archives of the Jewish Historical Institute in Poland', in ibid., p. 258). In their bibliography Marty Bloomberg and Buckley Barry Barrett list 18 published diaries (*The Jewish Holocaust: An Annotated Guide to Books in English*, San Bernardino, CA: Borgo Press 1991); Alexandra Zapruder names 66 'young diarists of the Holocaust' in Appendix I of *Salvaged Pages*; while Laurel Holliday includes a further eight in her anthology *Children's Wartime Diaries* (London: Piatkus 1995).

15. Anne Frank, *The Diary of a Young Girl*, Definitive Edition (ed. Otto H. Frank and Mirjam Pressler, trans. Susan Massotty, New York: Doubleday 1995 [1947]; all references in the text are to this edition).

16. Langer, ed., *Art from the Ashes*, p. 153.

17. Gérard Genette uses these terms to discuss the diary's division between historical (documentary) and subjective (testimony) record (*Paratexts: Thresholds of Intrepretation*, trans. Jane E. Lewin, CUP 1997 [1987], p. 395).

18. Grinberg, 'Unpublished Diaries', p. 260.

19. Nechama Tec, 'Diaries and Oral History: Reflections on Methodological Issues in Holocaust Research', in Shapiro, ed., *Holocaust Chronicles*, pp. 270–2.

20. Marian Turski, 'Individual Experience in Diaries from the Lódz Ghetto', in Shapiro, ed., *Holocaust Chronicles*, p. 119

21. Ibid., p. 159.

22. Grinberg, 'Unpublished Diaries', p. 264.

23. As well as Young, *Writing and Rewriting the Holocaust*, and, in more extreme vein, Patterson, *Along the Edge of Annihilation*, see David Roskies, 'Yiddish Writing in the Nazi Ghettos and the Art of the Incommensurable', *Modern Language Studies* 16(1), 1986, pp. 29–36.

24. Mary Berg, *Warsaw Ghetto: A Diary*, trans. Norbert Guterman, ed. S.L. Shneiderman, New York: L.B. Fisher 1945; all page references are in the text. Berg's name, Miriam Wattenberg, was shortened and Americanized

on publication of her diary partly to protect relatives left behind in Poland (see Susan Lee Pentlin's essay on Berg in S. Lillian Kremer, ed., *Holocaust Literature: An Encyclopedia of Writers and Their Work*, London and New York: Routledge 2003, p. 138).

25. Zapruder, ed., *Salvaged Pages*, p. 444.
26. S.L. Shneiderman, 'Preface' to Berg, *Warsaw Ghetto*, p. 9.
27. Thanks to Liz Stanley for this point.
28. Although the 1968 French translation was simply called, *J'ai quartorze ans à Auschwitz* (Paris: Julliard), as was a 1982 reprint (Paris: Presses de la Renaissance), the 1992 edition has the more stylized title *Les Beaux Jours de ma jeunesse* (Paris: Editions Balland 1992). All French quotations are from the 1982 edition.
29. Genette, *Paratexts*, p. 395. Genette uses the term 'paratext' to mean the 'accompanying productions' of a text, including a writer's journal.
30. Primo Levi, *The Voice of Memory: Interviews 1961–1987*, Marco Belpoliti and Robert Gordon, eds, Cambridge: Polity Press, 2001, p. 251.
31. Philippe Lejeune, *On Autobiography*, trans. Kathleen Leary, Minneapolis: University of Minnesota Press 1989, p. 58. Margaret-Anne Hutton argues that the majority of the French texts she discusses are written in the historic present (*French Women in the Nazi Camps: Testimonial Texts, forthcoming*), while Andrea Reiter notes the same of German testimonies (*Narrating the Holocaust*, trans. Patrick Camiller, London and New York: Continuum 2000, p. 153); paradoxically, use of the present tense in a diary, where events are very recently past, seems stranger than its use in these memoirs.
32. A Lagerkapo at Plaszow asks her, ' "By the way, how is your novel coming?" ' (138).
33. Anne Frank ends her entry for 11 July 1942 with, 'Someone's calling me' (*The Diary of a Young Girl* p. 27); once more, this moment marks the cross-over of conventional adolescent and Holocaust diary – Anne does have to observe the commands of adults, but as we know she is living in hiding we cannot be sure what their summons means.
34. The list is translated thus: 'Jew, detainee, whore, witch'.
35. Theresa I. Cahn, 'The Diary of an Adolescent Girl in the Ghetto: A Study of Age-Specific Reactions to the Holocaust'; *Psychoanalytic Review* 75(4), Winter 1988, pp. 589–617: p. 604.
36. The French version of this scene differs significantly from the English; Zimra simply tells the balladeer that Villon died some time ago immediately after her remark about 'Camp B' (*J'ai quartorze ans*, pp. 230–1).
37. Jean Améry, *At the Mind's Limits: Contemplations by a Survivor on Auschwitz and its Realities*, trans. Sidney and Stella P. Rosenfeld, Bloomington and Indianapolis: Indiana University Press 1980, p. 16.
38. The phrase is that of Judah Marton, editor of Heyman's diary, from his intro-duction (*The Diary of Éva Heyman*, trans. Moshe M. Kohn, New York: Shapolsky 1973, p. 7; all further page references are in the text).
39. It is on the basis of possible additions by Éva's mother that Zapruder does not include extracts from *The Diary of Éva Heyman* in her collection (see *Salvaged Pages*, pp. 445–6).
40. Victor Klemperer, *LTI: Notizbuch eines Philologen*, Leipzig: Reclam 1990, p. 301, cited by Suzanne zur Nieden, 'From the Forgotten Everyday-Life of Tyranny', in Langford and West, eds, *Marginal Voices, Marginal Forms*, p. 152.
41. See Lawrence L. Langer's foreword, p. vii.

42. See Adelson's introduction, p. 15.
43. Dawid's ironic comparisons of unseasonably good weather with bad political news are a refrain throughout his diary (see for instance pp. 169, 250, 256).
44. For instance, on 1 June 1941 Dawid wonders why such great numbers of troops and vehicles keep passing by the ghetto, and is answered in a footnote by Adelson: 'In three weeks Hitler would shock the world by declaring war on Russia' (97). Sierakowiak does mention the Nazi–Soviet conflict on the appropriate date, but Adelson's note shows that as readers of diaries, we cannot be expected to wait till the right moment for answers to such historical questions: in a sense destroying what is distinctive about reading such a text, and pushing it away from testimony towards documentary.
45. Yitskhok Rudashevski, *The Diary of the Vilna Ghetto*, trans. Percy Matenko, Israel: Ghetto Fighters' House 1973; all page references are in the text.
46. Victoria Stewart, 'Anne Frank and the Uncanny', *Paragraph* 24(1), March 2001, pp. 99–113: 111. Even Arnost Lustig's Holocaust diary-novel plays upon this gap between the diary's last entry and its author's unknown or unimaginable fate; rather than ending with the writer's death (as Raoul claims can be the only 'conclusion' to the fictional diary, *The French Fictional Journal*, p. 5) its final entry concerns Perla's knowledge of her impending deportation from Theresienstadt to Auschwitz: 'I am about to go where almost everyone else has gone', *The Unloved: From the Diary of Perla S.*, trans. Vera Kalina-Levine, Evanston, Illinois: Northwestern University Press 1996 [1979], p. 172.
47. See also Zapruder's discussion of this technique, *Salvaged Pages*, p. 193.
48. Mikhail Bakhtin, 'Forms of Time and of the Chronotope in the Novel', in *The Dialogic Imagination: Four Essays*, trans. Caryl Emerson and Michael Holquist, Austin, Texas: University of Austin Press 1981, p. 84.
49. Zapruder discusses the transformation of the Young Pioneers, a Soviet youth organization to which Yitskhok belonged, into the resistance movement which he referred to as the 'pioneer project'; but the liquidation of the ghetto prevented the group's members taking any action (*Salvaged Pages* pp. 195–6).
50. Haman's villainy is described in the Biblical Book of Esther, and is thought to date from some time between 480 and 590 BC. The vanquishing of Haman is a common trope in children's representations of the war; see a child's drawing of Haman on the gallows reproduced in Frederik van Gelder, 'Trauma and Society: Debate about psychological consequences of the Second World War in the Netherlands and Germany', *Forschung Frankfurt* September/October, 1971, p. 4. The '*Vrais Riches*' diarist also looks forward to 'the celebrating of our second Purim' (Zapruder, ed., *Salvaged Pages*, p. 393, entry for 31 July 1944 in Hebrew).
51. *Pace* Zapruder, who claims that the writer's gender is known 'only' from the 'masculine forms of verbs in Hebrew and Polish' (*Salvaged Pages*, p. 362).
52. This is a 'virtual' order as the pages of the diary itself are clearly unnumbered; it would consist of, for instance, noting the location of the first page of the boy's diary (on p. 3 of Coppée's novel). See the appendix, where I have listed this virtual sequence.
53. The sequence is interrupted between 35 and 37; 36 is missing either through error or because of a missing page. Coppée's page numbers are respectively 18 and 253.

54. Versions of some of the text appear in Adelson, *Lódz Ghetto*, most of it in Zapruder, ed., *Salvaged Pages*, and brief extracts in Holliday, ed., *Children's Diaries*.

55. It is often literally repetitive, marking not 'progess' but preoccupation, disbelief and rethinking. As Zapruder points out, the boy refers to the 7000 Jews sent to Chelmno 'no fewer than six times in six sequential entries written over the course of two days' (*Salvaged Pages*, p. 366), and then again in a seventh. In the diary's original form, these 'sequential' entries are in fact scattered over the text; indeed, Zapruder presumably only points out their sequential nature because of the scattered impression a reader of the orginal text would receive.

56. Of the deportation of the 7000 Jews in July, despite the war reaching its 'last minutes', the diarist remarks, 'They are "plein d'esprit" the German gentlemen ain't they?' (17 July 1944); and of the phrase 'modern Gettos' he singles out the word 'getto', 'There is no proper plural indicated in nonHitlerite grammar' (12 July 1944).

57. Langford and West, eds, *Marginal Voices, Marginal Forms*, p. 13.

58. 'You have the power with one word to make me the happiest of men'; p. 261 in Coppée's novel.

59. Entry in Polish, 3 July 1944, Zapruder, ed., *Salvaged Pages*, p. 377.

60. This central phrase is unclear in the original. Zapruder simply terms it 'illegible', while Loewy's edition of the text transcribes it as, 'Hitleria Kapta' – it appears, rather, to be ' "Hiteria kapta" ' – and translates it into the German phrase, 'hitlerische Kapitulation' (i.e. Hitler's capitulation).

61. Zapruder, *Salvaged Pages*, p. 376.

62. Abraham Katsch, introduction, *Scroll of Agony: The Warsaw Diary of Chaim A. Kaplan*, ed. and trans. Abraham I. Katsch, New York: Macmillan 1965, p. 14.

63. Lejeune, 'The Practice of the Private Journal', p. 189.

64. Yitzhok Niborski, 'Preface to the Yiddish Edition', Rozenberg, *Girl with Two Landscapes*, p. xi. On differing notions of the 'trace', see Paul Ricoeur, *Time and Narrative volume 3*, trans. K. Blamey and D. Pellauer, Chicago and London: Chicago University Press 1988, pp. 119–26; and, for the most similar usage to the present one, Robert Eaglestone, 'Identification and the Genre of Testimony', in Sue Vice, ed., *Representing the Holocaust: Essays in Honour of Bryan Burns*, London: Vallentine Mitchell 2003, p. 137.

65. Introduction to *The Diary of Dawid Rubinowicz*, trans. Derek Bowman, Washington: Creative Options 1982, p. x; all further page references are in the text.

66. Loewy, ' Saving the Child', p. 159.

67. Young, *Writing and Rewriting the Holocaust*, pp. 27–8. Revealingly, in his blurb for Moshe Flinker's diary, Aryeh Newman says exactly the opposite: 'The one [Anne] saw catastrophe, the other [Moshe] redemption.' In fact, the binary is less clear-cut than either Young or Newman suggests – Flinker sees the possibility of messianic redemption within catastrophe, while Frank comments at different times on people's innate 'goodness' but also on her wish to live in isolation from any other human – but the point remains that facts are not recorded or perceived by either diarist in a 'pure' form.

68. Ibid., p. 371, entry for 12 June 1944, in Yiddish.

69. Ibid., entry for 31 July 1944, in Hebrew.

70. Lawrence Rosenwald, *Emerson and the Art of the Diary*, New York: Oxford University Press 1988, p. 5, cited in ibid., p. 132.
71. Syrkin, 'Holocaust Diaries', p. 96.
72. Patterson claims such distinctiveness for the Holocaust diary, *Along the Edge of Annihilation*, p. 25.
73. Order in which the diary was written.
74. Order in which the diary is read.
75. All dates from 1944.
76. E = English, H = Hebrew, P = Polish, Y = Yiddish
77. In the German translation, Loewy and Bodek order these entries in reverse, as if the diarist had started writing at the bottom of the page.
78. Loewy and Bodek date this entry as 25 August 1944, which I think is a misreading.
79. Loewy and Bodek date this as '10.[?].7.44'; I think the date should be 20 July 1944.

Fragmentary narration

1. Dori Laub, 'Testimonies in the Treatment of Genocidal Trauma', *Journal of Applied Psychoanalytic Studies* 4(1), January 2002, pp. 63–87: 73.
2. Hedi Fried, *Fragments of a Life: The Road to Auschwitz* (trans. Michael Meyer, London: Robert Hale 1990); Hana Greenfield, *Fragments of Memory: From Kolin to Jerusalem* (Jerusalem and New York: Gefen 1998).
3. Marga Minco, *Bitter Herbs*, trans. Roy Edwards, Harmondsworth: Penguin 1991 [1957], all page references are in the text.
4. Shoshana Felman and Dori Laub, *Testimony: Crises of Witnessing in Literature, Psychoanalysis and History*, London and New York: Routledge 1992, p. 5.
5. Francine Christophe, *From a World Apart: A Little Girl in the Concentration Camps*, trans. Christine Burls, Lincoln, NE: University of Nebraska Press 2000 [1996]; Isabella Leitner and Irving A. Leitner, *Isabella: From Auschwitz to Freedom*, New York: Doubleday 1994 [1978, 1985]; Jona Oberski, *A Childhood: A Novella*, trans. Ralph Manheim, London: Hodder and Stoughton 1983 [1978]; Binjamin Wilkomirski, *Fragments: Memories of a Childhood, 1939–1948*, trans. Carol Brown Janeway, London: Picador 1996. Page references to all four works are in the text. I have chosen to discuss *Fragments* as a work of fiction throughout this chapter, although its genre is problematic because of its history (see the introduction).
6. The unnamed child in *A Childhood* seems to have been born in 1938, the same year as Oberski himself, and was therefore five when deported to Belsen; Wilkomirski's fictional Binjamin was, as the novel's subtitle emphasizes, born in 1939 and four when deported to Majdanek.
7. One might argue that it is the present-time childhood perception which is episodic, rather than adult memory, but even if this were true, it would be impossible to represent it in texts with an adult narrator. As Cathy Caruth points out in her introduction to *Trauma: Explorations in Memory* (Baltimore and London: Johns Hopkins University Press 1995), trauma consists not in the nature or distortion of an event, but 'in the *structure of its experience*' and the event's belated reception (p. 4): these two features characterize the texts

discussed here, which are 'structured' in fragments and narratable only in adulthood.

8. The term is Gérard Genette's, used to refer to any difference between the time of the plot and that of the story; see his *Narrative Discourse*, Ithaca: Cornell University Press 1980, pp. 77–182.

9. Jonathan Kozol, 'Children of the Camps: Review of *Fragments* by Binjamin Wilkomirski', *The Nation*, 28 October 1996.

10. Gérard Genette, *Paratexts: Thresholds of Interpretation*, trans. Jane E. Lewin, CUP 1997 [1987], p. 395.

11. Indeed, the term appears *passim* in historical, testimonial, psychological and critical Holocaust literature; see for instance Jane Marks, *The Hidden Children: The Secret Survivors of the Holocaust*, London: Bantam 1995, p. xxv; Robert Krell, 'Reverberations of the Holocaust in Survivor Families', in Krell, ed., *Memories and Messages: Reflections on Child Survivors of the Holocaust*, Vancouver: Memory Press 1999, p. 25; Robert Krell, 'Hiding During and After the War', in ibid., pp. 34, 36; Sarah Moskovitz and Robert Krell, 'Child survivors of the Holocaust: Psychological adaptations to survival', *Israel Journal of Psychiatry and Related Services*, 27(2), 1990, pp. 81–91: 89; Ruth Kluger, *Landscapes of Memory: A Holocaust Girlhood Remembered*, London: Bloomsbury 2003, p. 33; W.G. Sebald, *Austerlitz*, trans. Anthea Bell, London: Hamish Hamilton 2001, p. 200.

12. Laub, 'Testimonies in the Treatment of Genocidal Trauma', p. 63.

13. The relations between the Holocaust and postmodernism are discussed by, among others, Jean-François Lyotard, *The Differend: Phrases in Dispute*, trans. Georges Van Den Abbeele, Minneapolis: University of Minnesota Press 1988; Ann Parry, 'The caesura of the Holocaust in Martin Amis's *Time's Arrow* and Bernhard Schlink's *The Reader*', *European Studies* xxix 1999, pp. 249–67; and Elizabeth Bellamy, *Affective Genealogies: Psychoanalysis, Postmodernism, and the 'Jewish Question' after Auschwitz*, Lincoln and London: University of Nebraska Press 1997.

14. Dori Laub and Nanette C. Auerhahn, 'Knowing and Not Knowing Massive Psychic Trauma: Forms of Traumatic Memory', *International Journal of Psycho-Analysis* 74, 1993, pp. 287–302: 290.

15. Jean-François Lyotard, *The Postmodern Condition: A Report on Knowledge*, p. 37. Lyotard mentions the role of the Second World War in hastening 'the decline of narrative' (ibid.).

16. David Harvey, *The Condition of Postmodernity*, Oxford: Blackwell 1989, p. 45.

17. Lyotard, *The Postmodern Condition*, p. 81.

18. This is Henry Raczymow's phrase, from 'Memory Shot Through with Holes', *Yale French Studies* 85, 1994, pp. 98–105, about his third-generation Polish ancestry. There are of course Holocaust works, usually novels, which are recognizably postmodern in denying 'the solace of good forms ... to impart a stronger sense of the unpresentable' (Lyotard, *The Postmodern Condition*, p. 81). Parry's example of Amis's *Time's Arrow* ('The caesura of the Holocaust') seems paradigmatic; although it might offer some formal 'solace', this does not derive from high modernist 'consistency': rather, *Time's Arrow* owes a formal debt to Philip K. Dick's science fiction and works of popular history (see the chapter on *Time's Arrow* in my *Holocaust Fiction*, London: Routledge 2000).

19. The French original is entitled *Une Petite fille privilégiée: Une Enfant dans le monde des camps, 1942–1945* (Paris: Éditions L'Harmattan 1996). The title

refers – both ironically and accurately – to Francine's and her mother's 'privileged' status in Bergen-Belsen as the family of a French prisoner of war. As the older Francine points out, 'Someone said that when your name is CHRISTOPHE, you don't need to declare yourself as a Jew, but Mother replies that she has always obeyed the law' (14).

20. Philippe Lejeune, 'W or the Memory of Childhood', *Review of Contemporary Fiction* 13(1) 1993, pp. 86–97: 97.

21. Paul Valent, 'Child Survivors: A Review', in Judith S. Kestenberg and Charlotte Kahn, eds, *Children Surviving Persecution: An International Study of Trauma and Healing*, Westport, CT and London: Praeger 1998, p. 111.

22. The two original volumes are *Fragments of Isabella*, ed. and with an epilogue by Irving A. Leitner, London: New English Library 1980; *Saving the Fragments* by Isabella Leitner with Irving A. Leitner, introduced by Howard Fast, New York: New American Library 1985; some new 'fragments' have been added to *Isabella*, the last one of which is entitled 'Fear', emphasizing the traumatic past's persistence even in the context of American 'freedom' (see Adrienne Kertzer, *My Mother's Voice: Children, Literature, and the Holocaust*, Ontario: Broadview Press 2002, pp. 87, 93).

23. Laub, 'Testimonies in the Treatment of Genocidal Trauma', p. 64.

24. Dori Laub, 'Truth and Testimony: The Process and the Struggle', in Caruth, ed., *Trauma*, p. 66.

25. Ibid., p. 71.

26. Jean Laplanche and J.B. Pontalis describe a 'defence' as a 'group of operations *aimed at* the reduction and elimination of any change liable to threaten the integrity and stability of the bio-psychological individual' (*The Language of Psychoanalysis*, trans. Donald Nicholson-Smith, London: Karnac 1988, p. 103).

27. Despite the ambiguous tone of this apostrophe – 'May you rest in peace' sounds like an epitaph, the reference to Romeo and Juliet suggests doomed love – Leitner's sister did marry her 'Romeo'. *Isabella* contains other citations which bolster its literariness, for instance, 'tread gently as you pass me by' (10), apparently a reference to W. B. Yeats's line 'Tread softly because you tread on my dreams', from his poem 'He wishes for the cloths of heaven'; and a quotation from *Macbeth* (205).

28. The same disordered narration occurs in Art Spiegelman's *Maus*; despite his son's urgings to keep the narrative 'straight', Vladek does narrate events at the moment they happened rather than when he found out about them – for instance the death of his son Richieu (Art Spiegelman, *Maus: A Survivor's Tale: My Father Bleeds History*, Harmondsworth: Penguin 1986, p. 108).

29. A less coherently fragmentary text could represent this collision of chronology and memory more effectively; see for instance Alina Bacall-Zwirn and Jared Stark, *No Common Place: The Holocaust Testimony of Alina Bacall-Zwirn* (Lincoln and London: University of Nebraska Press, 1999), in which a chronology is fashioned out of accounts given at different times. Here, there is a radical disjunction between the singular story of Bacall-Zwirn's experiences and the repeated plot of her narration. However, the disorder is that of the interviewer, Stark, and not the survivor, Bacall-Zwirn.

30. Valent, 'Child Survivors', p. 114.

31. During the Nazi occupation the theatre was renamed 'Joodsche Schouwberg' (Jewish Theatre) and limited to Jewish productions for Jewish audiences; from

summer 1942 it was requisitioned as an assembly-point. From Westerbork, prisoners were sent by train to one of several concentration- or death-camps.

32. The family leave Westerbork in 'Assembly' (38–43), for a camp with barbed wire and watchtowers (61–2); the camp is only named as 'Bergen-Belsen' by the boy when he and his mother leave (85).

33. Viktor Shklovsky, 'Sterne's *Tristram Shandy*: Stylistic Commentary', in *Russian Formalist Criticism: Four Essays*, trans. and eds Lee T. Lemon and Marion J. Reis, Lincoln and London: University of Nebraska Press 1965, p. 31.

34. See Blake Eskin, *A Life in Pieces: The Making and Unmaking of Binjamin Wilkomirski*, New York: Norton 2002; Philip Gourevitch, 'The Memory Thief', *New Yorker*, 14 June 1999, pp. 48–68; and Elena Lappin, 'The Man with Two Heads', *Granta* 66 (Summer 1999), pp. 7–65.

35. See, respectively, Mary Jacobus, 'Border Crossings: Traumatic Reading and Holocaust Memory', in her *Psychoanalysis and the Scene of Reading*, Oxford: Oxford University Press 1999; and Stefan Maechler, *The Wilkomirski Affair: A Study in Biographical Truth*, trans. John E. Woods, New York: Schocken 2001.

36. As Andrea Reiter points out, this double-voiced effect exists only in the English translation. In the German original, the word 'Erwachsener' means simply 'adult' perspective (personal communication, 30 October 2003).

37. Mark Pendergrast cast doubt on the authenticity of *Fragments*, before Ganzfried's exposé, arguing that recall in the form of 'exact snapshots' suggested that these 'memories' were in fact 'delusions, created either alone or with the help of psychotherapy' ('Recovered Memories and the Holocaust', http://stopbadtherapy.com/experts/fragments/fragments.html).

38. On several occasions the child's eyes are dazzled on emerging from a hiding-place or prison into daylight, as if figuring his inability to 'see' what has happened (42, 48, 64).

39. See Walter Benjamin, 'The Work of Art in the Age of Mechanical Reproduction', *Illuminations*, trans. Harry Zohn, London: Fontana 1970.

40. Various critics have suggested intertextual sources for *Fragments*. Maechler, in *The Wilkomirski Affair*, mentions Jerzy Kosinski's novel *The Painted Bird*. Sue Vice, 'Binjamin Wilkomirski's *Fragments* and Holocaust Envy: "Why wasn't I there too?" ', in her edited volume *Representing the Holocaust: Essays in Honour of Bryan Burns*, London: Vallentine Mitchell 2003, cites Thomas Geve's *Guns and Barbed Wire: A Child Survives the Holocaust* (Chicago 1987 [1958]); and Carl Friedman's *Nightfather: A Novel*, trans. Arnold and Erica Pomerans, New York: Persea Books 1994 [1991]). It seems likely that Doessekker was influenced by details from Oberski's *A Childhood* itself, and Jeroen Brouwers' first-person novel about a six-year-old boy in a Japanese prisoner-of-war camp, *Sunken Red* (trans. Adrienne Dixon, New York: New Amsterdam 1988 [1981]) – thanks to Nigel Clark for this reference.

41. Quoted in Harvey, *The Condition of Postmodernity*, p. 82.

42. Dorota Glowacka says the following of *Fragments*, although, as I have argued, the opposite is in fact the case: 'the fragment foregrounds the process of recollecting...and it incessantly cancels out its own promise that this memory can be perfected and fulfilled' ('The Shattered Word: Writing of the Fragment and Holocaust Testimony', in F.C. DeCoste and Bernard Schwartz, eds, *The Holocaust's Ghost: Writings on Art, Politics, Law and Education*, Alberta: The University of Alberta Press 2000, p. 51). While this may be true

of Leitner's *Isabella*, which Glowacka also discusses, she seems to forget that *Fragments* is not a factual testimony (p. 48).

43. Harvey, *The Condition of Postmodernity*, p. 59.
44. Quoted in Eskin, *A Life in Pieces*, p. 230.
45. Ida Fink, *A Scrap of Time and Other Stories*, trans. Madeline Levine and Francine Prose, New York: Schocken Books 1987; *Traces: Stories*, trans. Philip Boehm and Francine Prose, New York: Henry Holt 1997.
46. Cathy Caruth, *Unclaimed Experience: Trauma, Narrative and History*, Baltimore and London: Johns Hopkins University Press 1996, p. 7.
47. Gilles Deleuze, cited in Jean-François Lyotard, *Heidegger and 'the Jews'*, trans. Andreas Michel and Mark S. Roberts, Minneapolis and London: University of Minnesota Press 1990, p. 12.

Conclusion

1. W.G. Sebald, *Austerlitz*, trans. Anthea Bell, London: Hamish Hamilton 2001; all page references are in the text.
2. Jean Améry, *At the Mind's Limits: Contemplations by a Survivor on Auschwitz and its Realities*, trans. Sidney and Stella P. Rosenfeld, Bloomington and Indianapolis: Indiana University Press 1980; Dan Jacobson, *Heshel's Kingdom*, London: Hamish Hamilton 1998.
3. See Geoffrey Hartman, *Scars of the Spirit: The Struggle Against Inauthenticity*, Basingstoke: Palgrave Macmillan 2002, p. 79.
4. W.G. Sebald, *The Emigrants*, trans. Michael Hulse, London: Harvill 1996 [1993].
5. See Michiko Kakutani's complaint about the 'gratuitous device of the narrator' in *Austerlitz* ('Life in a No Man's Land of Memory and Loss', *New York Times*, 27 October 2001: E 40).
6. Maya Jaggi, interview with W.G. Sebald, 'The last word', the *Guardian*, 21 December 2001, p. 5.
7. Jaggi, 'The last word', p. 4; see Jeremy Josephs with Susi Bechhofer, *Rosa's Child: The True Story of One Woman's Quest for a Lost Mother and a Vanished Past*, London: I.B. Tauris 1996; *Whatever Happened to Susi*, BBC 2.
8. Saul Friedländer, *When Memory Comes*, trans. Helen R. Lane, New York: Farrar Straus Giroux 1979, p. 52.
9. Georges Perec, *W or the Memory of Childhood*, trans. David Bellos, London: Harvill 1996 [1975], p. 54.
10. David Bellos, *Georges Perec: A Life in Words*, London: Harvill 1995, pp. 58, 547.
11. Perec, *W*, p. 80.
12. On this point in relation to *The Emigrants*, see Katharina Hall, 'Jewish Memory in Exile: The Relation of W.G. Sebald's *Die Ausgwanderten* to the Tradition of the Yizkhor Books', in Pól O'Dochartaigh, ed., *Jews in German Literature Since 1945: German-Jewish Literature*, Amsterdam and Atlanta: Rodopi 2000.
13. Friedländer, *When Memory Comes*, pp. 155–6.

Bibliography

Diaries

Berg, Mary, *Warsaw Ghetto: A Diary*, trans. Norbert Guterman, New York: L.B. Fisher 1945.

Flinker, Moshe, *Young Moshe's Diary: The Spiritual Torment of a Jewish Boy in Nazi Europe*, trans. unnamed, Jerusalem: Yad Vashem 1971 [1958].

Frank, Anne, *The Diary of a Young Girl*, Definitive Edition eds Otto H. Frank and Mirjam Pressler, trans. Susan Massotty, New York: Doubleday 1995 [1947].

Heyman, Éva, *The Diary of Éva Heyman*, trans. Moshe M. Kohn, New York: Shapolsky 1973.

Holliday, Laurel, ed., *Children in the Holocaust and World War II: Their Secret Diaries*, London: Piatkus 1996.

Loewy, Hanno and Andrjez Bodek, eds, *'Les Vrais Riches' – Notizen am Rand: Ein Tagebuch aus dem Ghetto Lódz (Mai bis August 1944)*, trans. Esther Alexander-Ihme *et al.*, Leipzig: Reclam 1997.

Novac, Ana, *The Beautiful Days of My Youth: My Six Months in Auschwitz and Plaszów*, trans. George L. Newman, New York: Henry Holt 1997.

Rozenberg, Lena Jedwab, *Girl with Two Landscapes: The Wartime Diary of Lena Jedwab, 1941–1945*, trans. Solon Beinfeld, New York: Holmes and Meier 2002.

Rubinowicz, Dawid, *The Diary of Dawid Rubinowicz*, trans. Derek Bowman, Washington: Creative Options 1982.

Rudashevski, Yitskhok, *The Diary of the Vilna Ghetto*, trans. Percy Matenko, Israel: Ghetto Fighters' House 1973.

Sierakowiak, Dawid, *The Diary of Dawid Sierakowiak: Five Notebooks from the Lódz Ghetto*, trans. Kamil Turowski, London: Bloomsbury 1997.

Zapruder, Alexandra, ed., *Salvaged Pages: Young Writers' Diaries of the Holocaust*, New Haven and London: Yale University Press 2002.

Memoir and testimony

Breznitz, Shlomo, *Memory Fields: The Legacy of a Wartime Childhood in Czechoslovakia*, New York: Alfred A. Knopf 1993.

Brostoff, Anita, ed., with Sheila Chamovitz, *Flares of Memory: Stories of Childwood During the Holocaust*, Oxford and New York: Oxford University Press 2001.

Christophe, Francine, *From a World Apart: A Little Girl in the Concentration Camps*, trans. Christine Burls, Lincoln and London: University of Nebraska Press 2000 [1996].

David, Janina, *A Square of Sky: Memoirs of a Wartime Childhood*, London: Eland 1992 [1964].

Dubner, Stephen J., *Turbulent Souls: A Catholic Son's Return to His Jewish Family*, New York: Avon Books 1998.

Durlacher, Gerhard, *Drowning: Growing Up in the Third Reich*, trans. Susan Massotty, London: Serpent's Tail 1993.

——, *The Search: The Birkenau Boys*, trans. Susan Massotty, London: Serpent's Tail 1998.

Edvardson, Cordelia, *The Burned Child Seeks the Fire: A Memoir*, trans. Joel Agee, Boston: Beacon Press 1997 [1984].

Fersen-Osten, Renée, *Don't They Know the World Stopped Breathing? Reminiscences of a French Child During the Holocaust Years*, New York: Shapolsky Publishers 1991.

Friedländer, Saul, *When Memory Comes*, trans. Helen R. Lane, New York: Farrar Straus Giroux 1979.

Geve, Thomas, *Guns and Barbed Wire: A Child Survives the Holocaust*, Chicago: Academy Press 1987 [1958].

Hemmendinger, Judith, *Survivors: Children of the Holocaust*, Bethesda, MD: National Press Inc. 1986.

Iglinski-Goodman, Leah, *For Love of Life*, London: Vallentine Mitchell 2002.

Kisliuk, Ingrid, *Unveiled Shadows: The Witness of a Child*, Newton, MA: Nanomir Press 1998.

Kluger, Ruth, *Landscapes of Memory: A Holocaust Girlhood Remembered*, London: Bloomsbury 2003.

Kofman, Sarah, *Rue Ordener, Rue Labat*, trans. Ann Smock, Lincoln and London: University of Nebraska Press 1996.

Leitner, Isabella and Irving A. Leitner, *Isabella: From Auschwitz to Freedom*, New York: Doubleday 1994 [1978, 1985].

Lobel, Anita, *No Pretty Pictures: A Child of War*, New York: Greenwillow Books 1998.

Morhange-Bégué, Claude, *Chamberet: Recollections from an Ordinary Childhood*, trans. Austryn Wainhouse, Evanston, Illinois: Northwestern University Press 2000 [1987].

Perel, Solomon, *Europa, Europa*, trans. Margot Bettauer Dembo, New York: John Wiley 1997.

Samson, Naomi, *Hide: A Child's View of the Holocaust*, Lincoln and London: Nebraska University Press 2000.

Spiegelman, Art, *Maus: A Survivor's Tale. My Father Bleeds History*, New York: Pantheon 1986.

—— *Maus: A Survivor's Tale. And Here My Troubles Began*, New York: Pantheon 1991.

Walker, Fay and Leo Rosen, with Caren S. Neile, *Hidden: A Sister and Brother in Nazi Poland*, Wisconsin: University of Wisconsin Press 2002.

Wiesel, Elie, *Night*, trans. Stella Rodway, London: Fontana 1972 [1958].

Winter, Miriam, *Trains: A Memoir of a Hidden Childhood Before and After World War II*, Jackson, Michigan: Kelton Press 1997.

Interviews and oral history

Eisenberg, Azriel, *The Lost Generation: Children in the Holocaust*, New York: Pilgrim Press 1982.

Fisher, Josey, ed., *The Persistence of Youth: Oral Testimonies of the Holocaust*, New York: Greenwood Press 1991.

Gershon, Karen, *Postscript: A Collective Account of the Lives of Jews in West Germany Since the Second World War*, London: Victor Gollancz 1969.

—— ed., *We Came as Children: A Collective Autobiography*, New York: Harcourt, Brace and World 1966.

Grudzinska-Gross, Irena and Jan Tomasz Gross, eds and compilers, *War Through Children's Eyes: The Soviet Occupation of Poland and the Deportations, 1939–1941*, trans. Ronald Strom and Dan Rivers, Stanford: Hoover Institution Press 1981.

Grynberg, Henryk, ed., *Children of Zion*, trans. Jacqueline Mitchell, Evanston, Illinois: Northwestern University Press 1997.

Harris, Mark Jonathan and Deborah Oppenheimer, eds, *Into the Arms of Strangers: Stories of the Kindertransport*, London: Bloomsbury 2000.

Leverton, Bertha and Shmuel Lowensohn, eds, *I Came Alone: The Stories of the Kindertransports*, Sussex: The Book Guild 1996.

Marks, Jane, *The Hidden Children: The Secret Survivors of the Holocaust*, London: Bantam 1995.

Vegh, Claudine, ed., *I Didn't Say Goodbye*, trans. Ros Schwartz, London: Caliban Books 1984.

Wasilewska, Irena, *Suffer Little Children*, London: Maxlove Publishing 1946.

Fiction

Asscher-Pinkhof, Clara, *Star Children*, trans. Terese Edelstein and Inez Smith, Detroit: Wayne State University Press 1986 [1946].

Begley, Louis, *Wartime Lies*, London: Picador 1991.

Federman, Raymond, *The Voice in the Closet/ La Voix dans le Cabinet de Débarras*, Madison: Coda Press 1979.

Fink, Ida, *The Journey*, trans. Joanna Wechsler and Francine Prose, Harmondsworth: Penguin 1992.

Gille, Elisabeth, *Shadows of a Childhood: A Novel of War and Friendship*, trans. Linda Coverdale, New York: New Press 1996.

Grynberg, Henryk, *Child of the Shadows*, including *The Grave*, trans. Celina Wieniewska, London: Vallentine Mitchell 1969.

——, *The Victory*, trans. Richard Lourie, Evanston, Illinois: Northwestern University Press 1993 [1969].

Lustig, Arnost, *The Unloved: From the Diary of Perla S.*, trans. Vera Kalina-Levine, Evanston, Illinois: Northwestern University Press 1996 [1979].

Manea, Norman, *October Eight O'Clock*, trans. Cornelia Golna *et al.*, London: Quartet 1993.

Minco, Marga, *Bitter Herbs*, trans. Roy Edwards, Harmondsworth: Penguin 1991 [1957].

Nyiri, János, *Battlefields and Playgrounds*, trans. William Brandon and János Nyiri, Hanover and London: University Press of New England/Brandeis University Press 1994 [1989].

Oberski, Jona, *A Childhood: A Novella*, trans. Ralph Manheim, London: Hodder and Stoughton 1983 [1978].

Perec, Georges, *W or the Memory of Childhood*, trans. David Bellos, London: Harvill 1988 [1975].

Roth-Hano, Renée, *Touch Wood: A Girlhood in Occupied France*, New York: Four Winds Press 1988.

Sebald, W.G., *Austerlitz*, trans. Anthea Bell, London: Hamish Hamilton 2001.

Weinstein, Frida Scheps, *A Hidden Childhood: A Jewish Girl's Sanctuary in a French Convent, 1942–1945*, trans. Barbara Loeb Kennedy, New York: Hill and Wang 1985.

Wilkomirski, Binjamin, *Fragments: Memories of a Childhood, 1939–1948*, trans. Carol Brown Janeway, London: Picador 1996.

Wojdowski, Bogdan, *Bread for the Departed*, trans. Madeline G. Levine, Evanston, Illinois: Northwestern University Press 1997 [1971].

History

Adelson, Alan and Robert Lapides, compilers and eds, *Lódz Ghetto: From a Community Under Siege*, Harmondsworth: Penguin 1989.

Bentwich, Norman, *They Found Refuge: An Account of British Jewry's Work for Victims of Nazi Oppression*, London: The Cresset Press 1956.

Berghahn, Marion, *Continental Britons: German-Jewish Refugees from Nazi Germany*, Oxford: Berg Publishers 1988.

Dwork, Debórah, *Children with a Star: Jewish Youth in Nazi Europe*, New Haven and London: Yale University Press 1991.

Endelman, Todd, *Radical Assimilation in English Jewish History 1656–1945*, Bloomington and Indianapolis: Indiana University Press 1990.

Klarsfeld, Serge *et al.*, eds, *French Children of the Holocaust: A Memorial*, New York: New York University Press 1996.

Lattek, Christine, 'Bergen-Belsen: From "Privileged" Camp to Death Camp', *Journal of Holocaust Education* 5(2&3), Autumn/Winter 1996, pp. 37–71.

Lukas, Richard C., *Did the Children Cry? Hitler's War Against Jewish and Polish Children, 1939–1945*, New York: Hippocrene Books 1994.

Paulsson, Gunnar, *Secret City: The Hidden Jews of Warsaw 1940–1945*, New Haven and London: Yale University Press 2002.

Reilly, Joanne, *Belsen: The Liberation of a Concentration Camp*, London and New York: Routledge 1998.

Sosnowski, Kiryl, *The Tragedy of Children Under Nazi Rule*, Poznan/Warsaw: Zachodnia Agencja Prasowa 1962.

Tec, Nechama, *Resilience and Courage: Women, Men, and the Holocaust*, New Haven and London: Yale University Press 2003.

Turner, Barry, *And the Policeman Smiled*, London: Bloomsbury 1990.

Wasserstein, Bernard, *Britain and the Jews of Europe 1939–1945*, London: Institute of Jewish Affairs/Oxford: Clarendon Press 1979.

Psychology and psychoanalysis

Cahn, Theresa I., 'The Diary of an Adolescent Girl in the Ghetto: A Study of Age-Specific Reactions to the Holocaust', *Psychoanalytic Review* 75(4), Winter 1988, pp. 589–617.

Felman, Shoshana and Dori Laub, *Testimony: Crises of Witnessing in Literature, Psychoanalysis and History*, London and New York: Routledge 1992, p. 5..

Freud, Sigmund, *The Standard Edition of the Complete Psychological Works of Sigmund Freud*, trans. James Strachey, London: Hogarth Press and Institute of Psycho-Analysis, 1953–74..

Gampel, Yolanda, 'I Was a Shoah Child', *British Journal of Psychotherapy* 8(4), 1992, pp. 391–400.

Hogman, Flora, 'The Experience of Catholicism for Jewish Children During World War II', *Psychoanalytic Review* 75(4), Winter 1988, pp. 511–32.

Keilson, Hans, *Sequential Traumatization in Children: A clinical and statistical follow-up of the Jewish war orphans in the Netherlands*, with the collaboration of Herman R. Sarphatie, trans. Yvonne Bearne, Hilary Coleman and Deirdre Winter, Jerusalem: The Magnes Press 1992.

Kestenberg, Judith S., Flora Hogman, Milton Kestenberg and Eva Fogelman, 'Jewish–Christian Relationships as Seen Through the Eyes of Children, Before, During and After the Holocaust', in Yehuda Bauer *et al.*, eds, *Remembering for the Future: Working Papers and Addenda. Volume 1. Jews and Christians During and After the Holocaust*, Oxford: Pergamon 1989.

—— and Charlotte Kahn, eds, *Children Surviving Persecution: An International Study of Trauma and Healing*, Westport, CT and London: Praeger 1998.

Krell, Robert, ed., *Memories and Messages: Reflections on Child Survivors of the Holocaust*, Vancouver: Memory Press 1999.

Kristeva, Julia, *Powers of Horror: An Essay on Abjection*, trans. Leon L. Roudiez, New York: Columbia University Press 1984.

Lacan, Jacques, *Écrits: A Selection*, trans. Alan Sheridan, London: Tavistock 1977.

Lane, Christopher, ed., *The Psychoanalysis of Race*, New York: Columbia University Press 1998.

Laplanche, Jean, *Life and Death in Psychoanalysis*, trans. Jeffrey Mehlman, Baltimore: Johns Hopkins University Press 1976.

—— and J.-B. Pontalis, *The Language of Psychoanalysis*, trans. Donald Nicholson-Smith, London: Karnac 1988.

Laub, Dori, 'Testimonies in the Treatment of Genocidal Trauma', *Journal of Applied Psychoanalytic Studies* 4(1), January 2002, pp. 63–87.

—— and Nanette C. Auerhahn, 'Knowing and Not Knowing Massive Psychic Trauma: Forms of Traumatic Memory', *International Journal of Psycho-Analysis* 74, 1993, pp. 287–302.

Luel, Steven A. and Paul Marcus, eds, *Psychoanalytic Reflections on the Holcaust: Selected Essays*, New York: KTAV 1984.

Ostow, Mortimer, 'The Psychological Determinants of Jewish Identity', in Mortimer Ostow, ed., *Judaism and Psychoanalysis*, New York: KTAV 1982.

Psychoanalytic Review, special issue 'Child Survivors of the Holocaust', 75(4), Winter 1988.

Riviere, Joan, 'Womanliness as a Masquerade', in H. Ruitenbeeck, ed., *Female Sexuality*, New Haven: College and UP 1963 [1929].

Rustow, Margrit Wreschner, 'From Jew to Catholic – and Back: Psychodynamics of Child Survivors', in Paul Marcus and Alan Rosenberg, eds, *Healing Their Wounds: Psychotherapy with Holocaust Survivors and Their Families*, New York, Westport and London: Praeger 1989.

Santner, Eric, *My Own Private Germany: Daniel Paul Schreber's Secret History of Modernity*, Princeton, NJ and London: Princeton University Press, 1996.

Literary and cultural criticism

Astro, Alan, 'Allegory in Georges Perec's *W ou le souvenir d'enfance*', *Modern Language Notes* 102(4), September 1987, pp. 867–76.

Bakhtin, Mikhail, *The Dialogic Imagination: Four Essays*, trans. Caryl Emerson and Michael Holquist, Austin, Texas: University of Austin Press 1981.

——, *Problems of Dostoevsky's Poetics*, trans. Caryl Emerson, Minneapolis: University of Minnesota Press 1984.

Bellos, David, *Georges Perec: A Life in Words*, London: Harvill 1995.

Berger, Alan L., 'Jewish Identity and Jewish Destiny, the Holocaust in Refugee Writing: Lore Segal and Karen Gershon', *Studies in American Jewish Literature* 11(1), 1992, pp. 83–95.

Bernard-Donals, Michael, 'The Rhetoric of Disaster and the Imperative of Writing', *Rhetoric Society Quarterly*, Winter 2001, pp. 49–94.

Bernstein, Michael André, *Foregone Conclusions: Against Apocalyptic History*, Berkeley and London: University of California Press 1994.

Bosmajian, Hamida, *Sparing the Child: Grief and the Unspeakable in Youth Literature about Nazism and the Holocaust*, New York and London: Routledge.

Caruth, Cathy, ed., *Trauma: Explorations in Memory*, Baltimore and London: Johns Hopkins University Press 1995.

——, *Unclaimed Experience: Trauma, Narrative, and History*, Baltimore and London: Johns Hopkins University Press 1996.

Cheyette, Bryan and Laura Marcus, eds, *Modernity, Culture and "the Jew"*, Cambridge: Polity Press 1998.

Douglas, Lawrence, 'Wartime Lies: Securing the Holocaust in Law and Literature', *Yale Journal of Law & the Humanities* 7(45), pp. 45–73.

Eskin, Blake, *A Life in Pieces: The Making and Unmaking of Binjamin Wilkomirski*, New York: Norton 2002.

Espen, Hal, 'The Lives of Louis Begley', *New Yorker*, 30 May 1994, pp. 38–46.

Ezrahi, Sidra DeKoven, 'See Under: Memory: Reflections on *When Memory Comes*', *History and Memory* 9 (1 & 2), Fall 1997, pp. 364–75.

Fine, Ellen S., 'Transmission of Memory: The Post-Holocaust Generation in the Diaspora', in Efraim Sicher, ed., *Breaking the Crystal: Writing and Memory after Auschwitz*, Urbana and Chicago: University of Illinois Press 1998.

Finkelstein, Norman, *The Holocaust Industry*, London: Verso 2000.

Friedländer, Saul, ed., *Probing the Limits of Representation: Nazism and the 'Final Solution'*, Cambridge, MA: Harvard University Press 1992.

Genette, Gérard, *Paratexts: Thresholds of Intrepretation*, trans. Jane E. Lewin, Cambridge: Cambridge University Press 1997 [1987].

Geras, Norman, *The Contract of Mutual Indifference: Political Philosophy after the Holocaust*, London: Verso 1998.

Gilman, Sander, *The Case of Sigmund Freud: Medicine and Identity at the Fin de Siècle*, Baltimore and London: Johns Hopkins University Press 1993.

——, *Freud, Race, and Gender*, Princeton, NJ: Princeton University Press 1993.

——, *The Jew's Body*, London and New York: Routledge 1991.

Girard, Alain, *Le journal intime*, Paris: Presses Universitaires de France, 1963.

Gourevitch, Philip, 'The Memory Thief', *New Yorker*, 14 June 1999, pp. 48–68.

Horowitz, Sara R., *Voicing the Void: Muteness and Memory in Holocaust Fiction*, Albany: State University of New York Press 1997.

Jacobus, Mary, *Psychoanalysis and the Scene of Reading*, Oxford: Oxford University Press 1999.

Kertzer, Andrea, *My Mother's Voice: Children, Literature and the Holocaust*, Ontario: Broadview Press 2002.

King, Nicola, *Memory, Narrative, Identity: Remembering the Self*, Edinburgh: Edinburgh University Press 2000.

Kremer S. Lillian, ed., *Holocaust Literature: An Encyclopedia of Writers and Their Work*, New York and London: Routledge 2002.

LaCapra, Dominick, *History and Memory after Auschwitz*, Ithaca, New York: Cornell University Press 1998.

Langer, Lawrence L., 'Damaged Childhood in Holocaust Fact and Fiction', in Michael A. Signer, ed., *Humanity at the Limit: The Impact of the Holocaust Experience on Jews and Christians*, Bloomington and London: Indiana University Press 2000.

——, 'Family Dilemmas in Holocaust Literature', *Michigan Quarterly Review*, 26(2), 1987, pp. 387–99.

Langford, Rachel and Russell West, eds, *Marginal Voices, Marginal Forms: Diaries in European Literature and History*, Amsterdam and Atlanta, GA: Rodopi 1999.

Lappin, Elena, 'The Man with Two Heads', *Granta* 66, Summer 1999, pp. 7–65.

Lathey, Gillian, *The Impossible Legacy: Identity and Purpose in Autobiographical Children's Literature Set in the Third Reich and the Second World War*, Berne: Peter Lang 1999.

Lejeune, Philippe, *On Autobiography*, trans. Kathleen Leary, Minneapolis: University of Minnesota Press 1989.

——, 'W or the Memory of Childhood', *Review of Contemporary Fiction* 13(1) 1993, pp. 86–97.

Lyotard, Jean-François, *The Differend: Phrases in Dispute*, trans. Georges Van Den Abbeele, Minneapolis: University of Minnesota Press 1988.

——, *Heidegger and 'the Jews'*, trans. Andreas Michel, Minneapolis: University of Minnesota Press 1990.

McCaffery, Larry *et al.*, eds, *Federman A to X-X-X-X: A Recyclopedic Narrative*, San Diego: San Diego University Press 1999.

Maechler, Stefan, *The Wilkomirski Affair: A Study in Biographical Truth*, trans. John E. Woods, New York: Schocken 2001.

Mazur, Zygmunt *et al.*, eds, *The Legacy of the Holocaust: Children of the Holocaust*, Kraków: Jagiellonian University Press 2002.

Motola, Gabriel, 'Children of the Holocaust', *TriQuarterly* 105, 1999, pp. 209–32.

Motte, Warren F., *Georges Perec: Traces of His Passage*, Birmingham, Alabama: Summa Publishers 1988.

O'Dochartaigh, Pól, ed., *Jews in German Literature Since 1945: German-Jewish Literature*, Amsterdam and Atlanta: Rodopi 2000.

Patterson, David, *Along the Edge of Annihilation: The Collapse and Recovery of Life in the Holocaust Diary*, Seattle and London: University of Washington Press 1999.

Pellegrini, Ann, *Performance Anxieties: Staging Psychoanalysis, Staging Race*, London: Routledge 1997.

Peskowitz, Miriam and Laura Levitt, eds, *Judaism Since Gender*, London and New York: Routledge 1997.

Pinfold, Debbie, *The Child's View of the Third Reich in German Literature: The Eye Among the Blind*, Oxford: Oxford University Press 2001.

Reiter, Andrea, *Narrating the Holocaust*, trans. Patrick Camiller, London and New York: Continuum 2000.

Roth, John K. and Michael Berenbaum, eds, *Holocaust: Religious and Philosophical Implications*, New York: Paragon House 1989.

Rothberg, Michael, *Traumatic Realism: The Demands of Holocaust Representation*, Minneapolis: University of Minnesota Press 2000.

Scullion, Rosemarie, 'Georges Perec, *W*, and the Memory of Vichy France', *SubStance* 87, 1998, pp. 107–29.

Shapiro, Robert Moses, ed., *Holocaust Chronicles: Individualizing the Holocaust through Diaries and Other Contemporaneous Personal Accounts*, New York: KTAV 1999.

Sokoloff, Naomi, 'Childhood Lost: Children's Voices in Holocaust Literature', in Elizabeth Goodenough *et al.*, eds, *Infant Tongues: The Voice of the Child in Literature*, Detroit: Wayne State University Press 1994.

——, *Imagining the Child in Modern Jewish Fiction*, Baltimore: Johns Hopkins University Press 1992.

Stewart, Victoria, 'Anne Frank and the Uncanny', *Paragraph* 24(1), March 2001, pp. 99–113.

Stone, Dan, 'Holocaust Testimony and the Challenge to the Philosophy of History', in Robert Fine and Charles Turner, eds, *Social Theory after the Holocaust*, Liverpool: Liverpool University Press 2000.

Syrkin, Marie, 'Diaries of the Holocaust', in Murray Mindlin and Chaim Bermant, eds, *Explorations: An Annual on Jewish Themes*, London: Barrie and Rockliff 1967.

Vice, Sue, ed., *Psychoanalytic Criticism: A Reader*, Cambridge: Polity Press 1996.

——, ed., *Representing the Holocaust: Essays in Honour of Bryan Burns*, London: Vallentine Mitchell 2003.

Wilczynski, Marek, 'Trusting the Words: Paradoxes of Ida Fink', *Modern Language Studies* 24(4), Fall 1994, pp. 25–38.

Young, James E., *Writing and Rewriting the Holocaust: Narrative and the Consequences of Interpretation*, Bloomington and Indianapolis: Indiana University Press 1990.

Art, photography and poetry

Stargardt, Nicholas, 'Children's Art of the Holocaust', *Past and Present* 161, 1998, pp. 191–235.

Vishniac, Roman, *Children of a Vanished World*, Berkeley and London: University of California Press 1999.

Volaková, Hana, ed., *I Never Saw Another Butterfly: Children's Drawings and Poems from Terezín Concentration Camp*, trans. Jeanne Nemcová, New York: Schocken 1993 [1976]

Index